Trevor Dannatt
works and words

Trevor Dannatt
works and words

Roger Stonehouse

black dog publishing

london uk

Contents

Foreword

When my future wife and I were undergraduates at Cambridge in the late 1950s, we yearned for the new in the buildings and the environment around us. We felt stifled by the architecture of the recent past, felt the potential of liberation that was realised in the Festival of Britain site and in particular by the Royal Festival Hall itself. But the revolution of the modern—I doubt if "modern-ism" was a phrase we used—seemed a long way away, though our Architectural Faculty contemporaries talked of Corb and Max and Jane endlessly—indeed some were related.

But the hope that this yearning for the new in buildings might become reality came to us through Trevor Dannatt. He designed a house in Clarkson Road, Cambridge for my History supervisor, the social historian, Peter Laslett and his wife Janet. When they invited us for Sunday lunch in their new house, the whole occasion was an eye-opener. It could not have been—and continues to be—more different from those roads of Cambridge Dons' houses, redbrick, bay windowed, gravelled drives, secluded behind hedges, excluding, exuding privacy.

Here was a house set back from the road but 'protected' only by a grass verge; instead of hedges, clumps of bullrushes and reeds; an open statement to the passerby, certainly not flashy but proud and distinctive—too distinctive for some Fellows and Cambridge burghers.

I do not need to describe the house. But when Ann and I went inside we both knew that the future we instinctively wanted was possible. Here it was, and here was someone living in it.

More amazingly still, Peter and Janet told us that the architect, one Trevor Dannatt, had lived with them for some time before designing the house to "see how they lived". This, too, seemed—was?—revolutionary but it also felt deeply right. This was how the world could be, should be.

The experience, of architect and his building, never left us; it represented an ideal of design and behaviour.

Trevor Dannatt's classical, harmonious, balanced modernism seems as attractive today as it did then. It is not showy and it is rooted in principle, but not theory; it is humane and at home with the places where his buildings sit and with the people who use them. These are enduring qualities.

My one regret—the fault is entirely mine—is that I did not probe Trevor's thoughts further over how he would have revivified the internal spaces of the Barbican. On the face of it, nothing could be further from the architectural values of the Royal Festival Hall than the Barbican. This was not Trevor's modernism. Yet he respected it and as his quizzical, humourous, architect's eye roamed searchingly over the Barbican's richly organised, complex internal volumes and spaces, I wondered—"What would you do to it?"

Well, the conversation never took place. I still wonder, because I like his mind, respect his eye and warm to his values. As Ann and I did when we first went in to Number 3 Clarkson Road, Cambridge all those years ago.

Sir John Tusa

The Complete Consort

Roger Stonehouse

> I start from a love of buildings.... Literature makes
> order, shows a whole view of human life, sets it in a
> matrix. Likewise architecture.[1]

Thus, Trevor Dannatt began to set out his position and
intentions at the RIBA in 1969, concluding, from TS Eliot's
"Little Gidding":

> And every phrase and sentence that is right
> (Where every word is at home,
> Taking its place to support the others,
> The word neither diffident nor ostentatious,
> An easy commerce of the old and new,
> The common word exact without vulgarity,
> The formal word precise but not pedantic,
> The complete consort dancing together).[2]

There can be no more precise a description of his intentions
in bringing an architectural/technical order to his buildings, to
the whole and to the parts, nor of the order and propriety he
seeks in architecture, art and life.

Prose and Poetry

In this context, it is fitting that this book should be subtitled,
works and words, not just because it contains some of Dannatt's
writings but because literature and architecture share the
common intention of helping us make sense of our world and
our place in it through creating a form of order and "a whole
view of human life". In prose and poetry, precision is paramount
in the choice and structuring of words relative to purpose and
occasion, just as in the choice and structuring of form and
material in architecture.

However, as with all artists, there is an ambivalence—on one
hand, a wish to be precise and a love of the deeply ordered
(but fear of producing the superficially orderly) whilst, on the
other, an internal rebelliousness and assertion of individuality,
here professed in a preference for the loose and expressed by

the use of a diagonal, which may appear wilful but is always
useful and spirited.

As will become clear, the subtitle is also a double-play on
words, for the works it refers to are not only Dannatt's works
of architecture but the works of art which he has habitually
collected and which have a deep affinity with his architecture.

Propriety and ambience

Eliot's distinction between those purposes and occasions which
require the "common word" and those which require the "formal
word" is also a necessary distinction in architecture but one
which is now often forgotten or neglected, though it has always
typified Dannatt's work. It embodies the sense of propriety which
is fundamental to his work but missing in most architecture of
today and the recent past. However, propriety is an ever present,
ancient need of which Vitruvius wrote—a sense of decorum, an
appropriate level of display, of strength of presence.[3] Without it,
as Colin St John Wilson identified, "there can be no architecture—
merely technology, sociology or formalism".[4]

But this need for propriety reveals deeper, associated
needs—for an appropriate character, presence, or, in Dannatt's
word, "milieu":

> ... we should be trying to create ambience beyond the
> lab[oratory] concept of environment. Something to which
> we respond beyond comfort and well-being, a *milieu*
> which connects us to the poetry of living, heightens our
> awareness of today as part of yesterday and the day
> before yesterday, rather than, say, romantically orientating
> to some quite unknown future.[5]

There is a strong functionalist basis to his approach but
that this is more than mechanical functionalism, is revealed in
the declared intentions "... to release the potentialities of a
situation or to develop a *milieu* that may produce interaction
and even some pleasure" and to create a "background that
responds to the deeper levels of human consciousness".[6] These

Balcony window with green table, St Ives, 1957.
The Estate of Patrick Heron/DACS, 2008.

'Pattern' of the three levels of the Laslett House, 1958.

are responses to the immeasurable matters of the human spirit, which Alvar Aalto had called for in his RIBA Gold Medal address in 1957.[7] But even at the practical levels, Dannatt was aware early of the shortcomings of functionalism: "Just at one moment, perhaps, our plans correspond to needs, but who knows the future? So we do perhaps begin to consider more the *milieu* creating role of architecture, the whole environment inside and out."[8]

Central to the idea of propriety, and the associated creation of an appropriate *milieu*, is formal significance—a sensibility of ordering, form, material, and detail, "the search for a certain inevitability at every scale" through "intensifying thought to find what can be discarded".[9] This is not the flaunted, self-conscious abstraction of minimalism but the editing out of all that is extraneous to leave only that which is appropriate—a process equivalent to that which will be seen in works in his art collection. As Eliot put it: "The word neither diffident nor ostentatious."

Propriety is also dependent on scale, a recurrent consideration, and on Eliot's "easy commerce of the old and new"—whether that be with a greenfield site or existing buildings—the latter providing a continuity in time and place and the possibility of 'being-at-home'.

Eliot's distinctions between "common word" and "formal word" are not necessarily rigidly categorical but, nevertheless, they do give a way of thinking about buildings and the occasions and situations for which they are required to form a setting. The same word might be common or formal depending upon the occasion of its use, conversely a building might be seen as either common or formal in its different parts or from different perspectives, and hence ambiguous; but what matters is that appropriate thought and form is given to the necessary propriety of an occasion or situation—the "common word" of housing, the "formal word" of places of gathering and ordered activity, such as schools, and of the special events of life, perhaps celebratory or spiritual. As Bronowski says "ambiguity lies in the very texture of all ideas".[10] As he shows, it is the means by which poetry, as all arts, can exist and communicate; it is inevitable in all social and cultural transactions, situations and occasions. This is not the imposed, contrived ambiguity of Venturi but arises from the careful consideration and subtle teasing out of the inherent activities of life, as Wilson puts it, that "search for the truth of each situation [whereby] a building... makes possible the happening of whatever is most

significant and appropriate to that occasion".[11] In other words, the deep consideration of that which is the business, motivation and stuff of literature and architecture (that which literature "sets in a matrix", and for which architecture is called upon to provide a setting).

Prose and Poetry
The references to poetry bring into play another significant literary distinction suggested by the philosopher Samuel Alexander, 1859–1938, who, as Leslie Martin put it, asked:

> Was it not possible that the great mass of architecture, with its link to practical purpose, should be the same kind of art as good prose writing? Could there not be two kinds of architecture, rooted in a common language, the one neither better nor worse than the other, but each appropriate for its particular purpose—a prose and a poetry in architecture?[12]

Thus the distinction between prose and poetry is one of purpose and mode not quality—"the one neither better nor worse than the other". The purpose of 'buildings of prose' is to provide an ordered, 'just so', everyday background to life—the means of being 'at home in our everyday world'—through the eloquence and fittingness of their language, perhaps even, making the ordinary special (ie. extra-ordinary, out of the ordinary) without making it extraordinary (ie. alien). On the other hand, 'buildings of poetry' are intended to heighten our awareness of ourselves and our being-in-the-world by taking us out of the everyday, whilst being rooted in our experience of the world—perhaps in response to uncommon events, such as acts of celebration, commemoration or worship, or uncommon historical or geographical locations. As Alexander says, these two kinds of architecture are rooted in a common language.

In such observations lies a major source of the value and significance of Dannatt's work and that of a number of his contemporaries in Britain—such as Colin St John Wilson, Denys Lasdun, Peter Moro, and James Gowan and, not least, his mentor and close friend, Leslie Martin, who developed Alexander's ideas as the basis for his paper, "The Language of Architecture", in 1955.[13]

Martin illustrated the difference by reference to Georgian London, the prose of the streets and squares and the poetry of the city churches—all within a common language. He stressed that architectural prose was not inferior: "that misconception at the bottom of all resistance to this idea". And he pointed out the problems of the loss of a source of a common language in modern architecture and of the new, highly repetitive building types, such as office buildings, which were "not a suitable subject for the individual types of expression that [architects] have been trained to provide"; with regard to the latter, though, he saw, in comparison with the problem solved by Georgian London, only a difference in technique and scale, not principle.

The consequences of neglecting the distinction between situations requiring architectural prose and poetry, and of a loss of language and a sense of propriety, are only too clear in today's Babel of stylistic fetishisms and the circus freakshow of so-called icons.

These continuing mores were evident in 1969, when, in contrast, Dannatt suggested that:

> As individuals and professionals we might know what we want to do ultimately, but meanwhile we might relax a little, forget our public image and make some prosaic buildings. Good prose is structured, cogent, lucid, without redundancies. Perhaps we should let poetry come of its own accord or at least think that art does not always have to be eloquent to endure.[14]

Thus, he picked up the distinction between prose and poetry and suggested that, on occasion, prose might raise itself to the expressive power of poetry. The relationship between the two, in spoken and written language, was set out wittily by Terry Eagleton:

> In ordinary speech we treat language as transparent, whereas poetry treats it as opaque. Rather than just stare through the language to its meaning, it savours words as a value in themselves. In fact, poetry is that strange kind of utterance in which such things as tone, mood, rhythm, rhyme, pitch, pace and texture are *part of the meaning*. It is the kind of language that makes it impossible for us to separate what is said from how it is said. There are several ways to say "I think I'll have the one with the squashy centre", but only one way of saying "Thou still unravished bride of quietness."[15]

Architecture is different—the effects of the elements of the language are so immediate, bearing so directly on the senses and thereby relating to bodily experience and memory, that they are always part of the meaning.[16] Conversely, the semantic content in architectural prose, ie. the everyday and ordinary, is usually so obvious, so known, that it does not mask the poetic, empathetic potential of the forms, nor does it mask the dire consequences of inappropriate forms.

To pursue Eagleton a little further:

> While mature men and women use language to buy shares and wage wars, poets love to relish the shape and flavour of words on the tongue—what Seamus Heany calls "mouth music". Poetry is a kind of primitive magic, in which words and things share a secret bond, In fact, it pushes words to the point where they are things—not just abstract tokens, but palpable experiences.

Here, spoken and written poetry seems to approach the modes of communication and experience in architecture. But the point is clear: the heightened, explicit poetic intent, of itself, inevitably brings a focus on form at the expense of an immediate revelation of content or meaning (though provoking subsequent, deeper readings of meaning). In the languages of words and of architecture, there are occasions for prose and occasions for poetry—though poetry may always be lurking in the prose and, thus, "may come of its own accord". But good, fitting prose is not easy.

In commercial, bureaucratic societies such as our own, language grows increasingly stale and abstract. Words become worn and tarnished, like coins passed too often from hand to hand. People who talk about the co-ordinated delivery of best-practice solutions for the dynamic enablement of cost-effective projects are poetic virgins. They have clearly never thrilled to the lilt and texture in their lives. The task of poetry is to bring a moribund language alive again in the minds and mouths of its users.[17]

The people who talk thus are those, including the architects, responsible for most office blocks, shopping centres, hospitals and much else. The question is how to rediscover the "lilt and texture" of life, to bring "a moribund language alive again" without the descent into the circus freakshow of 'icons'. It is with such questions that Dannatt and some of his contemporaries have been concerned and to which their architecture responds—in, as Dannatt puts it, "making good prose or poetry out of the flux of conditions"; the latter being the "needs", the "situation found" and the "means available".[18]

Wilson, a friend and contemporary of Dannatt, who like him was closely associated with Leslie Martin and who shared the same values and intentions, also wrote of the "private necessity" which architecture is required to fulfil.[19] This private necessity lies in our need to feel 'at home' in our world, and, therefore, to make sense of our world and our place in it; and beyond that, to make sense of ourselves and, on occasion, to be touched by our sense of the universal and eternal, by that which, whilst of our everyday life and experience, takes us out of the everyday—a need Wilson described by relating it to other arts, including prose:

> James Joyce once defined the aim of his art in terms of the word "epiphany". By this he meant the understanding by which the most ordinary acts of men could be shown forth—a sudden focus into depth, into naked revelation, of what has seemed to be trivial incident.... [In architecture] it is born of necessity, of ordinary acts: it must then grow to transcend them. That is the paradox of its nature, reconciling that which is measurable with the immeasurable.... This has nothing whatever to do with the search for the extraordinary; it has much to do with the enlargement and the celebration of the powers of life and their embodiment.[20]

It is those moments—occasional, but familiar to all—when, perhaps on the turning of a stair or at a window, in apparently ordinary circumstances, one is captured, taken out of oneself, seeing all in all—moments of epiphany, which Dannatt instinctively creates in response to his intention of creating "the background that responds to the deeper levels of human consciousness", quoting Maxwell Fry.

The Architecture

Two kinds of architecture

These dichotomies—common/formal, prose/poetry—underlie Dannatt's belief in the need for two kinds of architecture, as Colin Davies put it, or, perhaps more accurately, a belief in the need for a spectrum of architecture:[22]

> the sense that architecture exists at different levels of emphasis... for public buildings another order is attempted than, say, for housing or welfare buildings... a place for expressive architecture and many places for a high level of ordinariness... there are different levels of intensity of work and we must distinguish clearly what level is appropriate to each task.[23]

Leaving aside what might be meant by "expressive architecture", and, indeed, whether there can ever be an architecture which is not inherently expressive at some level or other, the general distinction drawn here remains valid and significant. It is a position shared with Leslie Martin, concerning:

> the different levels at which architecture should operate. All buildings are not solved in exactly the same terms. There are different degrees of emphasis. One may be public and give significance to an area: others may more appropriately be anonymous and may add to the general cohesion and environment for the community.[24]

This property of anonymity or ordinariness—that heightened ordinariness, making the ordinary extra-ordinary without making it extraordinary, described earlier, was explored by Alison and Peter Smithson in their book, *Without rhetoric: an architectural aesthetic 1955–72*, which Dannatt enthusiastically endorsed in his review "Out of the ordinary".[25] "... I found the book entirely sympathetic... I can only compare it with the delight I have had from certain, for me, extending books—for instance Adrian Stokes's *Smooth and Rough* or Michael Tippet's *Moving into Aquarius*. Each has a common characteristic—the compelling quality of literate artists writing about their art and other artists with sympathy and understanding."

> Of the different definitions of "rhetoric" it is, I think, that of 'language' characterised by artificial or ostentatious expression which the authors believe architecture in our time can do without. This is the underlying theme—the achievement of ordinariness (Auguste Perret's 'banal') using the word in a non-deprecatory way. Thus "... why we think about the Hochschule für Gestaltung at Ulm—of its ease, of its ordinariness that has a kind of understated lyricism which is full of potential and does not disturb the peace of the hillside...".[26]

The architect of the Hochschule was max bill, whose work Dannatt had published as editor of the *Architects' Year Book 10* in 1962, and whose prints and a painting he was later to acquire as the pinnacle of his art collection. The reference to Perret's use of the word banal (the original meaning of which is "common to all") came from a quotation of Perret in an essay by Ernö Goldfinger, which was published, in the *Architects' Year Book 7* in 1956, and in which Dannatt identified Perret's "continuing preoccupation with the constant".

There is an architectural density of great potency in the central space [of the Royal College of Physicians], a similar density in the core space of the National Theatre and, surprisingly, in the Claredale Street housing, where in the confluence of the access galleries there is an extraordinary poetry of space and material with slots of view extending into the city....[21]

He, who without betraying the materials nor the requirements of today, will have produced a work which seemed to have always existed, a work, which in one word is banal. I say, he will be able to consider himself satisfied. The object of art is not to surprise or move us... but to lead us dialectically on from satisfaction to satisfaction and beyond admiration to placid delectation.[27]

So, here can be seen not only a continuing preoccupation with continuity, the constant, the ordinary and the subtle, but also fertile, sustaining matrices of art, architecture and words and of personal acquaintance, often close friendship, with leading architects and artists.

Order of works
Significant as the distinctions within each of the dichotomies of common/formal and prose/poetry are in helping us make places through which we may make sense of the world—personal, social, natural and spiritual—they can never be absolute, as witnessed, for example, by the phenomenon of an epiphany. However, building functions and purposes are, to greater and lesser extents, typified by such distinctions and by Martin's "different levels of emphasis". So, within this book the buildings and projects are grouped by function and purpose, not because Dannatt has an explicit position relating building function to building form-type, as is the case with Martin and Wilson, but because of his belief in determining and realising an appropriate ambience, "pitch" or degree of "architectural density" for the purpose or function.[29]

In this publication a commentary introduces each group of buildings and projects, for which the architect has written the brief descriptions and selected the illustrations. The sequence in which the groups are arranged extends from those where the intention is one of an architectural prose— the "common word" of domestic and residential architecture and then the "formal word" of commerce, schools and universities—to those of a more poetic intention (implicit if not explicit) and greater architectural intensity—in the "common word" of a hotel and houses in the desert and the "formal word" of buildings for assembly, worship, and national and international institutions. This sequence reveals not only the nature of the work and how the architectural language responds to the different requirements but sheds light on the role architecture can play in helping us make sense of the

world and our place in it, and in building a world of sense (that which is innate in vernacular architecture).

Underlying this variation of response is a coherence, arising from a certain attitude, a certain sensibility and intention in architecture, with a constant approach which has matured over a long period of practice. The values, intentions, skills and knowledge which the works embody are now largely lost, or, at least, rare and disregarded but nevertheless essential. The works therefore carry lessons for today and the future. It is, however, intriguing that a significant number of the works confound the fact that they were designed and built some 30 to 50 or more years ago. Dannatt early established a language of architecture which has stood the test of time in what might be termed a "contemporary timelessness".

For instance, the building shown on the cover of this book—the Laslett House of 1958, and recently 'rediscovered'— might perfectly plausibly have been designed at any date since, as a fresh, new work of architecture; a statement validated by a house in East Lothian, the winner of the 2006 *Architects' Journal* Small Buildings Award, the architects of which, unsurprisingly, had not known of the Laslett House.[30] Reciprocally, the latter has great affinities with earlier houses, to be discussed later.

The question arises as to why certain forms, details, manner of use of a material—certain tropes, they would be called in literature—remain acceptable for much longer periods than others. Partly, it may be because they are manifestations of much deeper patterns of form, patterns which may satisfy Wilson's "private necessity" and, in so doing, may provoke a different sense of timelessness.[31] This, it is suggested, is the case with two of the tropes which will be explored when considering the Laslett House; the base-superstructure composition and the corner window.

As will be seen, a person sitting in the latter is in a situation which is simultaneously inside and outside, a part of the wider world yet apart from it. Such situations (and, relatedly, those which are liminal and/or layered in degrees of enclosure) have been found to be attractive in all cultures.[32] They are recurrent and attractive because they are found deeply satisfying by what Wilson termed the "natural imagination":

> that code [which] acts so directly and vividly upon us because it is strangely familiar; it is in fact the first language we ever learned, long before words... [It is] that symposium of shapes and meanings and phantasies experienced by the

Laslett House, 1958.

Paterson Architects, House in East Lothian, 2005.

... the Economist group—that diamond amongst the paste of commercial architecture of our time.[28]

infant in passing from its first stage of an all-embracing envelopment with the mother, a kind of fusion with what is most sheltering, to the later stage of separateness, exposed at arms length, to the otherness of objects "out there". The transition from one state of mind or "position" to another is overwhelming, and to find some mode of reconciliation between these poles is a dire necessity to be worked out by every individual. These states of mind are associated very directly with a wide range of sensual experience, of rough and smooth, resonant or muffled, light and dark, warm and cold, of being inside or outside or in-between, exposed or protected. But then it is these sensations in turn which are also the sole vehicle for architectural experience and uniquely so. [33]

Thus, as Wilson suggests, "in some way the buildings that elate us seem to be carrying out, in that code, some reconciliation of those primary poles of feeling, seem to make us, at last, at home in the world—our psychological states transcribe precisely into conjunctions of form in which the impossible happens, opposites are fused, envelopment and exposure reconciled in the portico and the aedicule, the loggia and the courtyard and the hanging garden".

Places and situations which appeal to the needs of this "natural imagination" and those which have a related sense of timelessness recur throughout Dannatt's architecture; places which may evoke a personal sense of permanence, the elemental, the eternal. They arise not only when consciously sought, where the purpose requires, in places of consciously poetic intent—places of worship, assembly and display, and at Kew Gardens and in his buildings in Riyadh—but also unbidden in quotidian moments of his domestic architecture and works for commerce, those moments of epiphany, where it is much more a consequence of his underlying attitude to life, of his "inner landscape" and intentions—of which more later. His use of material and detail is such as to support, not mask or confuse, the moment, the experience; but the materials and forms are never explicit, symbolic statements of timelessness—for such would destroy the moment, such experiences being personal and hence dependent on discovery. The subtlety, which Dannatt so often seeks, allows us to be taken unawares. Through using and reusing a limited pallette of materials and forms, he has been able to learn how to exploit the order they imply and their expressive potential.

The base-superstructure composition of the Laslett House is one of enduring relevance which, with its classical antecedents,

engenders a cultural timelessness, that continuity and sense of time, which he holds dear:

> We must... perhaps, look again at what is dubbed traditional. For such emphasis has been placed on what is different in our time that we have overlooked those depths that are essentially the same. [34] From even a small fragment of an old building we receive intense satisfaction, a sense of the depth and continuity of life... how can we not be dissatisfied with our own efforts... producing buildings without a sense of time or quality that fail to relate man to his environment? [35]

Such thoughts are directly related to propriety and rootedness, ie. making sense.

The value of much of his work, and that of some of his distinguished contemporaries, lies in its remaining true, fresh and relevant after the aberrations of postmodernism, High-Tech, Neo-this and Neo-that. In his best work it embodies the characteristics of what Michael Benedikt termed 'real' architecture in his 1987 manifesto, *For an Architecture of Reality*, which rails against such aberrations. [36] Benedikt commences with these moments of epiphany, quotidian moments of revelatory poetry within the prose of life:

> There are valued times in almost everyone's experience when the world is perceived afresh; perhaps after rain as the sun glistens on the streets and windows catch a departing cloud, or, alone, when one sees again the roundness of an apple. At these times our perceptions are not at all sentimental. They are, rather, matter of fact, neutral and undesiring—yet suffused with an unreasoned joy at the simple correspondence of appearance and reality, at the evident rightness of things as they are.... Such experiences, such privileged moments, can be profoundly moving; and precisely from such moments, I believe, we build our best and necessary sense of an independent yet meaningful reality. I should like to call them *direct aesthetic experiences of the real* and to suggest the following: in our media-saturated times it falls to architecture to have the direct aesthetic experience of the real at the centre of its concerns.

For Benedikt, there are four components to this "realness". All are present in Dannatt's works and therefore provide a context for their consideration, whilst their presence assert the works' timeless value. These four components, one of which is of two kinds, are:

- 'presence'—"analogous to the 'presence' attributed to certain people... or to 'presence of mind'... experienced not only visually, but also by coherent appeal to the other senses: to touch, movement, sound, smell... [where] every material and texture is fully itself and revealed... [and] stands by precisely where it needs to be and ends there.... A building with presence... seems attentive to *our* presence."
- 'significance'—"not achieved by the display of icons, signs and symbols... but by how buildings actually come to be and how they continue to be part of the lives of the people who dream them, draw them, own them and use them.... Buildings with significance show a fundamental seriousness—even when they are 'follies'—and a sense of magnitude independent of their actual size.... Effort, care, ingenuity (rather than cleverness), knowledge, ambition—these traits of its creators 'come through' in a building and tell us how it is to be taken."
- 'materiality'—"reflects our intuition that for something to be real it ought to be made of material having a palpability, a temperature, a weight and inertia, an inherent strength.... Clarity in what a building is made of, how it is made on that account, and how the way it looks reflects both..."
- 'emptiness'—"the most difficult component of realness with which to deal verbally, yet perhaps the most important one."
- 'emptiness one'—"approximated by words such as 'artlessness', 'innocence', 'suchness', 'quiddity', 'inevitability', 'unworldliness', 'purposelessness'... [It] implies that a building should not be slave to its programme, twisting and turning to accommodate every movement and wish... but rather should be formed according to innate principles of order, structure, shelter, the evolution of architecture itself—and accident. It should be *found* useful and beautiful, like a tree."
- 'emptiness two'—"much contemporary high-style architecture lacks emptiness two, by being quite literally full... if not of people and goods, then of Design... these buildings are full of themselves and their cleverness." Architecture with emptiness two is "always unfinished: if not literally, then by the space it makes and the potential it shows". In other words, it engages our presence.

Though these are qualities which Dannatt instinctively seeks, it is hard, as Benedikt realises, "to design egolessly; form without rhetoric, without artifice, pretension, or dragging surplus".

A further clue to the reason for the continuing relevance of the works through changing times is found in Dannatt's quotation of the art critic Bernard Berenson:

> Is it not precisely Piero's ineloquence, his unemotional, unfeeling figures, behaving as if nothing could touch them, in short, his avoidance of inflation, which in time of exasperated passions, rests, calms, and soothes the spectator and compels gratitude and worship?[37]

For Dannatt: "The same might be said of Seurat." Such calm and restraint can raise prose to the level of poetry.

Roots of the architecture

What then are the roots of this architecture and its architect's attitudes? They lie in the Janus-like times of his awakening interest in art and architecture. His architectural education at the Regent Street Polytechnic, where he went in 1938, coincided with the shift from architectural education grounded in the calm certainties of classical architecture to the Bauhaus-inspired, open-ended explorations of form, space, colour and structure from first principles. He was quickly captivated by Le Corbusier, who bestrode the classical and modern worlds; both by his architecture, closely explored in publications, and by his writings, in particular, *Vers une Architecture* with its seminal analysis of the correspondences between Greek architecture and modern engineering. This Janus position of the period plausibly explains Dannatt's immediate attraction to Seurat's *Bathers at Asnières* and the nature of his architecture—calm, ordered, quiet, sensitive to location and purpose, inventive in composition, structure and language, deeply considered in the qualities of material, colour and the play of light.

The most influential of his tutors was Peter Moro (whose own house, the design of which Dannatt was unaware, was contemporaneous with the Laslett House and another example of this powerful, deep-seated trope).

> Whatever the subject, his architecture was deeply rooted in the bedrock of the programme, where he sought to organise the plan three-dimensionally with space and volume for convenience and delight, aiming to create humane environments. He was deeply involved with the niceties of use, the pleasures of movement, the delight of material to sight and touch.

Peter Moro, House at Birdham, 1938.

Peter Moro's own house at Blackheath, 1958.

Royal Festival Hall, river front, 1951.

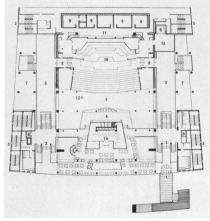

Royal Festival Hall, plan at front stalls level.

He pursued building design with a rare honesty of approach. He was rational, with a clear understanding of how to put things together and, perhaps, faith that in designing well, resonances would emerge from unconscious springs.[38]

Such "designing well" requires deep wellsprings of life-experience and a sensitivity to places. Thus, the creativity is inevitably permeated with the "natural imagination" and with rhythms and associations which chime with our inner being— the mode of poetry's "mouth music".

Just five years after qualifying, Moro ("I chose a handful of the best of my former students whose ideas of design were sympathetic to my own.") invited Dannatt to join the design team for the Festival Hall, which was opened in 1951 and renamed the Royal Festival Hall.[39] This, too, was somewhat Janus-like in nature, with the symmetry of its plan and ordering of its structure rooted in classicism whilst being the first major public work of the Modern Movement in this country (and many of us would say still one of the greatest). Its principal architect was Leslie Martin, thus initiating the acquaintanceship, later close friendship, which became the most significant influence on Dannatt's architectural development.

Previously, whilst working for Jane Drew (later Fry, Drew), she had asked him to assist in editing the first *Architects' Year Book* (1945) and, later, handed him the editorship, whence he published eight editions over the period 1949–1962, with the intention of "the presentation of current thought on the philosophy and practice in the art and technique of modern architecture (including the illustration of recently completed buildings)".[40] This editorship provided the opportunity to promote and pursue those aspects of architecture he considered important, which in turn led to contacts with leading architects and artists. Two areas were to prove particularly significant: first, an interest in Scandinavian architecture, especially the work of Aalto, Asplund and Finn Juhl; and second, the relationship between architecture and art.

The books were "much inspired by *Circle* in format and scope". *Circle; An International Survey of Constructive Art*, jointly edited by Martin, Naum Gabo and Ben Nicholson in 1937, had published contemporary works and essays in art, architecture and science. These were bound by a common spirit of a quest for "a sense of wholeness and a coherence of form", seeing the need "to consider once again the relationship between science and art".[41]

Each Year *Book* followed this breadth of approach in publishing developments not only in architecture but in art and in science and technology related to architecture. This breadth of approach, firmly rooted in rational enquiry and analysis, also benefited from, and reflected Dannatt's involvement in the MARS (Modern Architecture Research Group), of which he was Honorary Secretary from 1952 to 1957, when it was dissolved. This group, which had been founded in 1933, was the British arm of the Congrès Internationaux d'Architecture Moderne (CIAM), an organisation which had been established in 1928 by leading modernist architects, and which, through its debates and publications, promulgated many of the central tenets of the Modern Movement in architecture and planning, thereby influencing the form of cities and buildings across the world. His involvement coincided with the rift within CIAM between those architects wishing to maintain the earlier 'pseudo-rationalist' approach and those, including the Smithsons, James Stirling and Howell, Killick and Partridge in this country, who saw the need for a social and anthropological approach with its implications for place-making. These changes chimed with Dannatt's interests and thus were promoted through publication in the *Year Books* and in turn influenced his own architecture.

The *Year Books* were, as he wrote:

> also concerned with the past, not in an antiquarian sense but as a source of fundamental precepts, including studies in architectural history... and of the more immediate past, giving account of the development of modern architecture, offering new views on its nature and pointing out aspects which might inform our work today and be the source of further developments.[42]

He argued that much of the modern architecture in this country at that time was unconvincing and merely picturesque in nature, replicating the elements of the new architecture as pictorial elements without understanding or inner conviction about planning, space or form. Here is revealed the climate of 1953, a climate still prevalent in 1983, when, as he observed that "recently... we have seen a simplistic historicism (and/or vernacularism) promoted almost as a packaging solution to the problems of design and style", and still running strongly in 2007 in a 'me too' era of 'freaks', icons, blobs and overt technological expression.[43] All of which sets in context the value of the works seen in this book and of those architects pursuing associated lines of thought.

In the Spring of 1953 he was invited to curate the architectural section of the exhibition, *20th Century Form: Painting, sculpture and architecture*, at the Whitechapel Gallery in London. As Bryan Roberston, the Director of the gallery, wrote in the catalogue:

> The pictures and sculpture... have been chosen with three objects in mind. First, to provide a plain man's guide to some aspects of modern art. Second, to show that certain clear-cut and stabilised forms of pictorial or sculptural expression have influenced architecture, and vice versa. Third, to demonstrate to people who are not usually interested in or sympathetic towards the art of their own time, that a great deal of the aesthetic endeavour of this century is less remote from modern life than is often realised. We have, therefore, included architectural models and photographs in the exhibition, not in a subsidiary role but on equal terms with the pictures and sculptures.

Dannatt's deep interest in the relationship between art and architecture were already established as was his habit of collecting and he lent a Le Corbusier sketch and a Robert MacBryde still-life to the exhibition, which also included works by Arp, Braque, di Chirico, Feininger, Heron, Hitchens, Kandinsky, Wyndham Lewis, and Lowry.

Whilst the range of architecture selected—including works by Aalto, Le Corbusier, Mies van der Rohe, Frank Lloyd Wright, Sert, bill, Asplund, Eames, Gropius, Terragni, Lewerentz, Nervi—graphically illustrates the breadth of his interests and sources at this time; the roots of his own architecture.

The English Free School

In his Introduction to the architecture section, Dannatt evinces the contemporary, rather denigratory, orthodox position regarding nineteenth century architecture, even though, as a student, he had found Lethaby's recently published *Philip Webb and his work* "inspirational".[44] This position was all too understandable given the missionary zeal of the Modern Movement in promoting a democratic architecture of clarity and cleanliness to sweep away the oppressive, dirty, overcrowded consequences of the Industrial Revolution and the deprivations and ravages of two World Wars. Though in this piece he acknowledges that the new architecture did, in part, develop from the work of nineteenth century pioneers, it was to be more than another decade before the value of the English Free School of architects such as Street,

Butterfield, Webb and Waterhouse began to be recognised and valued.[45] This eventual recognition and acceptance of the value of the English Free School with its organic and inventive approach to form, its flexible planning in response to function and site, its development of a language from the nature of the materials and the means of construction, and its integration of services was perhaps inevitable, for many of those architects which Dannatt, Martin, Wilson and their like so much admired—such as Aalto, Asplund and Wright—had themselves been influenced by this movement, via, for instance, Herman Muthesius in Europe and Sullivan in the United States. Thus there was a generally unproclaimed, reconnection with a heritage, a way of thinking and making, embedded within, as it were, a cultural DNA, a way of making architecture which still distinguishes some architects in this country from those elsewhere in the world.

This heritage can be seen in many of Dannatt's residential and small scale works; in the asymmetrical and informal planning which is articulated to achieve human scale; the use of 'natural' and warm materials (brick and timber); variously pitched roofs and skylines; careful regard for orientation; relationship to site and landscaping; and variation of materials and dimensions to create an appropriate character in each part of a building as opposed to the sterile consistency of Gropius' functionalism. Notwithstanding this, Dannatt's asymmetrical compositions and interpenetrations seem to be more directly influenced by interests in developments in painting and sculpture and the nature of his inflections and articulations, Scandinavia, especially Aalto, and Wright.

Order and Precedent

It was, however, Leslie Martin (who acknowledged his own debt to the English Free School) who was the most consistent influence:

> ... as a student in the late thirties and early forties, I was stimulated by the first published buildings of Martin and Speight—two or three houses and the Northwich School, I had *The Flat Book* and, more important, *Circle* (where, perhaps, I 'read' the illustrations with more understanding than the text). He was one of the architects for whom I wanted to work, and did— followed by an association in work, friendship and shared interests over some thirty [to become some forty] years, a period which has seen the development

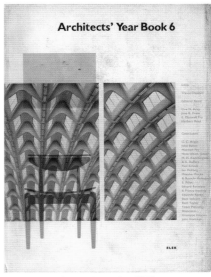

Architects' Year Book 6, dust jacket, 1955. Typography: Colin Forbes.

Leslie Martin and Sadie Speight, nursery school at Northwich (now Hartford, Cheshire), 1938.

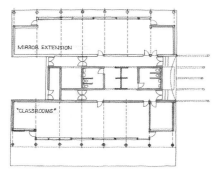

School at Northwich, plan.

Leslie Martin, Patrick Hodgkinson and Colin St John Wilson, Harvey Court, Cambridge, model, 1958.

of a grave and eloquent architectural language, personal yet within the developing movement (now a tradition) of constructive architecture.[46]

Peter Moro had grounded his student in "three-dimensional planning; in particular as to circulation, the needs of people and the means of realisation". But:

> Martin extended this and demonstrated the idea of a comprehensive architectural order that could be made eloquent by a sensibility to detail and material that reinforced the main idea rather than decorated it. At the same time, the order could be extended; one was not working in isolation and precedents were to be sought (not eschewed) and studied.[47]

Here are stated two ideas central to Dannatt's architecture: order and precedent.

With regard to Martin's philosophy and approach to order, Dannatt identified three aspects that are manifest in Martin's buildings and in each of which can be seen parallels in his own architecture:

> Firstly... needs have been analysed, digested and restated in total terms—the building is from early on seen as a whole rather than put together. The idea may often seem deceptively simple but behind it there is, among other things, a conceptual ordering that does not dismiss precedents but draws on and revitalises them.. Secondly... how the conception has been brought into a total system, a consistent formal and structural language to which all parts respond. Thirdly... a sureness and fine sensibility in the handling of elements and materials that can be enjoyed almost for their own sake... but enjoyed also because there is such a satisfying conjunction of whole and part. There is a sense of style that runs throughout from overall concept to, say, the way the doors are put into openings... all responding to the same aesthetic.[48]

Martin described his paradigm of architecture thus:

> first, the pattern of needs—that is the programme; second, the appropriate pattern of the built form (which [for each building function-type] has a range of its own); and, third, the technical means. These are inseparable, interacting and interlocking. The work of architecture is the 'fit' between them. And in all this there is no special need to search for expression or 'symbol'.[49]

However, the purity, clarity and harmony of form of many of Martin's buildings, such as Harvey Court (designed with Wilson and Patrick Hodgkinson, 1957–1962) betray more in intention than the discovery of a pattern resolving the constituent patterns, which Martin's description, with its undertones of functionalism and the mechanistic, would allow. There are obviously formal intentions beyond what might be considered to be any inherent expression and symbolism of the purpose of the building, which arise from the matching of the pattern of form to those of use and technical means. First, there is the intention to enable comprehension by working within traditions of form and language—both of building-type, eg. the court, and of architecture, subsuming relevant principles of composition and ordering, here, for instance, of Aalto, Le Corbusier, Kahn and Classicism. Second, there is the intention to develop forms which are perceptually and conceptually harmonious and complete, which arises from the conviction that the making of buildings and places inevitably creates a form of order within the world, and that that order should have repose and clarity, and, therefore, must be conceived with some form of coherence, inherently exhibiting balance and harmony.

These intentions show clear and illuminating parallels with Dannatt's summation of his own position, in which he quotes Norberg-Schultz:

> ... the creation of an organic entity... that structuring which is the essential basis of architecture... not statics, which has to be consonant with it, but that deeper structuring. The organisational pattern, no— not just that, the organisational/spatial pattern, the Swedish word 'formsprak', that which permeates a building (or environment) in all dimensions, transmutes the utilitarian into significant order to produce 'the architectural totality, the building task realised within a characteristic formal organisation' let us say—a style.[50]

For Dannatt, order is the *sine qua non* of architecture:

> Peresutti spoke well when he said the architect's job is to be 'the leader of a profound love of quality' ... [that] implies caring deeply about order, and about the structuring of the environment... buildings, spaces, secondary and tertiary objects fitting together. ... We should aim to clarify the nature of our task [in each project] and determine the importance as well as the relative value of its components, trying to find a life-enriching order... think of Bloomsbury....[51]

This conviction was shared with his late partner, Colin Dollimore, whose "architectural roots were in the Modern Movement and [who] like many then and now saw it as a continuing and evolving language of space and form matching needs with a coherent order inwardly derived, not imposed".[52]

Though there is a congruence of intention, Dannatt's eyes are gentler than Martin's, his order, though still rigorous, is less 'platonic', his view both more quotidian and more spiritual, more wry, more personal and, therefore, idiosyncratic—more the product of a literary mind—which is revealed in his discussion of another contemporary, Denys Lasdun, which also betrays a certain ambivalence. "Although my lazy predilections are for a looser sort of architecture, especially in the domestic field, I cannot but hold my breath in awe of [Lasdun's] achievements, his singleness of purpose, the outstanding ability to extract a formal architectural order out of so many diverse building tasks and to heighten it to the level of eloquent dominance, as is so evident at the National Theatre."[53] This is also a typically self-deprecatory, if a not a little knowingly disingenuous, statement, for Dannatt's predilection for a "looser sort of architecture" involves a similar intensity of thought to Lasdun's. Whilst he admires Lasdun's and Martin's forms of order, he pursues different objectives in the order he seeks in his own work—more open-ended, less suggestive of the authoritarian.

> There is a time to be noble and a time to be modest, or just innocent—which doesn't mean relaxing thought but possibly intensifying it to find what can be discarded and what is appropriate in a limited situation.[54]

His interests are more in the creation of *milieu*, something which for Martin was left to come of its own accord.

Precedent and the patterns of need, which are "sources of order" for Martin and Dannatt's architecture, come together in Martin and Wilson's analysis of Cambridge colleges, "The Collegiate Plan".[56] They saw that "the architectural idea of the court is fundamentally one of organisation", where: the enclosing wall of buildings around a private space identifies the college community; the courts of varying sizes and age give consistency and order to the buildings of the whole community, irrespective of styles; and around each court, staircases give access to landings, each landing having a group of rooms for students and a shared kitchen. Thus, social and conceptual relationships are established: between the individual and his or her room; between the rooms around a landing; between the landings linked by a staircase; between the staircases around a court; between the series of courts forming a college; and thereby, hierarchically, between each individual member of the college and the college itself. By subsuming the other functions of the college within the wall of building around each court, for instance, the chapel, library, and dining hall, these relationships are further strengthened.

Therefore, as Martin observed, "the built form (the court) embodies a pattern of use"; and, further, "if a social pattern has been observed to work there is no point in disturbing this. Nevertheless, the corresponding pattern of the form may be developed."[57] As will be seen, these patterns, which are embodied in this precedent, were developed by Dannatt in various forms in his collegiate buildings, on the first of which, at Leicester, he worked in association with Martin.

Dannatt also takes up the idea of pattern in his approach to work on existing buildings, seeing no difference, in essence, from the design of new buildings. In his essay, "Re-flections" on the work at the Greenwich Maritime Campus, he argues that in all buildings, humble and great, there is a discernible pattern of form and use, against which the discernible pattern in a potential new use can be matched, brought into 'sync'. In such work, and new build, the common denominators are the "organisation of space [and] the manipulation of form towards a coherent entity". Thus, as he identifies, "*the creative* [conservation] embraces what exists, as the springboard for a new order that identifies and respects an older one—to the advantage of both".

In these 'Re-flections' on working with existing buildings he also raises the question of representation and symbolism, observing that new uses may be housed in an existing building without changing the appearance, "the representative order", of that building. And how, it might be asked, does this observation also relate to that belief in functionalism—that the form of a building "follows", or arises from its function—which was so formative for architects of Dannatt's generation? In fact, of course, it undermines it—for as Peter Cowan so pithily determined, 80 per cent of all human activities can take place in a Georgian terrace house (including, for a number of years, Dannatt's office in Crawford Street).[58] In the fracturing of the belief in a single, inevitable, reductive relationship between a function and a form, that realisation of the importance of the ambience, or *milieu*, and of responding "to the deeper levels of

... most airport scenes show immense efforts to control and no corresponding significant order, We liked railways because they had just this, Termini, junctions, main stations, local stations, cuttings, tunnels, embankments, bridges, all spoke the same language. An ordered hierarchy of control, all fitted together. Even today the fragments show the relevant pattern. Clear, precise ordering of transport through the length and breadth of the country and a hierarchy of speed (train, horse carriage, bicycle, pedestrian).[55]

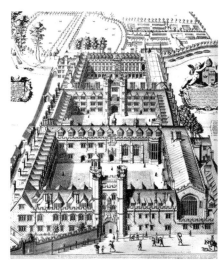

Logan's view of St John's College, Cambridge, 1690.

human consciousness", can flourish, as has been seen in the earlier discussion of 'propriety'.

Whilst Martin had seen "no special need to search for expression or 'symbol'" in the creation of architecture, Dannatt, quoting Adolf Loos and, again, Norberg-Schulz, raised the difficult question:

> What about the symbolising role? That which Loos saw so clearly when he wrote:"When we discover a mound in the woods six feet long and three feet wide and shaped in the form of a pyramid, we become serious and something inside us says "here someone lies buried, this is architecture". "Architecture becomes symbolic or monumental in giving visual expression to the constitutive ideas of a community or to the social structure." To cultivate the symbolic or monumental might be worse than ignoring it (for example, too many student residences have been college symbols rather than domestic buildings). On the other hand, there are moments when we have to raise the local into the national....[59]

Dannatt seeks his response in a typically perceptive, everyday, gentle, poetic—no less relevant—manner through the contemplation of Tower Bridge.

> It interests me to think of a basic statement such as a bridge. There is the functional-practical artefact, military or railway, any old bridge. Bridge as an incident. We can have a *milieu*-creating bridge, Ponte Vecchio or old London Bridge. And there are bridges as symbols. For instance, Tower Bridge—most powerful of examples, how well it works both ways—up the Thames under it, gateway to the port or the sea; across it, splendid entrance to the City. An architectural/engineering totality.[60]

"The unquantifiable quality"

But whilst a sense of propriety, discipline and a sense of order, and an inventive inquisitiveness are essential, they are not sufficient.

> Where does one start on a task? I still wonder. At the conscious level no doubt, the functional/practical—but at the same time maybe with the vision of a space and form, perhaps with a magic image of a conjunction of materials and light, or perhaps just the way a window is set in a wall might start the reaction.[61]

A sensitivity to place and form, not in the abstract but as experienced and as the 'matrix' of living, is required

apart from conscious sources, one draws on those unconscious sources that are part of one's personal equipment, nurtured over years since one began being an architect, through work, travel, buildings old and new, the arts and life itself. All that nurtures the creative imagination, enabling one to see things afresh and perhaps more whole. It is this unseen, almost unacknowledged because (in today's climate) unquantifiable quality, that ultimately constitutes our authority as architects and which seems to be forgotten in our pursuit of new passions such as sociology and technology.[62]

It is this "unquantifiable quality" which allows the recognition and resolution of what Aalto referred to a the immeasurable matters of the human spirit. For Dannatt, art has played an equal role with architecture in developing his sensibility, the particular nature of his "unquantifiable quality", and the "inner landscape" which nurtures that quality.

Art

The "inner landscape"

It was a student-teacher at Colfe's School, Alfred Hallet, who had first taken the young Trevor Dannatt to galleries and showed him "what paintings are about". But Mr Hallet did more than that—"look at that mosaic floor"—he started the opening of Dannatt's eyes; he taught him to look—something which made him such a good architect and teacher of architecture.

But the act of looking is not passive. Dannatt's father was a photographer who encouraged his sons to take photographs and showed him the significance of composition, that act by which we make sense of, and create sense within, the world in all thought and deed. Whilst Visiting Professor at the University of Manchester School of Architecture, 1975–1986, he spoke of the importance of each student's "inner landscape" of forms, patterns, ideas and experiences—not just of architecture but of all forms of art, particularly of painting, sculpture, literature and music. That sense we each seek and create is a product of our own "inner landscape".

His long-time friend, the artist Patrick Heron, recognised that: "Painting changes the landscape for us"—both our "inner landscape" and, thereby, the way we view the landscape of the world in which we dwell.[63] Thus Dannatt's "inner landscape", and its changing nature, is deeply structured by the art to which he is drawn and with which he chooses to live through its acquisition.

Involvement and collaboration with artists—including election to the Royal Academy of Arts in 1977—has been deeply influential in the development of his architecture and has led to the accumulation of a substantial collection of, mostly, twentieth century British and European paintings and works on paper, the major part of which will be bequeathed to The Whitworth Art Gallery at Manchester University and formed the *Now you see it* exhibition in 2006.

Dannatt the collector: art and architecture

Thus Alfred Hallet sparked a life-long affinity to painting, drawing, artists and exhibitions and, through introducing the schoolboy Dannatt to the works and writing of Le Corbusier ("the master"), a preoccupation with architecture. A last year at school was spent mostly drawing and painting, as was one day a week in his first year as a student of architecture. This developed a visual awareness and a lasting habit of painting and sketching. "Gallery going became a part of life"—with, for instance, the "very heady stuff" of a Henry Moore and John Piper exhibition visited in 1939/40 whilst a student—so that regular visits to exhibitions soon led to friendships with artists and the buying of paintings: early on (1944–1945), a Robert McBryde ("a major work for all time", admired because it "carries a calmness" which reflects the "calm buildings" he so much likes), a Robert Colquhoun, a Ben Nicholson and a small Reg Butler. "I bought only when touched by some quality in the work—probably colour/shape initially but later spatial qualities related to architecture. John Tunnard for example, I was keen on for his depth of space."

His friendship with a group of avant-garde, abstract artists in London, which included Adrian Heath, Robert Adams, Victor Pasmore and Eduardo Paolozzi, from all of whom he was to acquire works, led to his involvement in a series of small exhibitions of the group's work (1952–1955). These exhibitions provided the opportunity to experiment with unconventional installations which chimed with the nature of the paintings.[64] They displayed the balanced asymmetries which were the hallmark of the English Free School and a corner stone of the Modern Movement.

Subsequent to the 1953 *20th Century Form—Painting, sculpture, architecture* exhibition, discussed earlier, he again collaborated with Bryan Robertson at the Whitechapel Gallery in a major Jackson Pollock exhibition, for which he designed a highly innovative setting, recently republished as an exemplar.[65] Contemporaneously, his editorship of the *Architects' Year Book*, which brought together architecture, art and engineering, gave the opportunity to publish the work of over 40 artists, known and unknown, including bill, le Corbusier, Pasmore, Bacon, Butler, Paolozzi, Hilton, Léger, Mondrian, Pollock, Rietveld, Braque, Hitchens, Lanyon, Klee, Sutherland, Heron and Moore.

From this experience, he was to later reflect

> I wonder at the general effect in our time of the painter-dominated movement 'de Stijl'. The spatial thing was important, but was it not there already? Stylistically (at a superficial level perhaps) but immensely pervasive, the influence seems nothing but baleful, directing attention again away from buildings as constructed of tangible material exposed to weather and people, to building as plastic art, painting and eventually as graphics. At the end of the line as photographs, light and shade, pattern not form, surface, not structure and material.[66]

Here, by default, as it were, is a powerful statement of his architectural position and intent. For Dannatt, the influence of art is not through theory but through experience—the way of seeing, the possibilities of colour, compositions, space, pattern, light, and texture that paintings, prints and drawings reveal.

Therefore, it was inevitable that, whilst working at the Fry, Drew office, he should have formed his close and lasting association and friendship with Patrick Heron, an almost exact contemporary and, at the time, art critic for *The New Statesman*, whom he met through a mutual friend. Heron wrote two major pieces for the *Architects' Year Books*—"The Visual Arts", quoted earlier, and "Space in Painting and Architecture"—and was represented by a number of paintings in Dannatt's buildings but, more significantly, his paintings in the collection show many affinities with the developing architecture.[67] For instance, in *St Ives Window*, bought in 1951, the dynamism of the composition with its balanced asymmetries, interpenetrations and diagonals are means of composing and structuring building plans and forms which Dannatt was to develop in interplay with his continuing, regular, geometric ordering; an interplay which is so characteristic of his architectural language.[68] These means of composition are employed, not for their own sake but in response to location and the creation of an appropriate sense

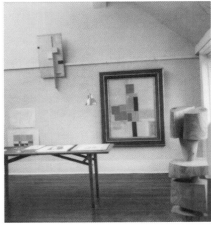

Weekend Exhibition at Adrian Heath's Studio, 1952. Works by Victor Pasmore and Robert Adams.

of place, as in the Riyadh Conference Centre and Hotel and the Victoria Gate building at Kew Gardens. The overlapping of planes and frames and transparencies and flows of light evident in Heron's painting are also equally strong characteristics of Dannatt's buildings. Last, but not least, Heron, "the consummate English colourist", in his paintings, and Dannatt, in his buildings, share a deep joy in colour, its choice and the precision in its use and placing—for "colour is the first thing I go for; colour turns me on" as Dannatt says about his attraction to any painting. Thus, he "sees Heron as 'representing an attitude to space and colour' that is directly relevant to architecture".[69]

But underlying all his architecture is that quiet repose—signalled by Piero della Francesca and Seurat and given presence in his everyday life through the acquisition of works as diverse as Robert Buhler's *The Moat at Hethel*—"a sensuous landscape, lake, reflections, trees sky merging in a slightly misty way... not architectural space... but space that holds mystery, and which might extend into the past"—and the sparse but rich geometric work by Patrick Scott at St Paul's School. This repose is related to the sense of permanence, the elemental, the eternal, noted before in relation to buildings such as The Society of Friends' Meeting House in Blackheath and the reordering of the chapel at St Paul's School, which incorporated a reredos composed by Scott of 15 panels, where only two are not identical.

Whilst the domestic interiors have the flows of space and light and the overlapping planes and transparencies to which Patrick Heron gives form in his paintings of interiors, they also have other qualities. These are embodied in the first painting he bought (in 1942), on impulse, an interior by Kenneth Rowntree, *Girl Drying Her Hair*—intimate, sensuous, sensual; a painting which is small but substantial in the evident substance of its paint and the weight of the figure and objects it portrays—tactile, architectural—yet alive with light, here interior light, the warm glow of an unseen gasfire. The painting is a domestic and English 'take' on Le Corbusier's definition of architecture as "the masterly, correct and magnificent play of masses brought together in light"—another pivot and continuity between the different worlds forming both his "inner landscape" and his architecture.[70]

There is a persistant fascination with the enduring nature of light, which is seen in the recent works of conservation and regeneration at Greenwich, which glow with the modulation and moulding of light shed against simple substantial forms (evoking Soane, perhaps). The effect of ever-changing but

constant light on thereby apparently ever-changing yet constant forms, chimes precisely with one of the more recent additions to the collection, max bill's *Strahlung aus rot*—for Dannatt, "The jewel in the collection—I would forsake all else for this." It is a picture about light, a picture reflective of the state of the viewer; a picture which, in its austerity and purity yet richness and brilliance of colour, illuminates a deeply engrained aspect of his "inner landscape" and character.

This aspect can be approached by comparing the Kenneth Rowntree and the max bill, for they exemplify not only the range of the collection but a shift in balance in the collecting from the painterly figurative via painterly abstraction to the minimalism of a 'hard-edged' abstraction. As Dannatt says, this is not a minimalism in terms of what is excluded (ie. the stripping out from the conventional or orthodox) but of what is included—of the choosing and placing of form and mark upon a blank canvas; one leaves emptiness, the other provides substance.

He is deeply aware of the question of communication which arises in these abstract paintings; paintings which are not abstractions from something (eg. nature) but abstract constructions, "appealing directly to spirit and eye and sensation"—the Constructive art of *Circle*. It is the same question which lies at the heart of the abstract, structural art of architecture.

There is a strong stream of the nonconformist (a Congregational upbringing with Quaker affinities) and hence the puritan (and thereby an affinity with the Purism of Le Corbusier and with Léger) in Dannatt's discussions of his collection—the interest in abstraction and light and the importance of the arts as a source of tranquility and contemplation, his oft used words, such as, wholeness, harmony (both within the picture and between the picture and its placing), calmness, profound calmness, infinite, authority, merging, reflection, and burden (of content and meaning, and therefore purpose).[71] All reflect a belief in a religious purpose and significance in life. Thus, art and architecture are seen as one, a consonance, and as a reflection of his deeper, religious roots in life. But for Dannatt, ever the nonconformist, that purpose and significance are seen in the everyday world—akin to an epithany: "One has a duty to look, a delight in looking and reflecting—the visual dialogue of the everyday... some anonymous work [seen] perhaps in a backstreet where you feel someone has thought

Kenneth Rowntree, *Girl Drying Her Hair*, 1942.
Courtesy The Whitworth Art Gallery.
© The Estate of the Artist.

and achieved poetry." No distinction need be made as to whether this refers to a building or a picture. Architecture (as all art), he says, has to be right, right the way through, not just a beautiful outside; "a building embraces all that can be described as mechanical, embodied in a formal language of space, form and material—that which can be described as poetic, and if need be, spiritual". Thus, he eschews the superficial and the self conscious search for the iconic.

Perhaps the most honorific place for a painting in any traditional home is on the chimney breast above the fireplace in the living-room—the hearth and heart, the place where the presentation of Dannatt's works will start—and here, Dannatt placed a painting by the Spanish artist, Francisco Lloréns, *Intimidad.* "Love at first sight, at an exhibition sponsored by BA at Olympia; I bought and carried away... and it found its true place here"; for others, at first sight, no more than a large, black square but, on contemplation, a painting which reveals great depth physically, in layers of paint, and metaphorically, in that the viewer may lose and find him or herself anew therein, with shifts of appearance and depth with shifting light; a painting created for contemplation, a painting, in Dannatt's phrase, of "high seriousness".

Conversely, rarely is a twinkle far from Dannatt's eye, a sense of irreverence and humour ("The Tate Modern—a building with ideas above its power station"—How true!) and a joy in the appetites of life, the pleasures of colour, form, geometry, light, pattern, texture.... So, a complex "inner landscape" is revealed, one within which the corporeal and the sublime, the quotidian and the heavenly are in constant interplay—to recall Eliot, "The complete consort dancing together"—and find expression in a quiet architecture of a timeless quality born of the act of building, for: "We must accept building as our bedrock, know it inside and out...."[72]

Left: Fernand Léger, *Woman's Head and Six Shapes*, 1952. Courtesy of The Whitworth Art Gallery. Private collection. © ADAGP, Paris, DACS, London, 2006.

Bottom: Robert Buhler, *The Moat at Hethell*, 1970. Courtesy of The Whitworth Art Gallery. © The Estate of the Artist/Bridgeman Art Library.

1. Dannatt, Trevor, "Architects' approach to architecture: Trevor Dannatt", *RIBA Journal*, March 1969, p. 98. (Available on the website www.trevordannatt.co.uk).
2. Eliot, TS, "Little Gidding", *Collected Poems 1909–1962*, London: Faber and Faber, 1963, p. 221.
3. Vitruvius, *De Architectura*, Bk. 1, Ch. 2, para. 5.
4. Wilson, Colin St John, "Sacred Games: The urn and the chamberpot", *Architectural Reflections: Studies in the philosophy and practice of architecture*, Manchester: Manchester Univerity Press, 2000, p. 193.
5. Dannatt, "Architects' approach", pp. 103–104.
6. Dannatt, "Architects' approach", p. 99; Fry, E Maxwell, "Housing and the Environment", *RIBA Journal*, August 1967, pp. 331–333.
7. Aalto, Alvar, "The RIBA Annual Discourse", *RIBA Journal*, May 1957, pp. 258–63.
8. Dannatt, "Architects' approach", p. 104.
9. Dannatt, Trevor, "Obituary: Denys Lasdun 1914–2001", *The Architectural Review*, February 2001, p. 27, p. 245.
10. Bronowski, Jacob, *The Identity of Man*, London: Heinemann, 1966, p. 48.
11. Venturi, Robert, *Complexity and Contradiction in Architecture*, New York: Museum of Modern Art, 1977; Wilson, "The ethics of architecture", *Architectural Reflections*, p. 41.
12. Alexander, Samuel, "Art and Instinct", *Philosophical and Literary Pieces*, London: Macmillan and Co., 1939, pp. 233–255; Martin, Leslie, "The Language of Architecture", *The Listener*, vol. 53, no. 1354, 10 February 1955, p. 233.
13. Martin, "The Language of Architecture".
14. Dannatt, "Architects' approach", p. 103.
15. Eagleton, like Alexander, Dannatt and this author, a professor at Manchester University, where Martin was a graduate; Eagleton, Terry, "How to read a poem", *The Times: Books*, 20 January 2007, p. 9; Eagleton, Terry, *How to Read a Poem*, Oxford: Blackwell Publishing, 2007.
16. Such a direct relationship may happen in speech as Eagleton describes in the shout of "Fire!"—where "the stabbing emphasis of the "F" consonant, followed by the long-drawn out wail of the vowels, mimics the motion of the fire itself, from its explosive beginning to the whoosh of its spreading".
17. Eagleton, "How to Read a Poem".
18. Dannatt quoted by John Welsh, *Building Design*, 21 August 1992, p. 21.
19. Stonehouse, Roger, *Colin St John Wilson: Buildings and Projects*, London: Black Dog Publishing, 2007; Wilson, Colin St John, "Architecture—public good and private necessity", *RIBA Journal*, 1979, vol. 86, no. 3, pp. 107–115.
20. Wilson, "Architecture—public good and private necessity", p. 115.
21. Dannatt, "Obituary: Lasdun".
22. Davies, Colin, "'Lambeth living, a community housing scheme", *The Architect*, August 1978, p. 27.
23. Dannatt, Trevor, "'Hourglass or quartz crystal?" *The Architectural Review*, December 1978, p. 370.
24. Martin, Leslie, "Notes on a developing architecture", *The Architectural Review*, July 1978, p. 17.
25. Smithson, Alison and Peter, *Without rhetoric: an architectural aesthetic 1955–72*, London: Latimer New Dimensions; Dannatt, Trevor, "Out of the ordinary", *The Architects' Journal*, 10 July 1974 (p. 249).
26. Dannatt, "Out of the ordinary".
27. Goldfinger, Ernö, "Auguste Perret 1874–1954", in *Architects' Year Book 7*, London: Eleka, 1956, p. 48.
28. Dannatt, "Out of the Ordinary".
29. Martin, Leslie, *Buildings and Ideas 1933–1983: From the studio of Leslie Martin and his Associates*, Cambridge: Cambridge University Press, 1983; Stonehouse, *Colin St John Wilson*.
30. Powers, Alan, "A House of Ideas", *Country Life*, 21 July 2005, pp. 66–69; Paterson Architects, "House at Three Seton Mains, East Lothian", *The Architects' Journal*, 9 January 2006, pp. 34–35.
31. Stonehouse, "Function-types, Formal Patterns, and Deeper Structures", *Colin St John Wilson*, pp. 35–37.
32. Stonehouse, Roger and Gerhard Stromberg, *The Architecture of the British Library at St Pancras*, London: E & FN Spon, 2004, pp. 46–48; Stonehouse, Roger, "Dwelling with the environment: The creation of sustainable buildings and sustaining situations through the layering of building form and detail", in *Dimensions of Sustainability*, Andrew Scott ed., London: E & FN Spon, 1998, pp. 127–131.
33. Wilson, "The Natural Imagination", *Architectural Reflections*, p. 12.
34. Dannatt, "Architects' approach", p. 104.
35. Dannatt, "Architects' approach", p. 98.
36. Benedikt, Michael, *For an Architecture of Reality*, New York: Lumen Books, 1987. pp. 2–4.
37. Dannatt, "Architects' approach", p. 103.
38. Dannatt, Trevor, "Peter Moro: an appreciation", *The Architects' Journal*, 22 October 1997, p. 28.
39. Powers, Alan, "Obituary: Peter Moro", *The Independent*, 21 October 1998.
40. Dannatt, Trevor, "Foreword", *Architects' Year Book 5*, London: Elek, 1953.
41. Martin, Leslie, "Introduction", in *Circle: constructive art in Britain 1934–40*, Jeremy Lewison ed., Cambridge: Kettle's Yard Gallery, 1982, p. 9; Martin, Leslie, "A Note in Science and Art", in *Architects' Year Book 2*, Trevor Dannatt ed., p. 9.
42. *Architects' Year Book 5*, p. 7.
43. Dannatt, Trevor, "Foreword", in Leslie Martin, *Buildings and Ideas*, p. 1.
44. Lethaby, WR, *Philip Webb and his work*, London: Oxford University Press, 1935.
45. MacLeod, Robert, *Style and society: architectural ideology in Britain 1835–1914*, London: RIBA Publications, 1971.
46. Martin, *Buildings and Ideas*, pp. 6–7.
47. Dannatt, "Foreword", *Buildings and Ideas*, p. 1; Dannatt, Trevor, in "Continuing Lines of Thought: The work and teachings of Sir Leslie Martin", Roger Stonehouse, *The Architects' Journal*, 5 October 1983, p.69.
48. Dannatt, "Foreword", *Buildings and Ideas*, pp. 1–2.
49. Martin, Leslie, "Architects' approach to architecture: Sir Leslie Martin", *RIBA Journal* May 1967, p.194.
50. Norberg-Schultz, Christian, *Intentions in Architecture*, London: Allen and Unwin, 1963; Dannatt, "Architects' approach", p. 103.
51. Dannatt, "Architects' approach", p.101.
52. Dannatt, Trevor, "Obituary: Colin Dollimore", *The Independent*, 20 August 1993.
53. Dannatt, Trevor, "Obituary: Denys Lasdun", *The Architectural Review*, December 1975, pp. 245–246.
54. Dannatt, "Architects' approach", p. 101.
55. Dannatt, "Architects' approach", p. 99.
56. Martin, Sir Leslie, and Colin St John Wilson, "The Collegiate Plan", *The Architectural Review*, vol. 126, July 1959, pp. 2–8.
57. Martin, *Buildings and Ideas*, p.20; Martin, "Architects' approach", p. 194.
58. Cowan, Peter, "Studies in the growth, change and ageing of buildings", *Bartlett Society Transactions*, 1962–1963, pp. 55–84.
59. Dannatt, "Architects' approach", p. 104.
60. Dannatt, "Architects' approach", p. 104.
61. Dannatt, "Architects' approach", p. 103.
62. Dannatt, Trevor, "A plea for quality", *Trevor Dannatt: buildings and interiors 1951/72*, London: Lund Humphries, 1972, p. 10.
63. Heron, Patrick, "The Visual Arts", *Architects' Year Book 3*, London: Elek, 1949, p. 21.
64. Grieve, Alastair, "Towards an art of environment: exhibitions and publications by a group of avant-garde abstract artists in London 1951–55", *The Burlington Magazine*, November 1990 , pp. 773–781.
65. Newhouse, Victoria, *Art and the Power of Placement*, New York: Monacelli Press, 2005, pp. 175–179.
66. Dannatt, "Architects' approach", p. 103.
67. Heron, Patrick, "Space in Painting and Architecture", *Architects' Year Book 5*, London: Elek, 1953, pp. 19–26.
68. In contrast, Martin maintained a regular 'classical' ordering and it is perhaps telling that Dannatt had tried to persuade him to commission Heron for a tapestry in the Royal Festival Hall, but Martin did not come to appreciate Heron until he started working with abstract squares.
69. Croft, Catherine, "Lifelong Collections", *Building Design*, 17 February 2006, p. 20.
70. Le Corbusier, *Towards a New Architecture*, London: The Architectural Press, 1946, p. 31.
71. A continuous affinity, from a Légeresque painting done at school to a Léger as one of the most recent acquisitions.
72. Dannatt, "Architects' approach", p. 104.

max bill, *Strahlung aus rot*, 1972/1973.
Courtesy The Whitworth Art Gallery. © DACS, 2006.

A Shilling Life [1]
Inner Landscape—Sacred Objects
Trevor Dannatt

Robson, Lyndale, London SE3, c. 1880.

The Sibelius sauna, Aino, Finland.

Lime works, North Downs, Kent, 1940.

"Inner landscape." A tenable notion but open to wide interpretation: it could be a pervading four dimensional panorama, embracing the close, the far, the broad and the intimate, all that the senses bring into one's conscious and unconscious being—sometimes clear, immediately available, sometimes veiled, censored perhaps, not so handy. All stashed away but hibernating for future use to fertilize and succour the creative process.

There are specific things, things seen whether forms or spaces, canvas or constructions and imponderables, flushes of feeling engendered, perhaps by words or music or the humbler senses, magic conjunctions and a surge of delight "the moment in the draughty church at smokefall".[2]

How far such residues affect the rational process of design (in so far as it is rational) remains an open question. Specific things can be tracked down, not so the resonances from the senses.

> The OED helps, defines what is sought, thus
> "inner" gives (2) "mental or spiritual—of thoughts, of feelings not expressed".
> "landscape" gives (3) "the distinctive features of a sphere of intellectual activity".

Fine definitions but one questions whether it is germane to explore architectural consciousness and sources; better perhaps just to quote Wordsworth:

> Who knows the individual hour in which
> His habits were first sown, even as a seed,
> Who that shall point as with a wand and say
> This portion of the river of my mind
> Came from the yon fountain?[3]

How far can one explore? Dispatches often seem after the event. All that pertains to the senses, all may be mustered in the design process, thus the sensuous conjunction of materials, the sound of a surface, the spill of light, the flow of space, the play of forms, the galb of a pot or a profile of a table edge or a moulding.

Maybe the caves and grottos of the inner landscape are best left alone, it is easier to remain with the more exposed features, identifying only some that have shaped one's consciousness, informing a general direction rather than specific projects.

Like any landscape there is terrain, natural features and climate and there are growths from seeds and cuttings. A rich, diverse, often seemingly contradictory assembly. Can George Borrow co-habit with Hawksmoor?

In the nature of things the tendency is toward autobiography—upbringing, education and experience. So one muses over the landscape and the empathy that has stored certain features, willy-nilly.

At school, fourth form, a holiday task to read *Lavengro*.[4] I was captivated, the spell of words…. "There's night and day, brother, both sweet things; sun, moon, and stars, brother, all sweet things; there's likewise a wind on the heath…."

Two years later, in a school play 'Old English' a simple stage direction.[5] "[Meller, who has drawn back the curtain and opened the window disclosing the shapes of dark trees and the grape bloom sky of a mild moist night….]" At chapel a children's address. "The beautiful silver vessel shining without, but neglected and unclean within." (Interpret as you will!)

The earlier landscape is perhaps the more interesting. There are people, words, ideas, paintings, music, places and buildings, lists might be prepared but there must be honesty, avoiding the 'conceit of knowing'.

These examples above were infusions and others followed, words and music, places and structures. Hearing Schönberg's *Transfigured Night* in wartime, protected by a Morrison shelter, Sibelius discovered early in the war when the Soviet Union was attacking Finland. "Rarely, rarely comest thou spirit of delight" and also much later hearing broadcast Eliot's *Four Quartets*. Or the other pole, the delight of the vernacular of a Kent lime works, under the North Downs. A greenhouse or a garden building, the Saltash bridge. A shed in the Pyrénées, the lake journey to Jyväskylä with the silence of the forest edge landing stages. Discovering Piero della Francesca and Seurat, twinned in my consciousness, Goya's *Fourth of May*. Corbusier receiving the Royal Gold Medal at the RIBA. The first visit to Christ Church, Spitalfields, in 1942 dusty autumn light and the overwhelming impact of that majestic interior of european scale. Then six years later Torcello Cathedral, after Brunelleschi in Florence. But also Street's Law Courts, Comper's St Cyprians, Clarence Gate, Westminster Cathedral, Villa Savoye and Fallingwater. Many others.... Different qualities abiding but common to all poetry and the poetry of structured space, form and the magic of light.

In an exhibition catalogue introduction I attempted an account of formative things that led to the appreciation of painting and sculpture, in particular I wrote of Alfred Hallet a student art teacher from the Royal College at school who became a friend and who encouraged me, and who revealed the Impressionists, and all that followed, took me to galleries, told me of Le Corbusier and *Vers une Architecture*, a revelation.[6] However, I think my awareness of 'fine buildings' had already begun. Living in Blackheath I was familiar with its individual Georgian houses, groups such as The Paragon and the earlier Morden College and of course the Queen's House and the Royal Naval College buildings. We were very proud of our buildings, our Heath and Park which I traversed daily, enjoying the enclosure of the Park and in contrast the open Heath crossed to Lewisham and the "School on the Hill".

The Blackheath years were punctuated by Easter visits to Yorkshire centred on Pudsey, my mother's home. The grimy but lively contrast was enjoyed—steam trains, gas lighting, big mill buildings, and mill dams, channels running with vivid dye colour set in fields of rhubarb. For summer holidays Father always launched out and we went regularly to the Grand Hotel Britannia at Vlissingen in south Holland, which was good Dutch bourgeois sophistication in a richly cultivated island where in sober contrast farmers, wives and children still wore traditional clothes and went to market in Middelburg every Thursday. Surely for me leading to the love of de Hooch and the church interiors of Saenredam, a clarity first sensed in the fine church at Veere.

IK Brunel, Royal Albert Bridge, Saltash, 1859.
© University of Aberdeen. Wilson Archive.

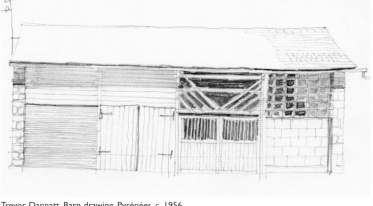

Trevor Dannatt, Barn drawing, Pyrénées, c. 1956.

Nicolas Hawksmoor, Christ Church,
Spitalfields, 1714–1729.

Torcello Cathedral, Veneto, eleventh century.

Brunelleschi, Pazzi Chapel, Florence, 1420.

Ninian Comper, St Cyprians, Clarence Gate,
London NW1, 1902–1903.

Alfred Hallet, *Landscape*, c. 1938.

Inigo Jones, Queen's House, Greenwich, 1617–1663.

Roan School, Greenwich, Sir Banister Fletcher and PB Dannatt, 1926.

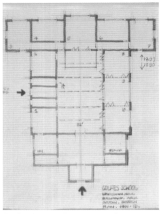

Colfe's School, plan, nineteenth century.

Pieter de Hooch, *A woman and her maid in a courtyard*. © The National Gallery.

Pieter Saenredam, St Adolphus Church, Assendelft, 1649, Rijksmuseum.

Church of Our Lady, Veere, Holland, fifteenth–sixteenth century.

Closer to home we had the Royal Observatory and Vanbrugh Castle and nearby my architectural uncle PB Dannatt had been co-architect with Banister Fletcher on the new Roan School building, 1926. At Greenwich the Queen Anne Court of the Royal Naval College had a much visited ship model gallery and then there was the river providing endless interest, tugs, lighters, sailing barges, steamers constantly passing.... The docks across the river seen from Maze hill displayed the elegant livery of the Union Castle Line ships. In the park one was always discovering new areas, mysterious reservoirs, conduit heads and secret exits, grotesque ancient Spanish chestnuts Returning from school in winter the darkening park resounded with the Park Keepers' cries of "All out." A distant street light gave me a fix to Maze Hill gate and so home.

Later years, bussing from New Cross station, the 53 breasted Blackheath Hill, a refreshing moment, the Heath spread out before one. To the east, the Park walls and the Ranger's House, the vast expanse of sky and Shooters Hill beyond, with its modest but memorable water tower, breaking the skyline.

The whole area, the then Boroughs of Lewisham, Deptford, Greenwich and Woolwich, partly on the Thames flood plain, partly on the Blackheath eminence; was an extraordinarily rich urban area, with its congested housing and industry and considerable open spaces on the edge of Kent where one could see blue hills beyond, pierced by the twin towers of the Crystal Palace.

Hallet brought painting and all that richness into my life and encouraged by example to see, draw and paint, so that my last year at school was mostly art room. Starting at the Polytechnic School of Architecture in 1938 with some smattering of the subject, within a few weeks I knew it was what I wanted to do. I was "summoned by buildings".

In retrospect I think we enjoyed a good course and were brought forward, as it were, from raw beginnings. Some lecturers leavened the technical bias, more so in later years though in the first year the ex-Cambridge architect Peter Smith (who employed me for a few weeks at the end of first year) pointed us in the direction of history and the literature of architecture.[7] First year was livened by freehand drawing one day a week at the Victoria and Albert and *plein air* in summer term and there were regular sketch design days with subjects varied between the constructive and the expressive.

My first year reading included Lethaby's *Life of Philip Webb* which I found inspirational, Summerson's *John Nash*, Kenneth Clark's *Gothic Revival*. But there were "picture books"—Antonin Raymond's work in Japan, Harada's *Lesson of Japanese Architecture*, Lurcat's book on *Groupe Scolaire de Villejuif*, then *Church Builders of the 19th Century*—quite a mix up really, but *Vers une...* held one, that most vibrant work, and needless to say, Le Corbusier was a profound influence through his 'works and words', extended over the years through the *Oeuvre Complete* volumes. These I perused thoroughly, explored plan, section, elevation, checking the position of every photograph, every detail.

Alfred Roth's *The New Architecture* provided an antidote with its catholic selection of Modern Architecture, and I was engaged by the Dutch publication of Van Loghem through which I discovered the Berlage building in London, still a sacred object![8]

In second year there was ex-Liverpool PG Freeman, a great perspectivist and runner up in the Bexhill Pavilion competition. An admirable teacher. Briefly Hubert Bennett (too handsome), much later architect to the LCC, George Pace (who brought us to All Saints, Margaret Street). Emil Scherrer (ex-Manchester, dapper and civilised) who in third year taught theory based on *Space, Time and Architecture*, published in 1941, and especially Peter Moro who joined the school when I was in third year with his house at Birdham as his passport to our respect and who five or six years later impressed me and other contemporaries into the London County Council's Architects' Department Festival Hall group under Leslie Martin and himself.[9]

The School of Architecture was close to the RIBA and its library. We enjoyed its freedom, the foreign journals and the most helpful librarians presided over by the distinguished and somehow glamourous Edward Carter, in his way a role model.

The Architectural Review provided a heady mix of information and opinion, even in wartime. JM Richards, Morton Shand (the Finnish connection!) John Betjeman, Paul Nash, Robert Byron et al, and published the most interesting new work with some attempt at critical analysis. Highlights being Highpoint 1 and 2, Richmond School, (Denis Clarke-Hall), Impington Village College, Chermayeff's house at Halland. Many other modern houses were featured, and there was Simpsons Piccadilly, the Gilbey building and so on.

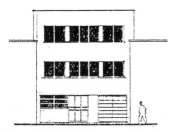

Peter Chandler Smith, house in Albion Mews, London W2, 1936.

House detail (from Harada, *The Lesson of Japanese Architecture*).

Antonin Raymond, fireplace, detail.

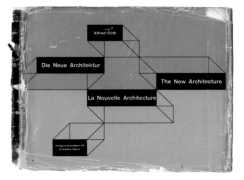

Alfred Roth, *The New Architecture*, dust jacket, 1945.

Berlage, WH Müller Building, London, 1915.

Peter Moro, house at Birdham, 1938.

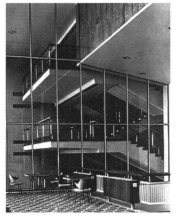

LCC Architects' Department, Royal Festival Hall, stair detail, 1951.

HT Cadbury Brown, railway ticket office, 1936.
Courtesy of the British Architectural Library.

Denis Clarke-Hall, school at Richmond, York, 1939. Courtesy of *The Architectural Review*.

Maxwell Fry, Sun House, Frognal, 1955.

EG Asplund, Stockholm Veterinary Institute, 1933–1937.

Robert MacBryde, *Mexican Table*, 1943.

Maxwell Fry, obviously a leader, engaged our imagination and the loose composition and charm of detail of the various houses I found very felicitous—balconies, screens, porches, sunrooms. Delicate secondary elements of architecture that through photography appeared to be primary. Not so with Lubetkin and Tecton and Peter Moro who provided the corrective to our rather wimpish planning and ordering. Like all students we were probably more influenced by journals than staff when it came to design, though journals then had more meat and were less celebrity oriented. Staff were equally committed and learning themselves and a London tour revealed pristine buildings in a grimy world. There was much to search out in the capital and Home Counties. New work was still being published in 1940 and later, editors were able to scrape up interesting war time buildings and notable histories, or obituaries, Morton Shand's of Asplund for instance.[10]

Graded medically low and uncalled up, after passing Part 2 and a diminished Part 3, I spent a year on the Polytechnic staff and then moved into practice at Jane Drew's office (soon to become Fry, Drew post-war) where we were engaged on work of doubtful national importance, that around 1944 included an officially approved post-war kitchens study and show when I moved briefly to the office of Bronek Katz, architect for the exhibition. At the Drew office I worked with the old but sprightly FL Marcus, the Berlin architect, an austere mentor, respected and revered.

More importantly I became involved in the *Architects' Year Book* established by the publisher Paul Elek, who scented out Jane Drew as a lively editor. I was quickly involved as assistant editor, corralling diverse contributors from home and abroad. In all I produced ten numbers taking over as Editor from volume 3 with an editorial board consisting of Ove Arup, Jane Drew, Herbert Read and Maxwell Fry.

Leaving Fry Drew in 1948 I joined the Festival Hall Group, where despite immense pressure there was a more reflective approach and a shared discipline and the high hopes of a group committed to the achievement of the first post-war major public building.[11] A joyous and widening experience under two fine architects.

After three years, in 1952 private practice, always my objective, began in earnest. I like to think, as a way of life rather than a means of life.

Kindly received in a corner of Gordon and Ursula Bowyer's Blandford Street Office, already established through their Festival of Britain commission (Sport's Section) but now with free space.

Gordon and I had travelled to Sweden together in 1946 on the pristine MV Saga from Tilbury, reached from St Pancras Station through the bombed east London landscape. Sweden was a test bed for the new architecture and we were not disappointed. Gothenburg first and its civic qualities the Concert Hall/Theatre Group with the Carl Milles fountain and then Asplund's Law Courts extension of reticent elevations and superb interiors.

Then Stockholm, the whole ambience of a fresh sparkling city. Ostberg first, then the Library and for me the more accessible Veterinary Institute and of course the Woodland Crematorium. Through the *Architects' Year Book* and other contacts we saw something of the everyday building scene as well as receiving fine entertainment, and returned to England inspired with a sense of standards to be achieved, and an art work each. We were both collectors and had already bought works by Nicholson, Colquhoun, and MacBryde. Others followed and over the years became a 'collection' of works, that now seem very much part of the inner landscape.

Starting seriously in practice, one might say the most formative period was over, the topography of the inner landscape was laid down. What followed was a period of modest commercial work, coffee bars, shop interiors, several years as designer at Dickins and Jones Store with the opportunity to try out ideas, both planning and visual. The break came later when Leslie Martin invited me to join with him in the development of a women's Hall of Residence at Leicester University which enabled me to take an office in nearby Crawford Street. To revert, briefly in the spring of 1947 I first visited Denmark as the guest of Finn Juhl whom I had met through the Fry Drew office leading to a close friendship. These were magic days of blue skies, gentle hills and the early green of beech trees. I saw buildings, old and new, Lauritzen's Radio House, early houses of Jacobsen and his Bellavista development, Kronborg Castle, Frendensborg Castle. I also learnt of the delightful summerhouse, Liselund, near Møn (only visited some years later) and, of course, Finn Juhl's own house in Ordrup. I appreciated the great gifts of Danish architects both in building and in the applied arts, and I was introduced to the fine paintings of such as Købke, Hammershøi, Lundstrøm and many others, unknown in the UK. Far from

Finn Juhl's own house, 1945.

Kronborg Castle, Denmark, Knight's Hall, sixteenth century.

Liselund, Möen, Denmark.

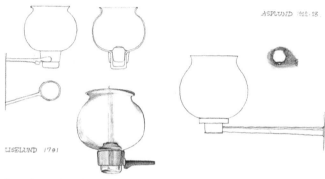

Trevor Dannatt, Light fitting from Liselund, 1791 (left), and by EG Asplund, 1922–1923, (right).

Vilhelm Hammershøi, interior, 1908, Åarhus Kunstmuseum, Denmark.

Vilhelm Lundstrøm, *Opstilling*, 1938.

being provincial there was a sophisticated, critical and popular visual culture extending from the public domain to the intimate domestic scene.

Finland had already made its mark pre-war through the Museum of Modern Art publication on Aalto as well as Morton Shand's accounts in *The Architectural Review*, but it was not until 1956 that I went to Finland and soon after published accounts in *Architectural Design* and the *Architects' Year Book*.[12]

Scandinavia was a pervasive influence through many buildings, interiors, furniture and artefacts. All embodying thought, care for the human dimension, creativity and plastic imagination, always well put together with colour and tactile sensibility.

Aalto was surely exploring his inner landscape with his mountain doodling when developing the Viipuri Library, to me more valid than Mendelsohn sketching building types whilst Beethoven Quartets were played in the next room yet despite this I find a correspondence between music and architecture, qualities of order and development, of timeless presence inviting a sort of listening rather than just seeing.[13]

There must be different inner landscapes. At least one that can store the diversity of built form available to a perceptive and informed eye, and another that is more discriminating, discerns the underlying *geist* of something, whether ancient or modern

Buildings are infinitely interesting and it is not possible to move without assessing what is passing by, however grotty, however magnificent. Insofar as the inner landscape is laid down from diverse sources over various periods of work over time and through the senses, forming what one might call architectural consciousness, not concerned with procedures, for those come with apprenticeship, but deeply with values and judgment, aesthetic choice, the formation of a certain sensibility, a landscape of sacred objects, consciously accessible, others less specific, obscure, more geological.

I have tried to distinguish between the specific and the general. The illustrations however small indicate space and form but also are reminders of the numinous qualities of the originals.

"What I have written I have written" but I continue to question, while images kaleidoscope around when called in from some sort of mental space, let us call it an inner landscape, though perhaps not quite "the distinctive features of a sphere of intellectual activity".

Trevor Dannatt at Jyväskylä, Finland, 1998.

Derelict building, Hampstead Road, London.

1. Auden, WH, "A shilling life will give you all the facts".
2. Eliot, TS, "Burnt Norton".
3. *Wordsworth*, "The Prelude", Book 11, Harmondsworth: Penguin Books 1971, pp. 211–215.
4. Borrow, George, *Lavengro*, The People's Library, 1900.
5. Galsworthy, John, *Old English* (1924), *Ten Famous Plays*, London: Duckworth, 1941.
6. "Now you see it", The Whitworth Art Gallery, Manchester, 2006.
7. Peter Chandler Smith, architect and landscape painter, 1902–1983.
8. *bouwen holland-nieuwe zakelijkheid. kosmos*, Amsterdam, 1932.
9. *The Architectural Review*, 1941.
10. *The Architectural Review*, May 1941.
11. McKean, John, *The Royal Festival Hall*, London: Phaidon 1992.
12. *Architectural Design*, April 1957; *Architects' Year Book 8*, 1957.
13. Whittick, Arnold, *Eric Mendelsohn*, London: Faber and Faber.

Works

1 Hearth

Pitcorthie House, fireplace and living room.

Just as Dannatt's collection of works of art started with a private, prosaic moment in front of a fire, raised to poetry by Kenneth Rowntree, this collection of his works of architecture starts with the hearth, that once everyday place of intimacy, gathering, warmth, reflection and retreat for which the contemporary world of centrally-heated architecture has found no substitute but which is a constant in his domestic and residential works from the earliest to the most recent.

As the Smithsons wrote in *Without rhetoric: an architectural aesthetic 1955–72*, and Dannatt quoted in his review of their book: "Since the late middle ages the best architects have been able to deal with fire, the fireplace, as idea... the architecture of common eighteenth and nineteenth century English rooms is built up around the fire*place*; it orientates the user... [its] removal destroys the meaning of the English domestic room...."[1] For Dannatt, the fireplace is

Adrian Heath's Studio, Charlotte Street, Weekend Exhibition, 1952.

never a mere incident in the room, it is always a focus (though not necessarily symmetrically positioned) and always an integral part of the room's language of forms. As so often in these works, the compositional modes are Janus-like: either, as in the earliest fireplaces, classically trabeated with stripped elemental forms, which are clearly articulated and sometimes overlapping, and display to full advantage the nature of the materials; or, balanced asymmetries of notches, slots and overlapping blocks (and, later, diagonals as at Blackheath). These latter had their roots in Dannatt's earliest exhibition compositions for Adrian Heath—one of which, brought the existing fireplace in to play—and are either sculpturally incised within the fairfaced brickwork or a plastered surface or raised to the level of a sculptural object as a conversation-piece in the Ambassador's Residence in Riyadh.

Other fireplaces arise from a different tradition: the rustic ingle-nook, that intimate space within the wider space of a room, which had inspired Frank Lloyd Wright, as had the massive, associated chimney, with the "fire burning deep in the masonry of the house itself", the experiential and compositional anchor for the house.[2] The Leicester University Hall of Residence fireplaces are the most explicit examples; whilst at the Plante House, a quasi-ingle-nook fireplace is formed as a free standing object, mediating between inside and outside and providing both internal and external hearths; and at Pitcorthie House, the tall, dominant chimney, by contrasting with the house's low horizontal form, signals and pinions the house in the landscape and forms the pivot for the counterposed monopitch roofs.

Detail, mantel at Collin Home.

1. Dannatt, Trevor, "Out of the ordinary", *The Architects' Journal*, 10 July 1974.
2. Kaufmann Jnr, E, "Precedent and progress in the work of Frank Lloyd Wright" in Edgar Kaufmann Jnr. ed., *Nine Commentaries on Frank Lloyd Wright*, Cambridge: Architectural History Foundation and MIT Press, 1989; Wright, Frank Lloyd, "Prairie Architecture" in Edgar Kaufmann and R Raeburn eds., *Frank Lloyd Wright: Writings and Buildings*, Cleveland: Meridian, 1960.

Symmetrical and trabeated hearths

Fireplace at Collin Home.

Talfourd Road, fireplace 1.

Talfourd Road, fireplace 2.

St Mary's Grove, fireplace 1.

St Mary's Grove, fireplace 2.

Balanced asymmetrical

Wood burning stove, Bowman Studio.

Laslett House, fireplace.

Trinity Hall, fireplace.

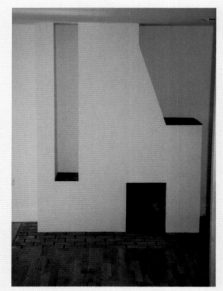

Blackheath, fireplace.

Embassy Residence, fireplace.

Blackheath, fireplace and stair.

Inglenooks

Plante House, interior fireplace.

Plante House, exterior fireplace.

Pitcorthie House, living room.

Hall of Residence, Leicester University.

2   Domestication

Studio extension, London N1, garden side.

The enduring qualities of the architecture were established quickly in the earliest domestic conversions and extensions—a simplicity of geometrical form, a play of horizontal and vertical, an openness and flow of space, washes of natural light, a lightness and sureness of touch, axial views through sequences of spaces and rooms, a rich but subtle use of colours, a totality of design including the design and choice of furniture, fabrics and fittings, and a considered and enriching placement of works of art. All are employed in the creation of places of a quiet, calming comfort; this is no self-indulgent, manifesto architecture, where form overrides practicality. All are to be seen in the context of the prevailing, upholstered fussiness of the late 1940s and early 1950s; and in this there is the bringing in to everyday form of the revolutionary transformations which had been published in *Circle* and have since become so commonplace as to be unremarkable.

The tone was set in 1950 in the completion of the conversion of an oasthouse, where Dannatt was fortunate in adding to the work of FL Marcus, the former Berlin architect, with whom he worked at Fry, Drew and who had developed a "clear and austere style... notable for its artistic economy and directness", as he put it in Marcus' obituary.

Throughout these conversions and extensions, the relaxed, "common word" is seen, and just as 'informal' is the literal opposite of 'formal', so, informality is the key. But this is not a casual informality—witness the carefully balanced asymmetries of the study for Dr Malnick, 1948–1949. The numerous, calming, horizontal planes are set against the single, taut, thin, white, vertical pole, which supports the flexible lighting. The horizontal, landscape-proportioned window is formed to create a view of the Greenwich Park landscape, its horizontality emphasised by the sliding, horizontally-louvred shutter.

The long, low, calming, horizontal plane is used again in the Sunhurst bedroom, but here set against an axially placed, veiled, rectangular window (its centrally placed mullion balancing horizontality with verticality), which, in turn, is set between, and within, continuous horizontal runs of vertically draped curtain, so that, when they are closed, the horizontal plane of the dressing table forms a continuous dado. This is good, well-structured prose of a high order. Like all good prose, it doesn't get in the way of living but yet it brings quiet delight. Only on analysis does the sophistication of its ordering construction become evident.

Everywhere the influence of contemporary art is evident, for instance: the Spry demonstration kitchen, 1954—a rigorous functional problem but, as realised, very reminiscent of Rietveld's three-dimensional, orthogonal interlocking of lines and simply-coloured planes; the interplay of the painting, its placing, and the architecture of its surroundings at Sunhurst, 1962; and the radiogram, 1950, where Ben Nicolson's Constructivist language of form raised the object to the status of a "formal word" as appropriate to an object of such contemporary reverence.

The Constructivist influence is also clear in the light fittings—simple, yet complex, geometrical forms arising directly from the function of masking and directing light and the means of construction. Whilst the outdoor terrace chair, 1949, takes the same separation of elements and materials but also brings into play the natural, reclining repose of the furniture of Dannatt's good friend, Finn Juhl, played against an appropriately athletic, dynamic structure.

As so often for architects, an extension to his own home provided the opportunity to extend and establish his formal language. Externally, the interplay of simply, but vigorously, modelled planes of brick and lead forms a robust object, which holds its own in scale with the much larger house and, in the tradition of all eighteenth and nineteenth century terraces, is formal at the front and informal at the back. Internally, there is a play of solid, void and screen, and a flow of space between levels, whilst a protected eyrie is formed, from which to look out reflectively into the trees.

House & Garden, cover, November 1956.

Talfourd Road, dining room, 1999.

One room flat, 1948.

Richard Church House
(completion)
Marden, Kent
1950

This house was originally an oast house group consisting of square and circular kilns with a connecting barn.

Partially converted in 1939 the completion was entirely concerned with the barn and consisted of planning new bedrooms and bathrooms in the upper part, a spiral stair to the second floor study and altering the ground floor to provide main entrance, etc..

The simple character and space of the old building was retained—by open planning with glazed screens and doors, by exposing much of the main structure and using everyday materials. The luxury is in spaciousness and clarity—qualities established in the original conversion by the architect, FL Marcus.

Section.

Above: Upper hallway.

Right: Bedroom and stair to the study at second floor.

Interiors at Eynsford
Kent
1962

The replanning of two separate first floor rooms in the home of Mr and Mrs JH Pedersen included the interior design and selection of furniture and furnishings.

The bedrooms have separate entrances from the hallway, but are connected by a wide doorway with pivoted panel, plus a narrow fixed strip of glass ensuring visual continuity. The separating wall forms a large cupboard to the main room. Opposite, the dressing table fitment extends the full width of the room. The centre has a flap-up top with mirror, revealing a two-depth compartment.

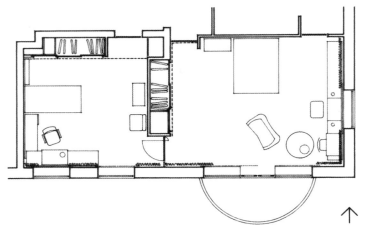

Clockwise, from top left: View from the small to main bedroom; Main bedroom, with dressing table; View from the main to small bedroom; Plan.

Bowman Studio, Twyford, perspective drawing, 1957.

Bowman Studio, gallery detail.

Doctor Malnick, interior, 1953.

Talfourd Road, room divider.

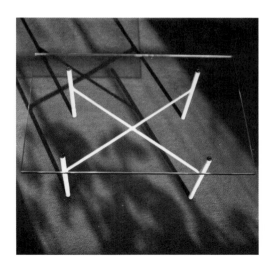

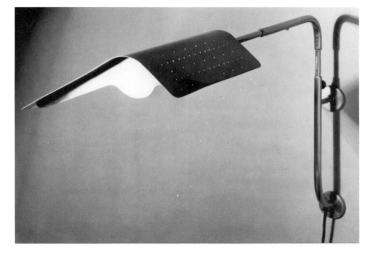

Clockwise, from top left: Furniture and
fittings—Glass table, 1955; Light fittings, 1947;
Radiogram, 1950; Terrace chair, 1949;
Spry Kitchen, 1954.

Studio Extension
London N1
1980

Built at the side of the early Victorian house, the extension partly embraces the existing porch and provides a garage with studio over. This is some 90 cm higher than the main floor of the house and reached by a landing and nicely adjusted steps within the room. On the street side there is a protected writing place with high level window and a narrow full height window alongside. On the other side there is a virtual bay window overlooking the garden with a solid door beside it to a small balcony and steel stair down. In contrast the glazing opposite the entrance is close mullioned. The flat roof is of timber construction and has a wide lead-clad fascia which forms part of the elevational composition with the porch.

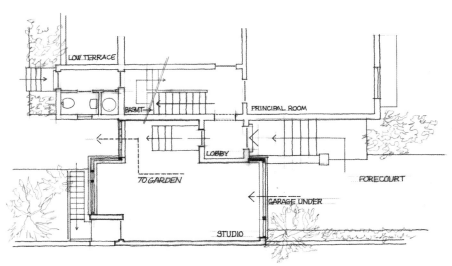

Opposite top left: Rear view and exit to
the garden.

Opposite bottom left: Plan.

Opposite right: View from the street.
Left: Detail of the rear window, with entry
steps on the right.

Right: Entrance to the studio from the
entrance porch, with view towards the front.

3   House

Pitcorthie House, junction of the gallery and main room.

Between his student project in 1941 and 2007, Dannatt designed over 20 one-off houses. All but two are the "common word" prose of everyday living—the exceptions being the arcadian villa of the Laslett House and, in Riyadh, the "formal word" of the Ambassador's residence (which will be considered as part of the Embassy together with the other houses for staff designed by Colin Dollimore). All are divided into two or more constituent block-like elements, which either intersect or slide by one another. By these means the scale of the building is broken down (often aided by giving the different elements counterposing mono-pitch roofs) and sheltered and differentiated outdoor spaces may be formed (sometimes on the flat roof of one of the elements), thereby integrating inside and outside spaces and house and garden.

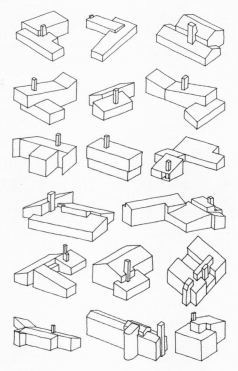

In these house designs, other recurrent compositional patterns (the tropes of literature) are established: the diagonal—either to open up and subtly orientate circulation or to react to the site geometry or both;

the split level—in essence, a diagonal used for the same purposes in section; the pinioning, large chimney stack; and the living space composed around the central or offset axis of the fireplace—to calm and control the room as a whole by means of the central axis or to form places of different milieu within one space by means of the offset axis.

The inevitable echoes from earlier reading and publishing are evident. For instance, in the proposed annex for the Laslett House, 1996, the overall parti, the use of the diagonal and the minor inflection of the east, datum wall, are all to be seen in a small house in Noordwijk by Brinkman and van der Vlugt, published in *Circle* in 1937—"where, perhaps, I 'read' the illustrations with more understanding than the text".

Whilst, at the Plante House, 1960, its parti of grouped, monopitched blocks is seen in a house at Ordrup Krat by Finn Juhl, which Dannatt included in the *Architects' Year Book 2*, in 1947.

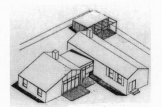 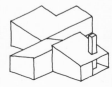

The Plante House's bedroom block and livingroom block are linked by a separately expressed kitchen and entrance, ie. the social, functional and formal hub of the house, with an associated courtyard formed between the elements as the building steps gently up the contours of the site. The offsetting of this hub allows the house to be entered in the middle, separating but linking the private and communal areas. The quasi-ingle-nook fireplace terminates the sequence of movement through the house in the house's lowest, most contained space, as the ceiling slopes down with

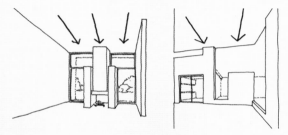

the roof, whilst giving views and access to the garden through the inside-outside space of a protected terrace (the view to the outside world emphasising, by contrast, the protective containment, as is the way with all true ingle-nooks). This containment is also contrasted within the room, as the ceiling slopes away and up to the soaring, full height, cutaway, south-facing corner—a form of conservatory—as the sun floods in and the space flows out to the courtyard beyond and to the adjacent open-plan kitchen, through a sliding glass screen. All is calm, quiet, unflamboyant, commonplace, ordinary, yet that heightened sense of ordinariness, which awakens the senses and satisfies the needs within a house for a feeling of protection and the reflective raising of the eyes to the outside world.

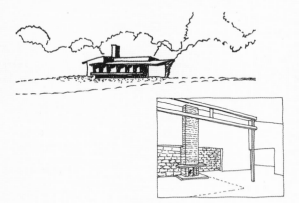

Pitcorthie House, 1965, takes a very different approach in its composition of elements. Whereas Plante rambles gently, but purposefully, through a suburban garden, Pitcorthie, on its exposed Scottish site with sweeping views to the sea, gathers its blocks of accommodation together for protection, huddled around a core of fireplace, kitchen, and bathrooms, and

pinioned by a great chimney stack, all set on a podium (the site of an earlier house). Oversailing roofs and walls extending out into the landscape to form protected outside areas recall Frank Lloyd Wright, as do the hearth and stack at the heart of the house—but there is something else. As Hildebrand describes, the attraction of many of Wright's houses can be attributed to the layering of space in degrees of enclosure, resulting in the ability to look to the outside from the protection of the hearth.[1] An attraction and satisfaction which Wilson so plausibly explained through the "natural imagination".[2] Here there is both the containment around the fire, signalled by the single column and the change from painted to natural stone, yet with layered views to the outside, and a 'long gallery'.

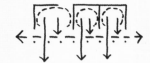

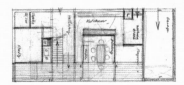

This latter, another transformation of a traditional element, Elizabethan in origin, is a kind of glazed veranda or loggia, which links a sequence of rooms, allowing a flow of space through the house, an open, horizontal sweep of view to the level horizon of the sea beyond, and, crucially, a mediating layer, inside yet seemingly also of the outside, which increases the sense of containment with retreat into the dining room, study or bedroom.

The precursor of this gallery is to be found in a sketch scheme for the Pappworth House, 1960. This was cousin of the Laslett House, one of only two exceptions to the extensive and extended family of houses formed of juxtaposed mono- or dual-pitched elements.[3] The Laslett House, 1958, also departs, appropriately, from the informal, "common word" of the domestic language of the other houses, in being a formal, arcadian pavilion, originally surrounded by meadow. It has the contemporary timeless quality discussed in "The Complete Consort". As a free-standing single cuboid, it is, again, Janus-like—both Palladian and Corbusian. Palladio is also evident in the ground floor's axial planning in an a-b-a composition (also used by Martin in a 1938 vicarage in Rock, Northumberland—unknown by Dannatt—and, of course, by Le Corbusier, as Colin Rowe had shown in 1947).[4] And Le Corbusier's influence is also seen in the spatial interplay of levels within the taut surfaces of a box (the second of his four types of composition, as used for the Villa Stein).

> It was my second house commission... an opportunity to put ideals of architectural design into practice, ideals gained through student years in contact with Peter Moro and later in the Festival Hall Group, with him and under the creative, benign and refined eye of Leslie Martin. These ideals I think most concerned the resolution of the living needs of what I suppose Peter [Laslett] would have called a nuclear family, on a site with modest natural features (strip lynchets) and to a limited budget. I wasn't concerned with architectural rhetoric.

It is, perhaps, when not concerned with rhetoric that the shadowy patterns of former experiences most readily structure an architect's mind. In the resolution of the complex functional problem set by the Lasletts, who required interrelated family, parent's and children's zones, the simple egg-in-a-box of the Royal Festival Hall (which there, seemingly effortlessly, had resolved ferociously difficult functional and technical problems) rematerialises. In common with the Festival Hall, the principal space—the living room—is raised above ground level (here to capture the view)—but supported on cross-walls not *piloti*—the ground floor is a classical, symmetrical, a-b-a plan, and the staircase is not only used as a means of functional organisation but is a *promenade architecturale*, rising to an enclosure containing the principal function, which floats over a recessed base which has an expanse of full-height, openable glazing.

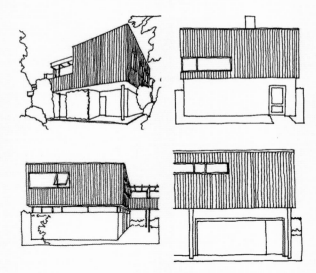

The connections are clear and direct but the most evident precedent, more evident than Dannatt's citing of Aalto's 1936 House and studio at Munkkiniemi, is stark—a house at Vedbæk in Denmark by Erik Sørensen, which Dannatt had published in the *Architects' Year Book 6* in 1955. As Gombrich explains, composition, whether in art or perception, is a process of pattern recognition, of "matching not making".[5] A mind tuned by Royal Festival Hall patterns recognised the match between the parti of the Danish scheme, a figure in Dannatt's "inner landscape" and the needs of this particular problem on this particular site. Such is the subconscious, contingent nature of design. Yet, there is another factor, for this floating box, and, in particular, this rendition as a timber box held aloft above a recessed masonry base with its vernacular roots, is a recurrent architectural form with constant appeal to some inner need. Patterns of base and superstructure, and, thereby of the mundane and transcendent, of heavy and light, enclosed and open, robust and yielding, rough and smooth, nature and man, rus and urbe, of the ground and, if not of the sky, then of the trees; all are characteristics embedded in this form-type. It is not surprising then, that, as has been seen, simultaneously but quite independently, Peter Moro should be adopting the same parti for his own house.

The stable security of the classical symmetry of the ground floor base gives way to the more relaxed, modern, balanced asymmetry of the first floor. The nature of the view, diagonal in plan and section, which links the two levels and traditions is rooted in a rich heritage: the developments in painting discussed earlier and marked by Le Corbusier, the Royal Festival Hall, and the domestic architecture of Adolf Loos (Dannatt having been introduced to the architecture of Loos by a fellow student, Rachel Wallis, who had lodged with Henry Kulka, Loos' Chief Assistant, when she had studied music in Vienna, and who recommended Dannatt to the Lasletts). Loos' raumplan approach—space planning involving the manipulation of levels—which Kulka described as "a veritable spatial fugue", prompted the resulting appropriately higher ceiling in the living room (the largest and principal space) over a partially sunken garage of low ceiling height.

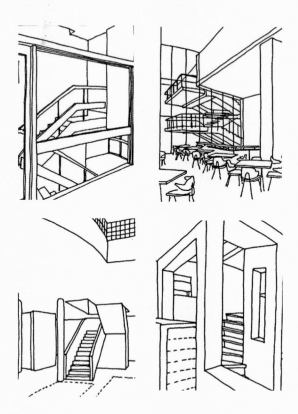

The elevations of the upper level also combine two traditions—the vertical windows of classical proportion and a horizontal, Corbusian strip window—not eclectically, but in a satisfyingly balanced composition (and so back again to the contemporary, developing modes of composition in art).

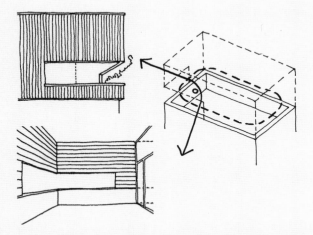

The horizontal strip window, which cuts through a corner of the livingroom, creates another satisfying, simultaneously inside and outside experience. A person sitting in this corner is in a situation which is at once protected and enclosed within the cube of the room, and exposed due to the the sweep of external space. It is a sensation somewhat equivalent to being in a tree— that satisfying, privileged situation of being able to look out and down, seeing without being seen. This experience is intensified by a 'nestling down' behind the protective, inward-projecting masonry dado/sill, which runs around the room as the floor level is dropped into the base.

The Loosian play of levels in the livingroom results in an inconsistency between external expression and internal form. But this is inconsistency with a purpose, intended or not, and of a kind shared with Lutyens, who in the circulation patterns of his country houses, on occasion, set up an external, formal expectation of symmetry, which is then refuted by the circulation pattern in the informal privacy of the domestic interior. Here, Dannatt plays a similar game, a composed formal, public persona and a private, relaxed, complex and

domestic retreat within—that exploitation of ambiguity which usually distinguishes poetry from prose.

1. Hildebrand, Grant, *The Wright Space: Pattern and Meaning in Frank Lloyd Wright's Houses*, Seattle: University of Washington Press, 1991.
2. Wilson, Colin St John, "The natural imagination", *Architectural Reflections: Studies in the philosophy and practice of architecture*, Second Edition, Manchester: Manchester University Press, 2000, pp. 1–19.
3. The other being the Ambassador's Residence
4. Rowe, Colin, "The Mathematics of the Ideal Villa", *The Architectural Review*, 1947.
5. Gombrich, Ernst, *Art and Illusion: A study in the psychology of pictorial representation,* Oxford: Phaidon, 1960.

House Plans

These four pages, apart from one school project, show 11 house studies of some 14 that were aborted for one reason or another. The plans all developed in response to particular needs and site conditions and in retrospect seem worth recording as brief case histories. It was decided to use original drawings rather than re-draw to a uniform style.

The school project (probably fourth year) House for an architect (bachelor?) clearly under Moro's influence (notably the plan shape) it seems well organised but inflexible. Random stone walling (Le Corbusier Villa at Mathes) plus something Japanese (a teak bath!). Ground and first floor plans. Ink drawing with Indian ink wash on heavy Whatman paper.

Dewar-Mills 'bungalow', c. 1940
Mills was a fellow student who left at the end of the third years to serve in the RAF. Back from the war he offered a house design to his prospective in-laws but coerced me, willingly, to do it. A simple two-wing design with differing ceiling heights, it was published in *The Architect* and *Building News*. The engagement and the house fell by the way.

House for VF Rees, 1946
In association with Peter Moro a two stage house was designed for an idyllic site in Berkshire. The single-storey first stage could have been realised despite early post-war restrictions, the two-storey second stage "in due course". Alas the site, with many other acres, was compulsorily purchased by the Atomic Energy Authority (Aldermaston)—the end of the project and briefly established practice.

Crooms Hill House, 1955
Just about to buy a lease in Canonbury a very secret site close to Greenwich Park was offered and 'put on ice' for future purchase. Planning permission was obtained for a split level house with a long wing parallel to the Park wall containing the entrance, living room/dining, kitchen and main bedroom. At entrance level a bedroom wing at right angles provided a first floor roof terrace at living room level with views over the Park, towards the Observatory. Later the vendor reneged on his offer and life took a different course.

Roffey House, c. 1950
A small house with studio for the Director of a firm of decorators and amateur painter. It owes something to the Rees House in the interplay of single end two-storey elements. A neat frugal plan, lopsided and a bit mean in not being truly symmetrical. Not built, maybe the Directorship lapsed.

Champneys House, 1955
Two wings at different levels slide together, bedroom and living room wings. Composed on the site with garage and projected cottage. Strong Danish influence, it would have been all white with white 'Eternit' roof (cf Juhl house in Ordrup). The client edited a journal devoted to the rose and the site was envisaged as a test bed for varieties. No house, no roses, no fee.

Pappworth House, two studies
First study: Two-storey elements about a central stair with semi-split levels. The first floor living room gave onto a terrace over the garage and access way below. At ground level on the garden side a gallery connects stair, dining room kitchen and playroom.

In the second study, a compact rectangular plan, with the gallery idea more fully developed, extending virtually along the whole front. The studies were done to show possibilities of an awkward site for friends who then decided to buy not build.

The gallery idea plan was to be fully developed at Pitcorthie House where it became the generator.

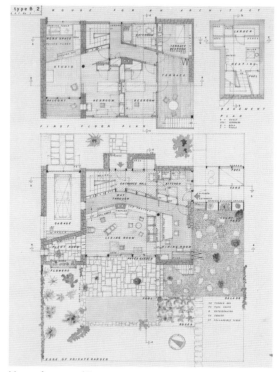

House for an architect.

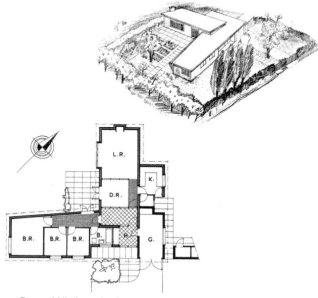

Dewar-Mills 'bungalow'.

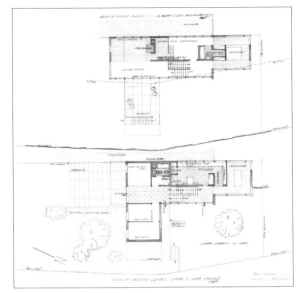

Crooms Hill House.

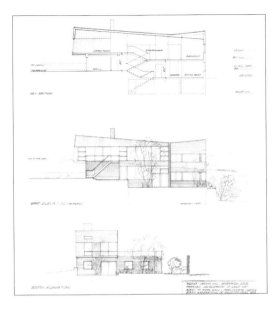

Rees House.

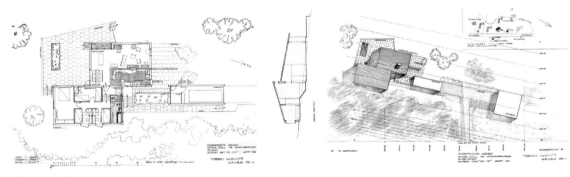

Champneys House.

Roffey House.

Pappworth House 1.

Pappworth House 2.

Hudhud House, Amman, 1975

An ambitious house for a Jordanian builder on a highly contoured site on the city outskirts. Complex plan relationships arose from the needs of the local pattern of family life as well as an office and private dining space requirement. The lowest level included a large recreation room opening onto a terrace and swimming pool (site plan to right). The family and the extended family were drawn in and it became impossible to resolve contradicting requirements and the opportunity to build receded. The experience of Jordan, its more open Society, the landscape and monuments was compensation.

Peter Woodward House, 1974

Designed as a gift for Arup's Senior Engineer in Riyadh who was totally involved in the realisation of the Conference Centre and Hotel project. A sloping rural site and specific husband and wife wishes gave opportunity for probably the most interesting interplay of plan, space and form in the main living areas.

Court House Tisbury, 1979

A small sloping site off a back road was developed in bedroom and living room wings, separated by dining/kitchen and loggia, forming a small courtyard and with southerly aspect. As at Crooms Hill it was not realised through entrepreneurial laziness.

Laslett Annexe, 1996

With the likelihood of the original now listed house becoming home for the succeeding generation, a single-storey one bedroom retirement house was developed on side land with generous living room and study. An interesting problem of privacy and architectural relationships. Planning permission was obtained.

Answood, East Hatch Wiltshire, 1999

A woodland site with a steep slope down from a narrow lane led to a set back building, primarily two-storey with an undercroft and bridge access to a car port at lane level. The stair extends to a third floor studio/music room.

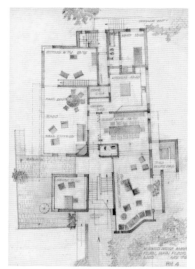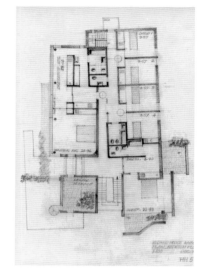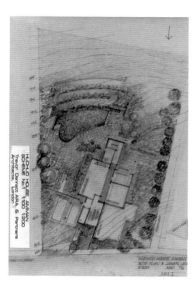

Hudhud House.

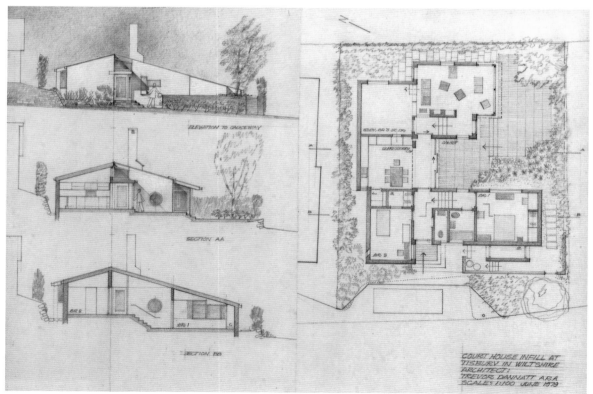

Court House Tisbury.

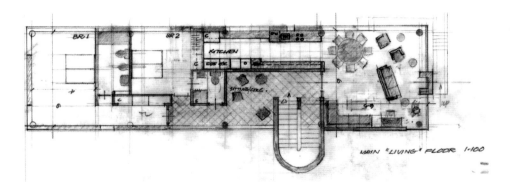

MAIN "LIVING" FLOOR 1:100

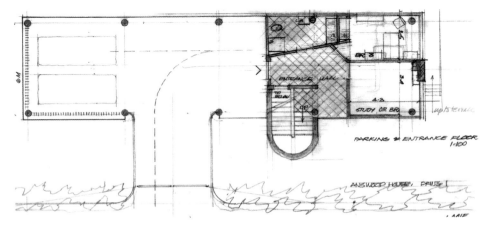

PARKING & ENTRANCE FLOOR 1:100

ANSWOOD HOUSE, DRWG 1

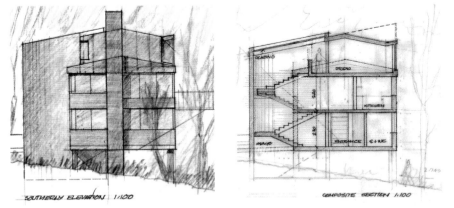

SOUTHERLY ELEVATION 1:100

COMPOSITE SECTION 1:100

Answood House.

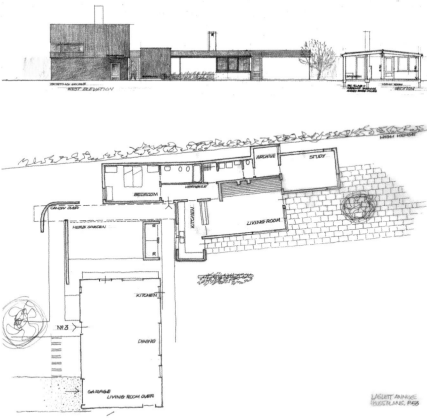

WEST ELEVATION

SECTION

Laslett Annexe.

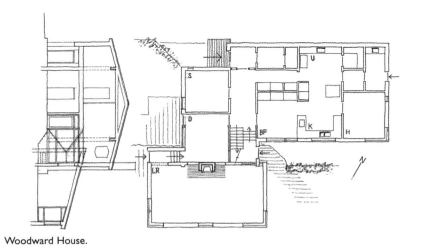

Woodward House.

Laslett House
Cambridge
1958

A preference for an upper level living room and a dip in the site, led to the sectional arrangement of garage slightly below ground floor level with the living room over. On the ground floor are entrance lobby, toilet, playroom, kitchen and the dining room out of which stairs lead, extending the space visually to the living room at half-landing level.

From there a shorter flight leads to the four bedrooms and bathroom. The upper ceiling level extends over the living room, giving extra height.

The lower walls are of insulating structural block which stop at first floor level. In the living room, the top of the wall extends round three sides as a continuous sill. The timber framed upper walls are built from this level and the form of the upper part of the house corresponds to the structural change which provides additional space at bedroom and living room levels.

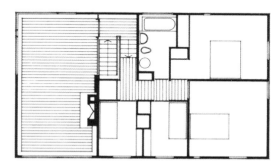

First floor.

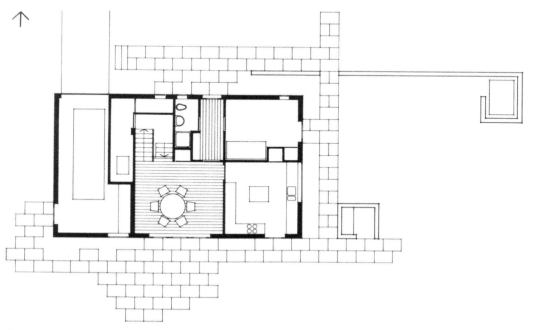

Ground floor.

Opposite: Clarkson Road elevation.

Opposite top: Garden side.

Opposite bottom left: Detail of the garden side.

Opposite bottom right: Detail of the front door.

Right: Detail of garden elevation, showing the dining room with glazing open.

Left: Living room corner window with the stair to the right.

Top right: View from the stair to the living room.

Bottom right: West side elevation.

Dobbs House
Hampstead, London NW3
1958

The site was formerly part of a large garden and the access road ends 3.7 metres lower than the adjacent side of the site of awkward shape, which with the need to screen from building to the south led to the T-shaped plan with the living room orientated east and west, to the garden on one side and opening on to the terrace over the garage on the other.

The approach to the house is by steps broken into easy stages with changes of direction. Past the north wall a turn through 180 degrees leads to the front door, recessed in a porch.

The house is divided by the hall and stairway giving access to all the rooms as well as to the garden. The formal arrangement and the structure follow this division on both floors.

First floor.

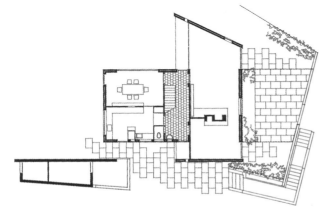

Ground floor.

Top: Garage level with the terrace over and the stair approach to the house.

Bottom: Garden view.

Plante House
Hampstead, London NW3
1960

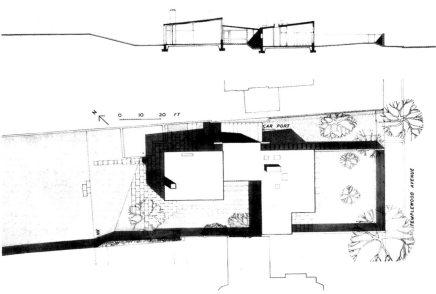

Site plan and section.

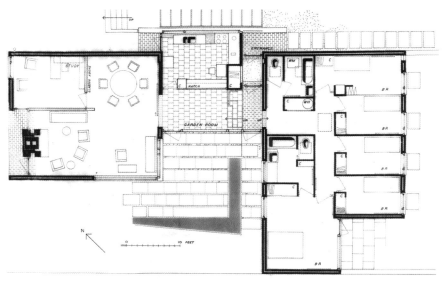

Plan.

The long site rises about ten feet from street to back. The clients' preference for living at one level, which, with the impossibility of maintaining the scale of the large houses on either side, and the need to give good orientation to various rooms while enjoying the garden, led to a one-storey, semi-courtyard plan.

The house 'looks in' but it exploits every 'outlook' with cross views from one part to another, giving a special interest and character. The approach to the house is by a screened drive-in, and the centre of the house breaks forward to form the main entrance.

An entrance lobby leads into the garden room where on one side a step leads up to the bedroom wing at front, on the other four steps lead up to the main level. The garden room links the wings but also serves as an informal dining area, with direct access to the courtyard.

The living-room wing is one space, with a high ceiling at the entrance, sloping towards the rear sub-divided by low solid walls, with glazing over to form an L-shaped room for dining and sitting and a separate study. Windows on two sides give excellent sunlight penetration and an intriguing variety of views.

View of the entrance drive, front door and carport.

Clockwise, from top: Garden room with, left, the south corner of the living room; Living room towards garden; Living room wing from the garden.

Opposite: Southerly window of the living room with garden court, right, and entrance, left.

Pitcorthie House
Colinsburgh, Fife
1966

Built on the ruins of an old house to take advantage of the landscaped view to the south with the sea beyond. The drive-in ends in a courtyard formed by rebuilt walls to the east and north, a new cottage to the west with the house to the south.

The main wing, in essence, consists of a core of service rooms surrounded by circulation or living space. The east end is a closed block containing three bedrooms, while the south side of the main wing, entirely glazed, is a gallery off which open bedroom, study and dining room.

From the dining and general area, with its 'gallery' extension, the effect of low horizontal interior space and view is succeeded by, on turning right into the living room, a secluded and different type of space with ceiling sloping down to windows overlooking terrace and garden to the west.

The living room has a generous fireplace, with stack which rises through the highest part to become, externally, a pivotal feature of the design.

The interior kitchen gains sunlight from the south clerestory but there is a broad lift-up shutter so that, if desired, the main outlook can be enjoyed across the dining space. The main bedroom and study have sliding doors drawn out from double partitions so they can become self-contained rooms—each with its part of the gallery space.

Left: South side of the house, seen from the park.

Below: West side of the main house, with the cottage on the left.

Top: Model showing the entrance courtyard, with the cottage to the left.

Bottom left: Plan.

Bottom right: Section.

Opposite, clockwise, from top left: West side showing the living room and terrace; Entrance side from courtyard; Cottage seen from the courtyard; End of gallery and corner living room detail.

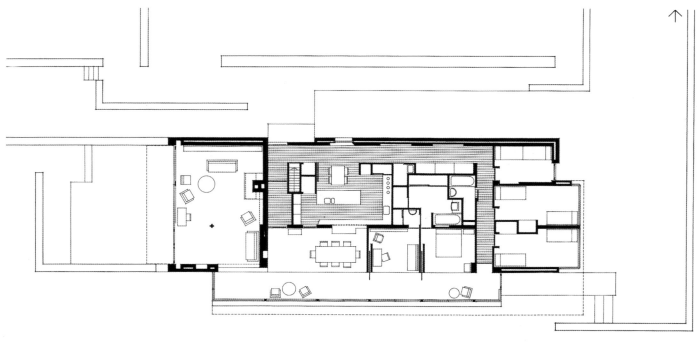

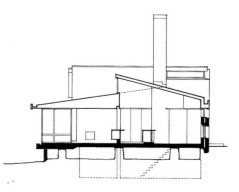

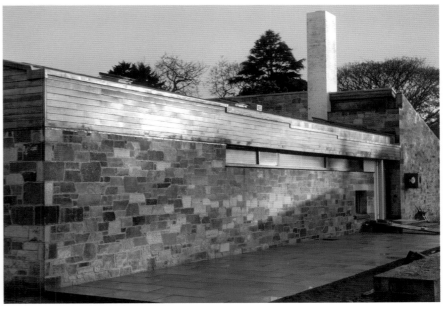

Opposite left: The gallery.

Opposite right: The dining room, with kitchen to the left and gallery to the right.

Above: Kitchen as seen from the dining room.

House No. 3
Blackheath, London SE3
2001

Three houses on a sequestered south sloping site adjacent Lloyds Place were developed by Dannatt, Johnson Architects for the Morden College Charity. For planning reasons two houses had perforce to follow prescribed formats but House No. 3 gave opportunity for a split-level plan with entrance area intermediate to lower living floor and bedroom floor. The central stair continues to serve a third bedroom and a generous roof terrace with extensive prospects. Load-bearing wall construction with reinforced concrete retaining walls, timber first floor and reinforced concrete roof terrace.

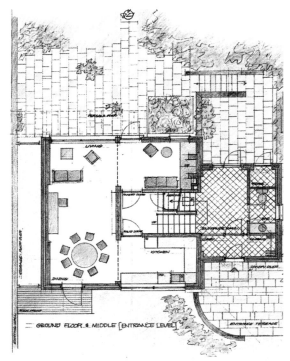

Ground and middle (entrance level) floor.

First and upper floor.

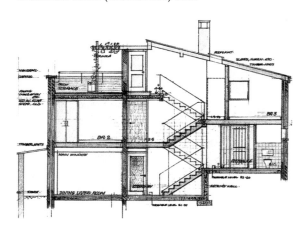

Section.

Garden side.

Entrance detail.

4   Communal House

Ebbisham Court, Felbridge.

These buildings, which provide communal accommodation for the young and the old, reveal two major considerations in their design. The first concerns the relationship between the individual and the group—the conflicting needs to provide privacy yet encourage social interaction. This is met by versions of that hierarchical ordering of groups of increasing size from the individual to the whole, which Martin and Wilson had seen to be so effective in the Cambridge court pattern discussed earlier. The second is the desire to make places in which people may be able to feel at home—to recognise a home. The response to this is a determined, but understated, vernacularism, the "common word" of everyday prose. The condescension of overt symbols and clichés is averted through the use of the locally established rhythms and patterns of solid and void, scale, punctured wall plane, and roof pitch—in terms of painting, abstract figurative as opposed to representational.

In Victorian times, buildings for such a purpose would have been required to express a paternalistic, charitable attitude of moral improvement, an attitude which prevailed well into the twentieth century; in contrast, by the 1980s such buildings were seen as too institutional, a view which had begun to dispense with such buildings, though without yet finding a means of meeting the needs they fulfil, and had arisen, in part, from an attitude born of a denial of the existence of Society. Dannatt's response was to seek an appropriate pitch of language and form between the assertively institutional and the domestic.

Three of the buildings are of courtyard form—the court performing its traditional roles of the gathering together of both the community and the building—social, symbolic, visual and formal gatherings. The first, Cedars Road, 1969, is a U-shaped building with a glazed gallery, which closes the south side of the court, thereby completing a continuous ambulatory, which ties together all parts of the building and provides a place for exercise and chance encounter. This ambulatory is a place of great variation: a glazed gallery looking onto courtyard and garden; then, at a corner, opening onto a garden Commonroom with

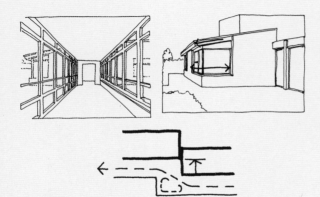

pitched ceiling; then becoming a single-sided, broad corridor looking onto the court, broken in its length by an inflection of the wing to form one of a series of resting places; then becoming an aisle to the dining room; before encountering the main entrance and a living room overlooking the entrance and the street; and, finally, before repeating the circuit, becoming a double-banked corridor leading to two, more secluded living rooms at the end of a 'cul-de-sac'. Although all the living rooms are different, each has the satisfying, life-enhancing situation of corner windows discussed in relation to the Laslett House, each of which is set back protectively under a projecting eaves or floor above. The roof pitch, the stock brick, the scale-modulating string courses, the window proportions and ratios of opening to solid, plane surface are all as the adjacent nineteenth century terraced houses. And, in the tradition of its neighbours, but with a more consistent language, which gives equal value to front and back, the building transforms from a formal, public-scale statement, addressing and responding to the street, to become informal and relaxed, and of gentle scale, as it opens to its garden.

The second, on a tight, triangular, urban site in Lambeth, Union Road, 1976, is designed as part of a housing development, with which it shares a common language, being distinguished only by its three-storey form. It is an example of a necessarily pragmatic design approach, which turns exigencies to advantage. Its form and appearance pose the question: is it one building or a group?—ie. just that ambiguity which is

needed to break down the institutional whole but to retain the communal identity. Each side of the court is of a different form but all are of a piece, and the corners of the court are closed, thereby asserting protection and unity. Again there is an ambulatory: variously, a sunny, glazed veranda in the court; a corridor; an aisle in the entrance hall; and then passing through the diningroom. This is that sensitive,

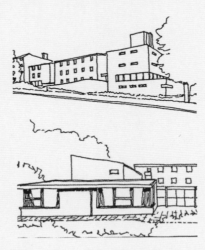

responsive, yet ordered, pragmatism which typified the English Free School of Butterfield, Waterhouse and Webb. For instance, the building is variously inflected to create windows capturing the sun or a view, or to create a resting place, or to control scale, or just to make a room more comfortable, functionally and spatially (eg. the angled cupboard and washbasin area in bedrooms). In the diningroom, which for financial reasons is subsumed rather than being in a separate block, the ceiling height is correspondingly lower than required for such a large space; this is turned to advantage by using the beams required to support the structural walls above to break down the scale of the room through forming bays, each orientated on a bay-window (identical to those in the adjacent houses).

Such is the changing nature of our society that both these buildings have now been converted into individual apartments with no communal function. At the third, in suburban, semi-rural Felbridge, 1978–1981,

another ambulatory becomes a glazed cloister, tying together single-storey, short, straight or staggered terraces of dwellings. One corner is chamfered with a Dannatt diagonal to form a social space. This brings into play the two adjacent sides of the cloister—those which extend to other parts of the development—to form wings embracing the court. Such plays of geometry and form are seen throughout, as they structure this relaxed ensemble (again a hallmark of good prose). The base-line formal, visual and social axis links an existing court to the new one. The echelon of a staggered terrace forms a partially contained intermediate court linking the old and new courts, and concentrates a distant view on one side, whilst, on the other, it forms a rest area in the quiet corner of the cloister, diagonally opposite the chamfer. The echelon also allows the expression of the individual homes within the whole and is the basis of the cluster which terminates the circulation in the second phase.

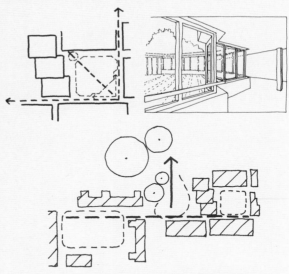

In contrast, two of the buildings, by John Shaw, who had been inspired by a visit to the Neolithic settlement of Scara Brae in Orkney, are of linear, attenuated, branching form with diagonal geometries. In each, the geometry and the branching allow the expression of individual rooms and flats and the various communal spaces within the whole. They also provide the means of inflecting the circulation spaces to provide rest and meeting places, to introduce light and to give variation to the form so as to reduce their apparent length. The diagonal branching also forms protected, partially enclosed, external spaces.

Additionally, at Greenwich, 1976–1977, on a narrow north–south site, at the scale of a room and window, the diagonal splays the wall to give a southerly aspect in the living area, whilst secondary windows provide alternative east or west views from the bed. The quasi-bay-window affords the sense of being partially inside and out, and splayed window reveals provide both a graded transition and greater level of light from the minimum sized windows. The internal complexity is held within the undulating wall of a continuous terrace.

These elements were all first established in Sumner Road, 1971, which had a more relaxed diagonal geometry. This allowed the building to exploit a more difficult north–south site and provided a more gentle, undulating form internally and externally in the three storey 'tail' of the building, whilst, in the 'head', it enabled the clustering of a 'village' of single-storey, pitched-roof communal spaces around a garden. Recalling the pinioning chimneys of Dannatt's houses, a dominant lift tower marked the entrance, which is situated at the junction of head and tail, the latter recalling a terrace of houses—its regularity arising from the ordered sets of repetitions which underlay the apparent organic fluidity of the planning.

On an adjacent site, and built contemporaneously, the remaining building, 1971, that for children "taken into care" is a 'big house', which is organised around a central stair hall, with the intention that this latter should have "the character of a place rather than a street—somewhere to linger—analogous to the stair hall of a country house... near to what might have been the ideal—a converted large house in the country". The stair is formed to encourage just such lingering, with a large plinth/landing at its foot, around which to gather, and a 'garden wall', against which to lean. True to the precedent, bedrooms are arranged in wings on the first floor, each for a different social grouping—usually a "family" presided over by a "house-mother"—and each linked to the whole by its own roof-lit sitting area at the head of the stair. Although a 'big house', encouraging connotations of community and protection, there is again present that useful, significant ambiguity, for the building can also be read, externally, as groups of smaller houses in the local terrace vernacular with its intimate, intricate urban complexity (which was fast being devoured by the adjacent modernist housing developments which Dannatt's buildings oppose).

1. Martin, Leslie, and Colin St John Wilson, "The Collegiate Plan", *The Architectural Review*, vol. 126, July 1959, pp. 2–8.
2. Stonehouse, Roger and Gerhard Stromberg, *The Architecture of the British Library at St Pancras*, London: Spon, 2004, pp. 75–76.

Old People's Home
Southwark, London SE15
1972

This building developed a plan form for an awkward site with a wish to avoid the institutional and provide diversity in the common parts of the building. This was designed by John Shaw, 1914–1984, a consultant partner in the Trevor Dannatt and Partners practice. Closely briefed by the Chief Welfare Officer of the Borough, certain ideas were developed following a visit to Scara Brae when a possible relationship between those vestigial dwellings and planning 60 residential rooms plus social accommodation on the long narrow north–south site was perceived.

The south end became a cluster of social rooms, including dining, related to the garden. At the north end a matron's flat and staff rooms were provided in two storeys, and between these two elements a longish three-storey link of resident's rooms was planned on a wide central corridor with islands containing WCs/bathrooms, etc.. The corridors expanded to give small sitting spaces with outlooks and the lift at the south end gave access near to the social rooms and the entrance. The narrow site indicated a saw tooth profile which allowed every room to enjoy sun at some time of the day.

Favourably received at the time and well run for some 30 years, the building fell victim to changing social policy and unlike the other two homes was not converted for alternative use, but demolished. For a comparable site at Greenwich John Shaw developed a similar idea for sheltered housing accommodation.

Housing for the Elderly and Disabled
Greenwich, London SE10
1978

As at the Old People's Home, the north–south site is long and narrow with a west frontage to Vicarage Avenue, an open space on the line of a railway tunnel. Vehicle access is to the south where planning requirements restricted building to two storeys.

The plan form is comparable to the Old People's Home with an articulated central corridor where the plan avoids long vistas and uninterrupted wall surfaces, while side lighting is gained by indents at two points. Flat entrance doors are deeply recessed to provide a threshold with some privacy and by the use of angled plans all principal rooms gain some southerly aspect.

There are 45 units which consist of bed sitting rooms and one bedroom apartments with a few family units which allow for wheel chair use. The Warden has a two-storey residence adjacent to the General Office and Visitor's suite at the south end by the suite of social rooms which have direct access to the southerly garden.

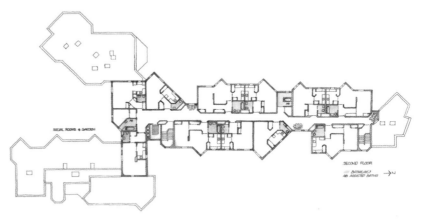

Left: Plan at ground floor, Southwark.

Right: Plan at second floor, Greenwich.

Old People's Home
Lambeth, London SW4
1969

Section through the courtyard, dining room and kitchen wing.

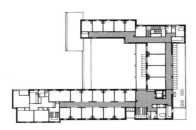

First floor.

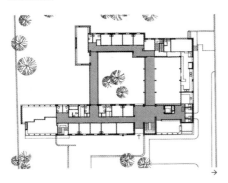

Ground floor.

Opposite, clockwise, from top to bottom: The east side seen from Cedars Road, with the staff accommodation on the left and main entrance in the recess to the right; View through the link towards the dining room; Detail of the garden room and link.

Right: Ambulatory on the courtyard (south) side of the dining room, with clerestory over.

There is room for 60 residents in single, single cubicle and double rooms.

The site falls to the north and kitchen, service, etc., are at a lower level than the main floor. There is a main wing on the east side with double-banked rooms while a second wing at right angles has double rooms on the south side only. The third wing (west) sets back in plan and is two-storey to open up the space around which the building is planned—a courtyard completed by the link which provides an ambulatory round the building at ground floor with widenings to provide resting places.

There are three sitting rooms within the main building, and a fourth at the end of the west wing overlooks the garden, and is of different character to the others, where one faces west while the other two (at either end of the main wing) face east, overlooking the road.

The highest point of the building comes at the lower end of the site on the road side, marking, with the indent in the main wall, the principal entrance. The projection at the other end marks the independence of the staff flats and separate entrance.

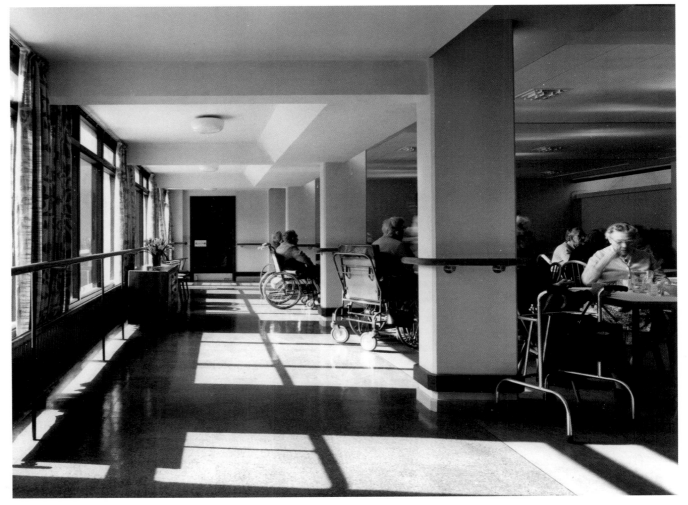

Old People's Home
London SW4
1978

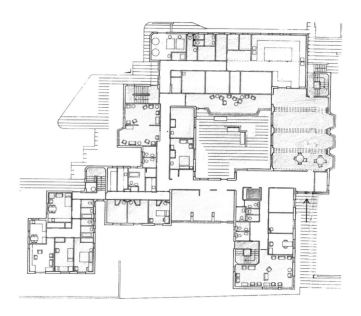

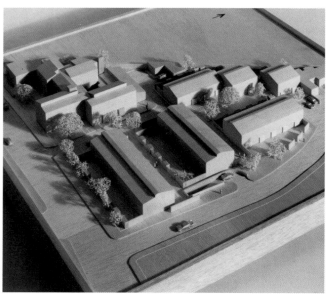

This old people's home is contiguous with the Union Road Housing scheme illustrated later. It is three-storey as opposed to the two-storey houses, but both are built in the same mode in recycled stock brick with common features such as sash windows, sometimes in bays. Whilst a three-storey building is not the ideal form, the site and cost-limits in this case dictated it. The plan is developed about a central courtyard but not rigidly so that corridors and facades step in and out, each common room has a different character, and where a link-corridor happens to have a south-facing aspect to the courtyard it also provides a sunny sitting space. The first and second floors are identical in plan, but have different spatial qualities, the latter having ceilings that follow the roof pitch and high level windows over the corridor.

For site and cost reasons the social rooms are within the main fabric and consequently have lower ceilings than might be expected. In the dining room, the low ceiling is relieved by the beams supporting the floor above which actually reduce the clear height, yet relieve the oppressive effect of a low flat ceiling, and three bay windows on the side, facing the public footpath, help to create the impression of a domestic front room. In general creating a friendly, non-institutional building.

Below, from left to right: Dining room bays; Courtyard with a sitting room window to the right; Interior with sitting room window.

Opposite, clockwise, from top left: Ground floor plan; Model showing the Old People's Home (top left), and housing scheme; The east side of Old People's Home, with housing terraces left and right.

Housing for the Elderly
Felbridge, Surrey
1977
(Ebbisham Court)

Trevor Dannatt and Colin Dollimore

Whittington College, of which the buildings at Felbridge are a part, dates from 1424 and was founded under the will of Sir Richard Whittington. The Charity is administered by the Mercers' Company and provides housing for elderly women in a collegiate-like group. In 1964 the College removed from Highgate and redeveloped at Felbridge with single-storey houses in groups with staff houses and a chapel, planned round a private road loop.

In 1974 the Trustees decided to provide for those elderly but still mobile yet needing occasional support, by the provision of self-contained flats with some common facilities and a matron's flat. A second phase has added seven more comparable units as well as an assistant matron's flat. There are several entrances, giving easy access to the grounds, but the approach from the old College was regarded as most important to encourage social links, and the plan results from a wish to form a linking court space common to both old and new developments. Thus one wing forms a base line, a return wing closes the space and is stepped to avoid a visual falling-away to the open side with its distant views.

The main group of flats is planned round a courtyard overlooked by an enclosed 'cloister' which offers access and walking space adjacent to the court garden, while one corner is expanded by a 45 degrees splay to provide a south-facing social space.

A further group of bed/sitting room flats are off the corridor of the wing which stretches towards the old group. Larger flats consist of sitting room, bedroom (with sliding door to the sitting room), kitchen, bathroom and lobby. Bed/sitting room flats are on a narrower frontage but with a comparable service area, the kitchen opening directly off a living space whose L-shape provides a large bed recess. Monopitch roofs allow clerestory light to service rooms.

Above: Site model, with the original development to the bottom.

Right: Perspective of the development in context, with the second stage top left.

Opposite, clockwise, from top left: General view; Service entrance with the matron's residence, left; Principal entrance from the original development.

Left: The courtyard and ambulatory, with sitting area.

Top: The ambulatory as seen from the courtyard.

Bottom: The matron's residence, with private garden.

Children's Reception Home
London SE15
1971

This is a short stay centre where children taken into care can live while their needs are assessed and until appropriate fostering can be arranged for them. It provides for the residential needs of about 30 children and a staff of about 15.

On the first floor the residential side consists of three groups of children's rooms integrated with houseparents' rooms, a cluster formation that decided the basic four-wing plan about a stair hall, also with a wing of staff flats with independent access, other staff rooms, sick bay, etc..

On the ground floor there is a dining room for the whole house and service accommodation. For work and play, two classrooms, games, hobbies, TV and quiet rooms are provided. The main entrance is in the centre of the fourth wing and has its own hall—which increases in width from the entrance to the space around the projecting foot of the pivotal stairs. Although the main ground floor rooms open off it, the hall has the character of a place rather than a street—somewhere to linger—analogous to the stair hall of a country house. This gave the key to the character of the building.

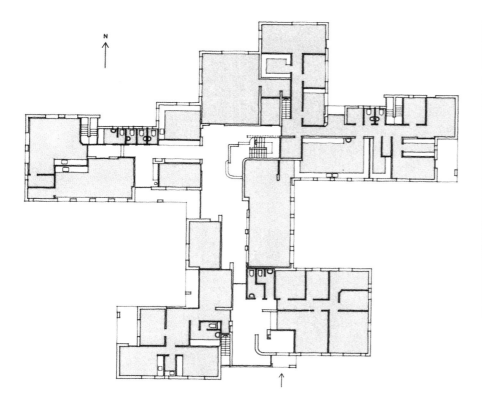

N

Ground floor plan and model.

Opposite: West side—classrooms, social and babies' rooms. Houseparents' and children's rooms are on the first floor.

Top: The first floor landing with clerestory lighting.

Bottom: The main stair with the lower landing projecting into the hall.

Opposite: The lower landing and communal space (photographed in 1970).

5   Housing

Union Road Housing.

The Sumner Road buildings for the old and the young, discussed in "Communal House", were designed and built in 1971, just five years after Dannatt's first housing project, at Poplar, and just five years before his second, Union Road. Taken together they embody remarkable continuities, variations and developments in approach.

When it was built in 1966 the Poplar housing was in a tough, industrial location of railway sidings, warehouses and cranes and adjacent to other four- and five-storey housing developments. It had a challengingly high density requirement of 136 ppa (337 pph) on a constricted site. The compositional device of the echelon is again a geometrical enabler—here, the overlapping of the staggered blocks enables an increase in frontage of the dwellings of 25 per cent, which gives better daylighting in the dwellings and wider, more comfortably proportioned rooms—which also brings visual delight through introducing rhythms and the interplay of complexity and simplicity. Whereas a conventional slab would have created two narrow tunnels of external space, the echelon also provided the means of bringing the existing buildings into play with the new development by the creation of partially enclosed spaces to east and west, addressing, respectively, the street and the sun. These interplays between density and form, built form and external space, and existing and new buildings were those central to the approach to architecture and planning of Leslie Martin, with whom Dannatt had worked in association on the student residence, Leicester University, in 1960.[1]

Poplar's urban complexity of form—a tough, outspoken, robust prose responding to its industrial setting—arises from the deeply modelled articulation of each maisonette, by the strongly expressed projection of its bounding crosswalls and concrete floor, and from the rhythmic expression of each section within the whole by means of the echelon and the interlocking roofs.

Union Road, 1976, arises from the same interests: the interplay between built form and urban space and, here, in this low-rise development, also the pattern of routes; the identification of each dwelling within the whole; an appropriate intricacy and complexity of form (but here intimate rather than robust, and not of a single building but of the layout of arrays of buildings and spaces); and a brick-and-tile language appropriate to the location. Surprisingly, it is the same density as Poplar. A four-storey maisonette development would have been the, then, conventional solution but Dannatt's response is a tightly knit interplay of two-storey terraces (each house with its own garden) with a network of paths and alleyways with small gathering and play areas, which retains the existing trees, and accomodates, scarcely-evident, sunken garaging.

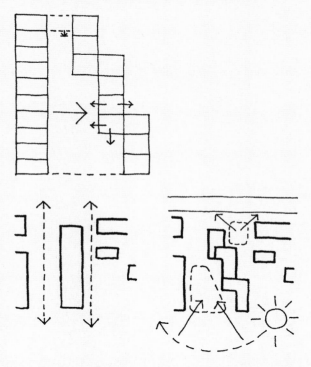

These Union Road houses are of "the common word"; as one reviewer says, approvingly, they are "ordinary enough" and, apart from the lack of chimneys and the split pitch of the roof to light internal bathrooms, they "might have been built at any time after the First World War".[2] In this, they are very much a part of their surroundings, but what distinguishes this housing, is the quality of thought and precision of form and detail: for instance, the recessed, protected porch and the projecting, protecting eaves; the apparently simple, asymmetrical bay window—straight

sided to lead into the porch, angled side to give a glancing view out and an enclosing space within; and the interplay of materials and detailing between house, garden and public areas. All these, and more, are again the simple, often neglected, often unrecognised elements which can bridge the gap between a soulless and, to use Eagleton's term, bureaucratic language and an inclusive, responsive, warm, welcoming language; the difference between a building which forever will be merely a house and that which can be recognised as, and may become, a home.

1. Martin, Leslie, *Buildings and Ideas 1933–83: From the Studio of Leslie Martin and his Associates*, Cambridge: Cambridge University Press, 1983.
2. Davies, Colin, "Lambeth Living", *The Architect*, August 1978, pp. 27–32.

Housing
Poplar High Street
London E14
1966

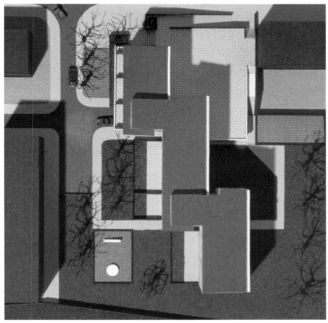

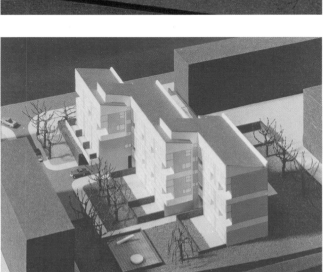

The form of this building is an answer to a particular problem, a response to an awkward site zoned at 136 persons per acre. The accommodation consists of 17 maisonettes, together with seven old people's two-room or one-room flats.

The staggered plan assists the density by the overlapping of flats where the building sets back; it respects light angles, providing excellent outlooks in both directions and prevents a tunnel effect next to the adjacent buildings by the creation of spaces which open out on both sides. Thus the existing buildings have been brought into relation with the new enhancing the setting of each and developing the open effect to the south, out of Poplar High Street.

At the north end a raised terrace with ramp and step approach from the street becomes the main access to the building. The fall of the site is such that a lower floor can be provided and here, under the terrace, are garages and service accommodation, and to the south three flats with private gardens.

The stepped plan engenders the overall form which has been emphasised by the arrangement of the one-way pitch roof and the projections of the maisonettes at the breaks. The roof pitch appears on all ends and break backs, while the long sides are divided up by vertical piers (corresponding to cross walls) and bands of concrete every other floor (corresponding to the living room floors). The brick used throughout is a semi-engineering red and there are correspondences with the Rosa Bassett Science Building mode.

Opposite: Part of the west side ground floor flats with maisonettes over.

Top left: Site model, plan view.

Bottom left: Site model, showing the west side.

Right: Detail of the two wing ends from the south.

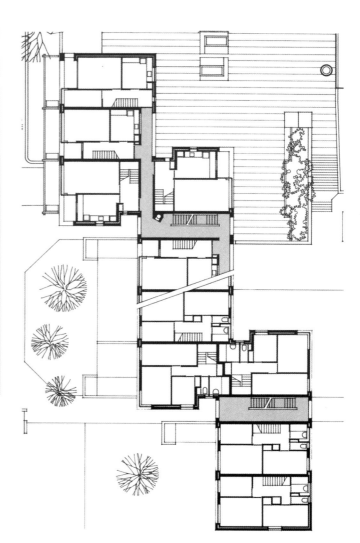

Opposite top: General view of the west side showing the staggered form of the building.

Opposite bottom: View of the east side of the scheme.

Above: The end of the building to Poplar High Street, with the ramp from the street level to the terrace over the garage and principal access.

Right: Plan (cut): bedroom floor, bottom; living room floor, top; access terrace over the garage.

Union Road Housing
London SW4
1978

The scheme comprises the three-storey old people's home already described and the two-storey housing group, mainly for large families. The houses are sensible, economical buildings using the characteristic Lambeth second-hand stock bricks, standard aluminium sash windows and concrete interlocking roof tiles.

Though they vary in size from five to seven person, the plans are virtually identical, with either a 4.9 or 5.5 metre frontage. They are disposed in a rectilinear formation on the triangular corner site. Living rooms face either west or south and each dwelling

has a small private garden. A single-storey disabled person's dwelling, the only non-standard house on the site, neatly turns the awkward acute angled corner at the northern extremity. The two-storey solution has created an intimate ensemble, with a network of footpaths rather than slabs of communal open space. The footpaths converge on a small play area in the middle of the scheme, like a miniature village green. Cars have been pushed out of the way in a set of underground garages using existing basements, under the terrace to the south.

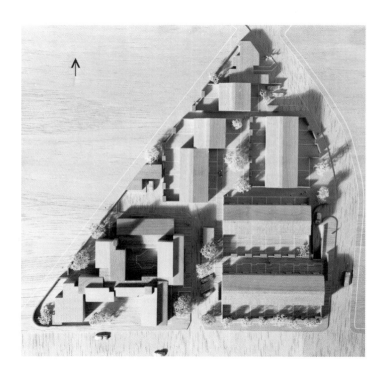

Left: Site model, plan view, with old people's home, bottom left.

Right: View down a terrace from the east side.

Opposite: The central courtyard, with the three-storey old people's home to the right beyond.

6 Commerce

Tea Bar, suspended ceiling detail.

The few works for commerce span, in their milieu, from the few 'playful words' of coffee bars to the more formal 'sober word' of a boardroom. All are interventions, conversions or extensions which exhibit Eliot's "easy commerce of the old and new...".

The Tea Bar, in the Power and Production Pavilion of the 1951 Festival of Britain, was a private commission designed and detailed over a four day Easter holiday, at a time when Dannatt was working for the London County Council. It was doubly formative: it lead to the commissions for coffee bars and works for Dickins and Jones, which, with the Blackheath Congregational Church, enabled Dannatt to establish his own practice; and it established enduring elements of his architectural language.

In the introduction of the white and coloured, solid and semi-transparent, overlapping, suspended ceiling planes, which demarcate different use areas of the bar and give the small bar presence within the large pavilion, Dannatt acknowledges the influence of Ben Nicholson and *Circle*. These were to become frequently used compositional elements, as was the related vertical, semi-transparent screen, here in the form of a freely suspended Venetian blind. These planes are played off against a line of angular, delicate, purpose-designed light fittings with asymmetrical conical shades, as if a Naum Gabo sculpture published in *Circle* had unfurled itself—they are born of Asplund at his Woodland Crematorium and his Bredenberg Department Store, and, by their uplight, emphasise the hovering and space-defining nature of the plane. The play of plane and taut line was to become another regular trope. All is set in motion by exploiting the serendipitous presence of the pavilion's diagonal geometry. This vigorous, but balanced, overlapping and interpenetrating of lines, semi-transparent and opaque planes, and solid geometrical forms, together with blocks of bold colour chime with Heron's paintings of the time.

The inventive, lively, playful interplay of line, plane and screen reappear constantly in the subsequent coffee bars. The influence of *Circle* is again evident: for instance, in the light fittings at the Benets Buttery coffee bar, 1955—a rectilinear, version of Calder's mobiles. Whilst at the Lancaster Coffee Grill, 1955, in the diagonal wedge of the screened staircase there is the first use of a strong, sharp diagonal in the vertical plane; another distinctive trope.

At Primavera, 1954, there is the first appearance of the balanced, asymmetrical interplay of solid, horizontal members (inspired by a visit to the cathedral of Santa Maria Assunta at Torcello) against taut, vertical lines forming a transparent screen: here, as a display screen which replaced a solid partition; and soon repeated in the form of a display window unit at Dickins and Jones.

The language of overlapping planes and suspended screens came together physically with the art to which it is related in the two reception areas for the then printers, Lund Humphries. In that in Bradford, 1955, a suspended horizontal plane of deep, vertical louvres hovers to lower the apparent height of the room, each louvre being divided into three sections, which are painted in different colours to an overall rhythm. The colours and rhythm relate to the richer colours of a collage by Eduardo Paolozzi, which terminates the perspective of the ceiling and is made of the printers' paper scraps and, thereby, itself relates to one of the inspirations for the louvres—the sheets of coloured paper which were hung over strings as a party decoration. In that in London, 1958, a suspended ceiling of slats at two levels and different spacings intersects with a commissioned mural panel by Patrick Heron, which rises through the plane of the ceiling—the bands of colour in the mural and the slats of the ceiling bringing the two elements into close relationship. In each case, there is an axis and termination—that connotation of arrival, appropriate to a reception area.

The 1964 works for J Walter Thompson in Berkeley Square, which included extensive reception areas and a private cinema, find Dannatt using similar elements but now far more restrained, even chaste; treading a fine line between the elegant and the sleek—reflecting, perhaps, the Mayfair setting and client's persona.

In contrast, the works for the long established, mutual Greenwich Industrial Building Society, the first of which was almost contemporaneous with J Walter Thompson, demanded a very different milieu. This first project, 1965, involved the design of a small banking

hall adjacent to the existing nineteenth century building. The fascia to the ground floor of this latter, three-storey building is extended to tie in the new single storey extension and link it to its single-storey neighbour. The fascia becomes a freestanding beam as the fully glazed front of the extension is set back behind the building line to widen the narrow footpath and form a full-width porch. Visitors are invited in by a flood of daylight from a long, tall clerestory at the rear of the building; the light cascading down and reflecting from a sloping, shaped ceiling and filtered by a screen which separates the banking hall from the offices. The roof of the banking hall is raised in accordance with the significance of its purpose, allowing a narrow, secondary clerestory to bring light into the depth of the extension, so the angled roof appears to hover. The spirit of contemporary Scandinavian architecture, in particular, that of Finn Juhl and Alvar Aalto, is rarely absent from Dannatt's work, and here Aalto is at his most evident.

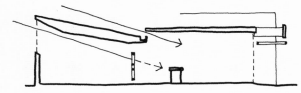

Ten years later, with the growing success of the Society demanding more space, the extension was demolished and the original building embedded within a new building which developed the site to the maximum floor area possible. The site conditions meant that the two embracing wings of the new building were of the same height and width on the street elevation but a symmetrical arrangement would have been pompously grandiose. Therefore, a balanced asymmetrical composition is used to relate existing and new, which are separated by full height narrow, glazed, shadow recesses which assert the repeated vertical emphasis necessary in a terraced street. The groundfloor fascia of the existing building is extended to the left to tie in that wing, relate to the fascia of the adjacent building and embrace the new entrance, which

is further marked by the off-setting of the windows above. This off-setting, in turn, brings the wing into a relationship with the existing building. In contrast, the wing to the right is at the end of the terrace and its windows are moved to, and extended around, the corner, thus terminating the terrace and turning the corner. The rear is a rational ordering of sash and pier—a sober ordonnance; a calmer, quieter descendent of the Rosa Bassett Science Building. The whole, in its 'just so'-ness and quiet, fitting, heightened ordinariness, belies, but is entirely dependent upon, the underlying sophistication of its "common word" prose.

Tea Bar
Festival of Britain
1951

Situated at first floor level in the middle of industrial displays, the design maintained the open feeling of the pavilion while establishing a different character appropriate to a refreshment area.

A stair and a balcony edge bounded the space on two long sides which was then articulated by suspended overlapping ceiling planes related to the different areas of use. Thus the entrance area, defined by the lowest canopy, was adjacent to the compact self-service unit. The main space divided into standing table area towards the balcony side and, nearer the stair side, the sitting area—this covered by the main canopy.

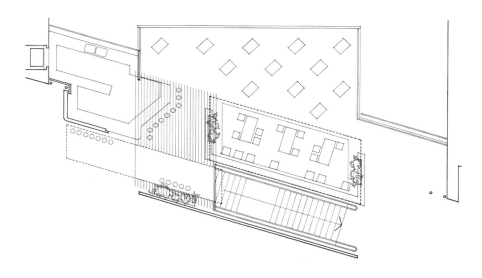

Left: Plan, showing service to the left and standing (top) and sitting areas (bottom).

Top right: Service counter.

Bottom right: General view of the sitting area.

Two Coffee Bars and Restaurant
for Wm S Ellis
London, 1953–1955

These were designed for the caterer who ran the Festival of Britain Tea Bar. The first, The Coffee Mill, giving on to a pedestrian way consisted of two small linked shops, one of which became the service and the other the main consumption area. With the experience gained from the '51 Tea Bar, the interiors and all fixtures were fully designed together with coffee-related mural panels, external signs, etc.. The second, Benet's Buttery, was within a small nineteenth century building set between Queen Victoria Street and Benet's Hill with views both ways and close to Wren's St Benet's Church. The service counter was at one end of the long high room with entrance on the main street set in a shop window wall which curved to meet the solid end and rear wall, where tall windows were fitted with coloured glass panels for horizontal and decorative effect. Free standing tabling and wall shelves were provided and the high ceiling allowed a 'constructivist' lighting feature with small 15 watts lamps on fine steel tubes attached to a larger steel tube armature.

Top left: View of The Coffee Mill entrance and service counter.

Top middle: Sitting area with coffee mural.

Bottom left: Signage detail.

Top right: General view of Benet's Buttery.

Bottom right: Detail of the low wattage lighting fixtures.

The restaurant was a total remodelling of a former ABC Café and named The Lancaster Coffee Grill. The basement included the main kitchen area and a traditional grill room. The ground floor devoted to coffee and light meals is divided by the servery and stairs to form a U-shaped seating plan with open and more intimate areas emphasised by the corresponding lighting feature. The stair wall of birch plywood screening the servery provided a central decorative feature and design work included all fittings and furniture.

The Lancaster Coffee Grill, general views showing the stairs and grill room.

Dickins and Jones
Regent Street, London, 1955

Extensive replanning, fitting out and decorative schemes, included features such as this window display unit for accessories (top and bottom left), redesigned suspended lighting (middle right), standard carpeting, in different colour ways and a special carpet runner.

Primavera
Sloane Street
London, 1954

This notable firm, founded by the discerning Henry Rothschild, centred on the shop, where the narrow interior at two levels was transformed by a new stairway linked with an open display unit facing both ways (left and right) where quality fabrics, glass and pottery could be displayed, with furniture at the upper level.

J Walter Thompson
Berkeley Square
London, 1964

Reorganisation throughout of what was a 1930s flat block included open floor entrance (left) and reception area. The perimeter of the space had a continuous recess formed by a fascia and wide cill (right) unifying the irregular main walls and allowing displays to be contained within a unifying architecture.

Lund Humphries
Reception areas

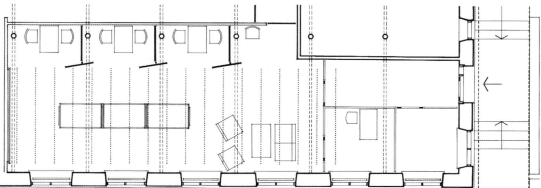

Bradford, 1955 (left)

Part of the ground floor of Lund Humphries' existing administration building re-planned as an entrance, waiting and exhibition space, etc.. The main area comprises a waiting area which extends into an exhibition space and interview bays which correspond to the structural grid and formed by L-shaped screens. Apart from natural side light, ceiling lighting consists of alternate lines of tungsten and fluorescent light, screened by simple hanging louvres between each row, each louvre is divided into three sections painted different colours to a particular overall rhythm. The colours are related to the richer colours in the collage (constructed from waste printed material) by Eduardo Paolozzi on the end wall of the room, terminating the perspective.

London, 1958 (right)

Reception, waiting and secretarial space was required within an existing room for Lund Humphries' London office. The room was restored as far as possible to its original Georgian character and new work inserted as free elements.

These consisted of: a shaped reception counter with a pass gate; a timber screen forming a sitting area with fixed seats and low table; a lowered ceiling over the public area consisting of slats at two levels spanning between deep side members.

A mural panel was envisaged as an area for applied colour in relation to the waiting space, rising through the 'open' ceiling. Patrick Heron's then work was in accord with the idea—bands of colour in the painting and the slats of the ceiling at two levels bring the two elements into close relationship. (The specially commissioned painting is now in the Tate Gallery.)

Top: Main reception, with interview bays, decorative ceiling feature and Paolozzi collage.

Bottom: Plan.

Opposite, clockwise from top left: View from the waiting area, showing slatted ceiling and mural panel; View to the rear office, with protected fireplace; Horizontal striped painting, *Horizontal Stripe Painting: November 1957–January 1958*, 1957–1958, Patrick Heron, © The Estate of Patrick Heron/DACS 2008, Courtesy Tate; Sitting area; Plan.

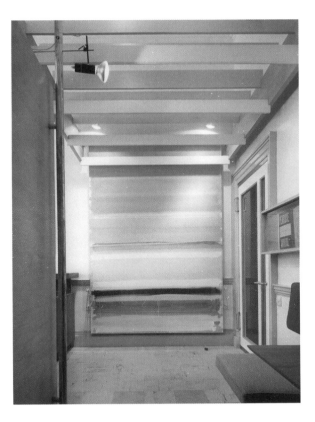

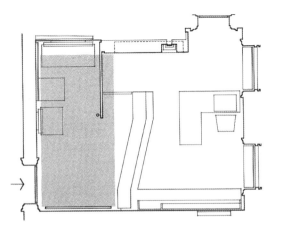

Greenwich Building Society
London SE10
1974

Original conversion, pre-1958.

Side extension and ground floor conversion, 1958.

Situated in the so-called 'Greenwich town centre', the offices for the Greenwich Building Society exemplify a type of development to be welcomed in an area suffering from neglect, showing how an existing building can be retained and extended to make a positive contribution to the urban scene. The nineteenth century, three-storey building was extended at the side and rear ground floor level in 1958—receiving a Civic Trust award in 1960. Additional floor space was required and it was decided to develop the whole site between the converging lines of the High Road and the railway cutting at the rear. On cost evidence and from sentiment, it was decided to conserve the main building which, although of no great merit, has a well-proportioned front of some dignity and had been the Society's premises for many years. Also, the space within the old building lent itself for use as a banking hall on the ground floor, general manager's office on the first floor and board room on the second. The old building is loadbearing brick with timber floors and this loadbearing wall character has been developed for the extension, although around the original building is a concrete beam/column system which isolates the old structure. This gives a clear internal articulation of space and form, which is expressed on the main front by the glazed slot each side of the old building. At second floor the separation of the two structures provides a glazed top light along the rear of the main office area. The building was fitted throughout to a high standard, including a number of rooms with special features, but towards the end of the century this local mutual Society was absorbed and became a branch outlet of a larger Society with adverse effect on the quality of the building in every respect.

Top and middle: Views of the rear offices, 1958.

Bottom: Section, 1958.

The 1974 scheme, showing the street frontage with the first and second floor extension embracing the existing building at either side and rear.

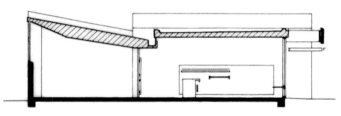

Detail of the front, showing the copper fascia over the entrance to the new offices and banking hall (right).

Return and rear elevation showing the main office extension and the caretaker's flat at third floor.

Clockwise from top left: Main stair detail; Director's dining room; Counter detail in the banking hall; Boardroom.

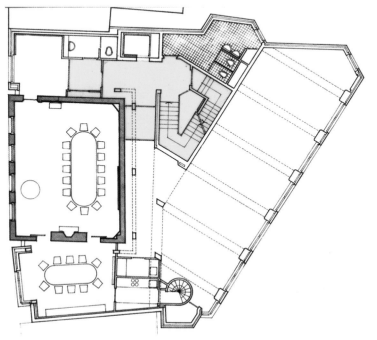

Second floor plan, showing the rear offices, boardroom and director's dining room.

7 Collegiate

Entrance court, Hall of Residence Leicester University.

A university college is necessarily formal in its nature—its activities are intended to be disciplined, ordered, structured and conducted in accordance with rules of convention and etiquette. At Knighton Hall, 1961—in association with Leslie Martin, and Needler Hall, 1964, this formal quality is embodied in the articulation of the structure of the buildings which accommodate the communal spaces, such as the dining halls and common rooms. There is a clear definition and separation of each structural member, a clearly established hierarchical ordering of the different types of member and a rational interrelationship of each, one to the next. Thus, unconsciously, the architecture of the structure echoes the hierarchy of roles in the life of the college, whilst the simple, solid, evidently weighty and strong elements confer an appropriate air of gravitas, and the ordered rhythms of repetition of the various elements contribute to an appropriately calm but rich milieu.

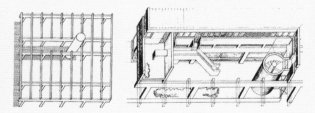

The communal spaces are at the heart of life in a college and here, in each case, they constitute the hub of the composition in the form of a rectangular podium of major spaces, upon which related accommodation sits in pavilions separated by terraces. From this hub, wings of student bedrooms and other accommodation stretch out to form a series of courts—radially at Leicester and bi-symmetrically at Needler. Thus the communal accommodation is not only socially and physically at the centre of the college, but it also forms a side of each court.

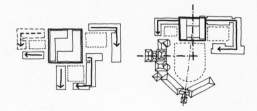

At Needler Hall, the hub also forms the side of a third court, which is bounded by existing buildings. The bedroom wings relate in height and scale to these latter, whilst their boldly expressed concrete spandrils and window heads, which link pairs of windows, chime with the rhythmical pattern of bay-windows in the existing buildings—an "easy commerce of the old and new".

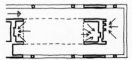 

Within the dining halls, symmetry emphasises the calm, formal milieu. At Leicester, a louvred ceiling hovers over the longitudinal axis of both the dining hall and the common room. Such ceilings had first appeared in the two reception areas for Lund Humphries but are now used in a more formal version. In the common room, the axis and ceiling terminate in ingle-nook fireplaces at each end—intimate, yet formal, retreats.

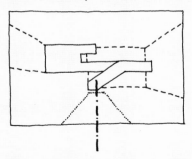

In the dining hall at Needler Hall, at the end opposite the high table, "below the salt", a simple, bold, solid, diagonal staircase rises from the room's central axis to set in motion a balanced asymmetry, which ties together the two different sides of the room; the release of tension occasioned by this visual movement leavening the room's static formality. A stair of similar form had been used at Knighton Hall, the bold diagonal deriving, perhaps, from the stair at The Lancaster Coffee Grill but now in a formal, as opposed to playful, mode. Such staircases become a familiar trope in various transformations and materials, for instance, at Vaughan,

 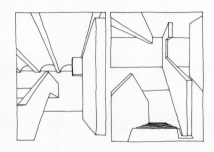

Leicester and Trinity Hall. Through being detailed as cut planes, these stairs are read in relationship to the adjacent walls rather than becoming busy, separate, eye-diverting objects. By such means they are able to maintain the necessary calm of the situations in which they occur. At Needler Hall, the stair in the dining hall returns along a balcony in a sweep of movement and planar form and material. A similar stair and balcony is repeated externally on the adjacent side of the dining hall and yet again, with its innate sense of embracing or wrapping, at Bootham School.

 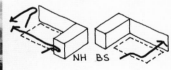

The trabeated structure seen in these college buildings is classical in origin. At Vaughan College, 1962, where the teaching and museum accommodation is wrapped around and raised above Roman archaeological remains, it is correspondingly raised to the level of poetry so that, in conjunction with the barrel vaulted structure it not only recalls Roman architecture but a cave (being an undercroft below street level).

> I went to see Ove [Arup] and explained what was growing in my mind, the need for a reaction to the ruins of a Roman building, its scale and grid and the idea of a massive structure for an open lower floor forming a table for a lighter structure of cellular spaces. There was immediate response, the offering of alternatives and a structural/architectural dialogue followed.... He

offered solutions that nourished one's tentative search for structural consonance and, in his words, did: "try to produce additional values by judicious disposition of the various parts".[1]

As at the Leicester Hall of Residence, the first floor accommodation, at street level, is treated as pavilions upon a platform. Here the horizontal layering of materials and rhythms arising from the trabeated structure is much richer and more satisfying than at the hall—perhaps, 'stratification', redolent of archaeological layers, would be a more appropriate word.

As discussed earlier, both Leicester and Needler Hall are transformations of the traditional college court form but with the bedrooms grouped along corridors rather than around staircases. At Burrell's Field, Cambridge, 1967, not only is there a court—though of a looser, more open form befitting the suburban site—but the rooms are also clustered around staircases.

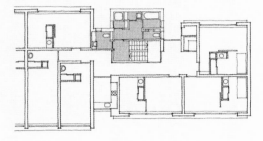

The Senior Combination Room at Trinity Hall, 1964,
—a place for meals, meetings, recitals and other social
events—also uses a formal, calming, ordered, articulated
structure to create a sense of an undercroft but, here, one
of a very different nature. On this hemmed-in site, daylight
is gathered by a linear conservatory through which the
internal space extends out uninterrupted to a narrow
external terrace. A continuous, scale-controlling, solid,
horizontal plane within this verdant side aisle/conservatory
reflects light onto the ceiling. Unlike the earlier suspended
louvred ceilings to which it is related in appearance, this
ceiling is substantial and structural—formal in nature but
also warm, rich, decorative and convivial with glowing,
patterned tungsten light shining from a random array of
intricate nests of timber slats set between the deep,
robust timber joists. It is, in effect, an arcadian grove of
academe. The horizontality, the flow of space out to one
side to a narrow terrace, and the concealed lighting
through richly patterned timber grilles all recall Frank
Lloyd Wright's Robie House.

supporting the stair and the edge of the floor above,
thereby creating an aisle of circulation, symmetrically
reflecting the conservatory/aisle, but such a line of
columns would have made the room too linear—
uncomfortably narrow in appearance. Dannatt's witty
response was to omit the offending lower portion of
each such column, which, thereby, becomes a concrete
tie (an architectural pun, even, to pun the pun, an
architectural malapropism) hanging from the roof
structure, so that space can flow under the stair to
another sitting area around a fireplace and defined by its
own ceiling plane; informality within formality.

1. Dannatt, Trevor, "Obituary, Ove Arup", *The Architects' Journal*, vol. 187, no.
   7, 17 February 1988, p. 26.

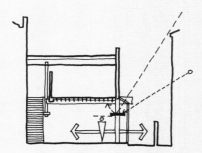

Rising, processionally on the axis of entry, an easy
staircase, of the now familiar form, sweeps up, if not to
heaven, then the haven of the Fellows' parlour, which is
replete with its antique port-table set before the fire.
Cutaway corner windows afford protected inside/outside
situations from which, at this upper level, to look out,
and reflect, upon the world. The windows are those of
the Laslett House, which two of the Fellows had seen,
thereby leading to the commission.

A game is played with the structure supporting the
staircase. The logic of the plan demanded a line of columns

Hall of Residence
University of Leicester
1960

Leslie Martin and Trevor Dannatt

Situated at Knighton, an inner suburb of the city not far from the faculty buildings. The group is planned as a self-contained Hall for 162 students in residence but with dining space for 250. An enclosed type of plan sheltered from the road was developed for reasons of control and economy as well as socially. Three residential groups enclose two linked courtyards which depend on the social building for their fourth sides.

Residential buildings are three-storey and contain study bedrooms of two types. South-facing rooms with balconies and with service accommodation on the north side: east- or west-facing rooms off a central corridor with service accommodation grouped at opposite ends. The residences are of load-bearing brick cross-wall construction.

In contrast, the social building is of reinforced concrete frame to permit wide spans and the general freedom of planning consistent with the use of various rooms together on social occasions. It is planned about an open internal court beyond the entrance hall on the axis of the approach through the first courtyard. Social rooms are arranged on either side of this and provide on the west side a junior common room looking on to the second courtyard, with library beyond. On the east side is the dining hall, the largest element of the plan, its length parallel to the court and mostly lit from it. South of this is the senior common room. Kitchen and service accommodation is on the east side.

The first floor of the social building includes residences for warden and staff. These rooms occupy only part of the first floor and there are a number of terraces. The principal one is planned in relation to a group of smaller social rooms which include music practice rooms and a recital room. Thus all the social rooms are planned in relation to the internal court, which extends right through the heart of the building and visually upwards to the terraces, giving these rooms a common relationship.

Left: Plan view of the site model, with the entrance court to the right.

Right: Entrance courtyard, formed of two residential buildings fronting the social building. Note the south-facing rooms with balconies.

Clockwise, from top left: Residential accommodation over the main social rooms, with service accommodation to the right; Inner courtyard of the social building with circular stair to the first floor social rooms. Common rooms on the left, with the dining room on the right, lit from the courtyard; The entrance hall with view to the inner courtyard, with common rooms on the right, and stair to first floor social rooms.

Opposite top: One of the common rooms (with fireplace recess).

Opposite bottom: The dining hall, with the interior courtyard to the right.

Hall of Residence
University of Hull
1964

Development of an existing hall at Cottingham (Needler Hall), providing 80 additional study bedrooms, dining hall, kitchen, staff and service accommodation, etc., in two storeys planned to one side of the old building and developed about two semi courtyards. The larger court gives access to the residential wings, the smaller forms an entrance court from which there is access to the main social rooms—that is, dining hall, senior common room, meeting room, music room in the new wing, junior common room, library in the old wing, as well as the warden's and existing accommodation. The senior common room on the first floor corner of the social group has access to a terrace which runs along the west side of the dining hall forming a colonnade below at ground level.

Student rooms are planned in groups, each with its own pantry but sharing sanitary accommodation generally at ground floor on the least favoured sides, with study bedrooms on the opposite side. On the first floor rooms are planned on both sides of a central corridor excepting five north-facing rooms which have narrow windows for outlook and high-level south windows for sunlight.

Opposite: View of the entrance court.

Left: Plan view of the site model showing the relationship to the existing buildings, with the entrance court at bottom.

Right: Residential court looking towards the original part of the old buildings.

Top: Detail of the residential building at the junction with the dining hall, with its first floor terrace linking to the senior common room.

Bottom left: Service side showing the access from the street, with some residential parts beyond.

Bottom right: Detail of the residential courtyard.

Left: Stair from the entrance hall of the social building to the senior common room, with the dining hall on the left.

Right: View of the dining hall towards the entrance, showing the laminated roof beams and the stair to the senior common room.

College and Museum
Leicester
1962

Vaughan College* provides non-vocational adult education and is built on the site of what is regarded as the 'forum' of Roman Leicester—to the north and west of the preserved foundations of a surmised Roman bath, forming a virtual courtyard that enhances the setting of the remains.

The building was a joint venture of the University and the City and it was thus that a Museum is included in the design, which is based on two levels. The museum at 'forum' level and at the upper level the main wing of the College is intermediate to the two floors of the classroom wing to the north.

The main floor of the College extends as a terrace, reached by steps from the street, open to the public to give a prospect as well as the approach to the entrance. A stair from the street leads down to a terrace at 'forum' level and the entrance to the Museum.

The more diverse elements of the college accommodation are planned in the main wing and these are linked by a flowing common space which varies in width according to different requirements and at the far end leads to the eight classrooms, which are on two floors approached by stairs beyond the common room, half a flight up or down.

The museum consists of the space between 'forum' level and the underside of the main wing of the college and is devoted to ancient and Roman history. It opens on to the 'forum' with its grassed spaces and looks towards the Jewry Wall and St Nicholas Church, seen through continuous glazing, breaking forward and back to avoid a straight demarcation between museum and site.

A total floor area of some 790 square metres is provided in one undivided space, which, architecturally, is dominated by a system of white-painted concrete barrel vaults carried on transverse double beams at 12.2 metre centres (the same bay as that of the Roman remains). The structure forms a 'table' from which the college part with its very varied spaces is built of load-bearing wall construction.

* Allaway, AJ, *Vaughan College Leicester 1862–1962*, Leicester University Press.

Opposite: General view showing the Roman walls, with the Museum at forum level and the College over. The classroom wing is in the distance.

Left: Rear view showing the double beams of the Museum, carrying the main floor of the College, library (left), and the end of the assembly hall (right).

Right: Junction of the main wing of the College with the classroom wing, right.

Top: Model of the scheme, showing the L-shaped building embracing the Roman forum with the Jewry Wall to the right.

Bottom: Aerial view of the scheme as built. Note St Nicholas' Church, top left.

Opposite top: The terrace in front of the Museum with the forum on the right.

Opposite bottom: View from the forum towards the Museum with the main wing of the College at upper floor level.

Main section looking towards the classrooms.

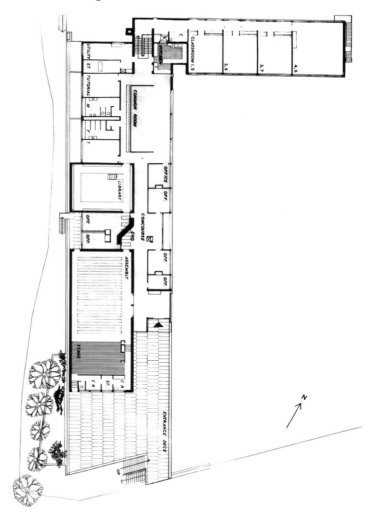

Plan at College level.

Left: General view of the Museum looking towards the main entrance.

Right: The stair from street level to Museum level.

Opposite left: Interior of the Museum with installation, including many Roman items.

Opposite top right: The College assembly hall, detail.

Opposite bottom right: Interior of the library.

Fellows' Social Building
Trinity Hall
Cambridge
1964

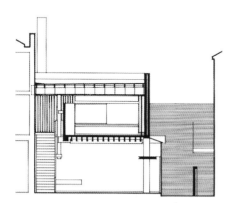

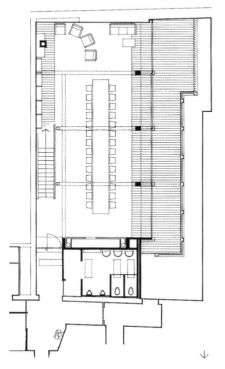

This new building provides a 'combination room' with 'parlour' over for the Fellows of the College, replacing a previous inadequate one-storey structure. The 'combination room' is used for meals, for committee meetings, social occasions, recitals, etc.. The 'parlour' is used as a retiring-coffee-reading room.

The site is very enclosed and natural lighting from the narrow courtyard was of particular concern. The 'combination room' is divided into four bays. Three relate to the dining area (and 'parlour' over), the fourth relates to a sitting space centred on a fireplace (and terrace over).

The main space defined on the court side by the columns extends beyond them into a continuous 'bay window' divided horizontally by an intermediate slab which, apart from its spatial purpose, helps screen the room from overlooking windows. Its top surface also reflects light into the room.

The structure is a concrete frame combined with existing walls. Columns on the window side support cross-beams between which span Oregon pine joists, carrying the boarded double floor of the 'parlour' over. The composite structure is exposed to view as the ceiling over the main part of the room. Between the joists lamps are fixed and screened by simple wooden louver nests. The combination of exposed concrete and timber structure integrated with lighting is richly decorative, giving a warm and convivial quality at night.

On the wall side of the room an easy stair (screened by a 'fence-like' balustrade) rises to the terrace and 'parlour' over. Despite the restricted site generous well-lit rooms with subtle spatial effects and character have been provided and opportunity was taken to realise a complete exterior/interior conception, including furnishings.

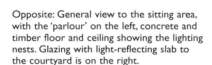

Opposite: General view to the sitting area, with the 'parlour' on the left, concrete and timber floor and ceiling showing the lighting nests. Glazing with light-reflecting slab to the courtyard is on the right.

Left: Plan and general section. The entrance is at the bottom with the sitting area at top.

Right: View from sitting area towards the entrance, with stair to the first floor.

Left: Detail of the external glazed wall with light-reflecting slab.

Top right: Parlour at the first floor, with void over the stair at left and terrace in the distance.

Right: Stair detail, with reinforced concrete hanger.

Left: View to the courtyard showing glazing and first floor terrace to the parlour, left.

Right: Detail of the glazed wall, with parlour windows at first floor.

8   School

Eltham Hill School, first floor link from the old building to the new classroom building.

All the school buildings are pavilions, each in a considered relationship—of siting, form and material—with an existing school. In each case, there is "an easy commerce of the old and new", in which the differences in style are the visible evidence of historical depth, change and continuity characteristic of a well-established school. In each case the nature of that "commerce", that transaction, is different but, inevitably, all are based on a figure-ground relationship between small pavilion and large existing school.

The basis of any figure-ground relationship is contrast. That contrast can take many forms: it can be dramatic, a conflict where each subjugates characteristics of the other, deflecting the eye and sensibilities; it can be eloquent, the figure made clear and pointed, "like bright metal on a sullen ground"; or it can be a subtle relationship, where the figure is designed to chime with and even bring out the latent qualities of the ground. It is in the latter two forms of contrast that Dannatt's intentions lie.

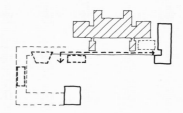

At Rosa Bassett, 1965, the science building interplays with the existing school to simultaneously form a court and terminate an axial route along the embanked terrace which fronts the school. It was proposed that this terrace would become the generating route for the expansion of the school, terminating, at the opposite end, in a group of pavilions clustered around a new court—of which, the gymnasium and changing rooms were the only ones built. The science building establishes a language of piers/pilasters, strong planes and deep modelling of the surface, which is related to the existing building in scale and character. The gymnasium then takes that language and transforms it in response to its very different functional and structural requirements. In both pavilions, the scale is broad and generous, the language open, regular, disciplined—characteristics of a milieu appropriate to a school.

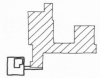

At Eltham Hill, 1969, the pavilion stands proud, elevated above falling ground, distinct from the existing school in language and form but related in scale and linked by a raised walkway.

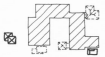

At St Paul's, 1983, designed by partner Colin Dollimore, the existing school is of a CLASP prefabricated structure clad in precast concrete—boxy, bland and flat of roof and elevation on a windswept and treeless site. The two pavilions were intended as indicators of the possible development of a 'crustaceous rim', roughening the edge of the box and mediating between it and the surrounding Victorian houses. They bring a solidity previously missing—and, in so doing, the new buildings figure against the 'neutral' ground of the existing building. The texture, tone, colour and strongly articulated detailing and form of the new buildings give them a feeling of quality and quiet strength which by contrast makes eloquent the repetition and 'flatness' of the existing building. The crispness of the white frames of the existing emphasises the depth, solidity and play of mass, void and shadow of the new, in which the feeling of strength and solidity is emphasised by largely imperforate walls capped by prominent, artificial stone copings.

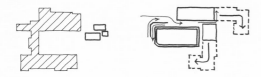

The Colfe's School Arts Lecture Wing, 1984, takes the nondescript language of the adjacent, brick-clad,

main building, with its thin, white trim and fascias, and raises it to an eloquent prose of movement and wit. Around the anchor of the lecture theatre, walls and teaching rooms overlap, slide and rotate and the stairs step forth and back, disposing to one side and the other as the levels of the site are exploited. These are all small but subtle shifts, which accommodate escape stairs, suggest further organic growth, and engender visual movement which brings the building to light-hearted life.

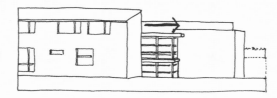

The circulation cheekily protrudes to form a welcoming timber porch with the covetable vantage of a glazed 'balcony' above, whilst the west elevation brings a similar smile to the face with the stepping down and up of its glazed quasi-colonnade supporting a deep, metal 'entablature'. This latter composition is an example of the inflection of an elevation by steps and slopes to accommodate internal variations—not a slave to a pseudo-rational grid but humanising and scale-adjusting in its ordered variation— which is also seen at Rosa Bassett and St Paul's.

Much further away from the existing building, the Colfe's Preparatory School, 1988, is an independent pavilion, which adopts the Arts Wing's language but adapts it to emphasise the horizontality of its form,

by means of which it consorts with that of the playing fields it edges; whilst the rhythms of the glazing bars acknowledge the framed elevations of the existing buildings in the distance.

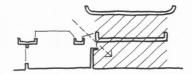

Even the Design and Technology Department at the City of London School, 1991, with partner David Johnson, may be considered as a pavilion, which is emerging from beneath, but ordered by, the structure of the existing building, from which it is separated by a strip of glazing. Again, it is of a related but different language.

In every case the pavilion is a distinctive, individual entity but also a part of the whole, maintaining and developing the coherence and character of the whole and that school's particular degree of formality—a, perhaps unconscious, metaphor for the ambition of every school with regard to the individual development of its pupils within its overall ethos.

Science Building and Gymnasium
Rosa Bassett School
London SW17
1965

The Science Building is sited east of the existing school and care has been taken to relate to it in scale and character. The two buildings define a courtyard open to the south and the field at lower level. The route from the old building is diagonally across this space, leading naturally into the recessed entrance.

The new building, by its projection, ends the terrace along the south front of the old building and in a future development this terrace could become a generating route, extending to further buildings and linking old with new. From this follows the siting of the Gymnasium, which enjoys a convenient position in relation to the old school and the games pitch.

The Gymnasium building consists of two elements—a low block (containing changing rooms, showers, etc.), and the gym hall itself. Clear, uninterrupted end walls are in red brick with concealed strips of top lighting. One side wall is in red brick up to three metres and above there is glazing on both sides with short returns on the end walls, breaking the rectangular box. On the changing room side the lower wall is faced with white painted boarding.

The science accommodation is organised on two floors about the rectangular stair hall and its extension.

The structural system of brick piers controls the design on three sides, on the east side the expressed roof pitches and lower height of the stair hall, etc., make clear the general arrangement.

The plan has four elements: the stair hall and ancillary accommodation; the north end; the centre section separated by the entrance; the south end. Windows stretch from pier to pier and, where required, brick is used as infill. The piers rise through the two storeys and carry up to grip the deep concrete roof fascia which aligns with the adjacent cornice while the piers reflect the old building.

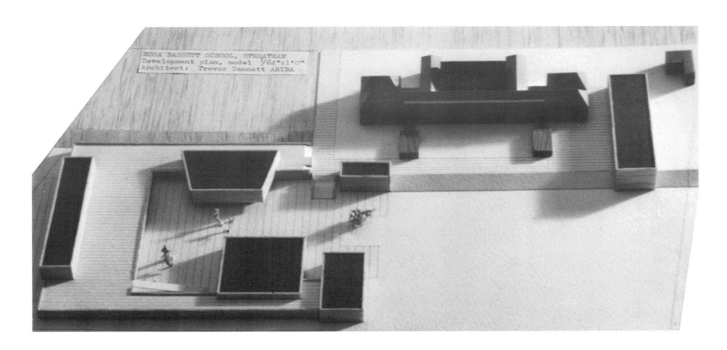

Opposite: View from the Gymnasium wing to the science building.

Right: Plan view of the site model, showing the relationship of the old building to the proposed development, with the science building, far right, and Gymnasium, bottom middle.

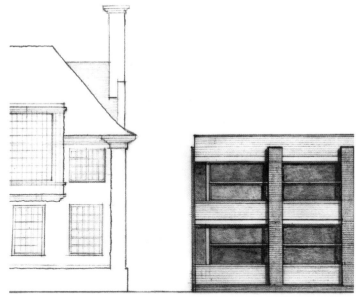
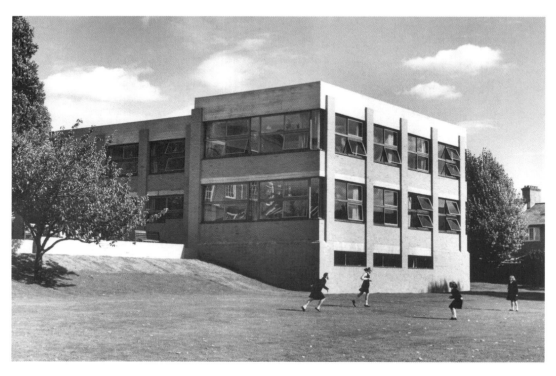
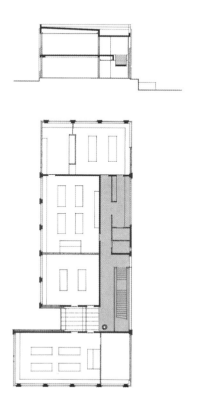

Opposite, clockwise from top left: The courtyard between the old building and the science wing with the entrance marked by a projection; Drawing showing the corner of the existing building in relation to the Science Building; Plan and section of the Science Building; The southern end of science wing looking onto the playing field.

Top left: Entrance and stair hall to the Science Building.

Top right: Side elevation of the Gymnasium.

Bottom left: End wall detail of the Gymnasium, with return glazing.

Bottom right: Gymnasium interior showing the return glazing and occasional outlook.

Classroom Building
Eltham Hill School
London SE9
1969

The existing school buildings are of the early 1930s, in the well-mannered brick, tile and timber window manner which was common to LCC buildings of the period. It was decided to extend laboratory and other accommodation within the old fabric and build to take the overspill and provide further rooms.

The new building had to be closely linked to the old without obstructing it or the adjacent field. This consideration, the levels of the site, and a wish for compactness, led to the architectural solution of a pavilion-like building pendant to the old.

The accommodation comprises general and specialised classrooms, a 'division' room and lavatories and stores. The main rooms are on three floors with two music rooms on a smaller fourth floor. The first floor is on the level of the terrace to the south of the old building and access is provided by a raised walkway, as well as at ground floor under it.

The architectural expression comes from the relationship of the solid load-bearing service block with the framed structure of the teaching spaces. The horizontally emphasised spandrel walls take the heating service and with set back windows provide secret gutters which take run-off from the building face. The profiling emphasises the pavilion-like character of the new building against the solidity of the old.

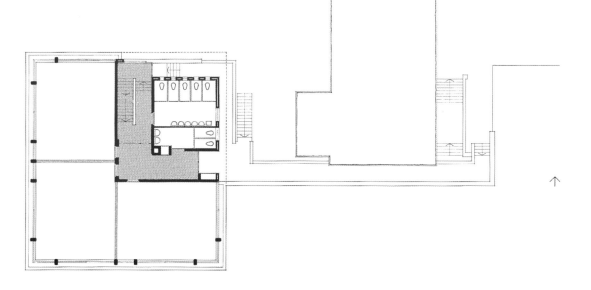

Opposite top: The new classroom pavilion in context.

Opposite bottom: View of the pavilion with the link to the old building on the right. Three floors of classrooms with the music room at upper level.

Left: Typical floor plan showing the link.

Right: The link seen from ground level.

Colfe's School
Lewisham
London SE12

Arts Building
1984

Built essentially for music and drama, the stepped hall seats 140 with more on the flat when the stage is dropped and high folding doors are opened to include the normally separate rehearsal room. A long stair hall gives access to two floors of music classrooms and there is a return to the rear of the hall for dramatic use. Three practice rooms are located under the stepped seating. The building is sited in a pendant relationship with the main building and its courtyard and capable of extension in two directions, eventually giving a more significant mass in relation to the existing building.

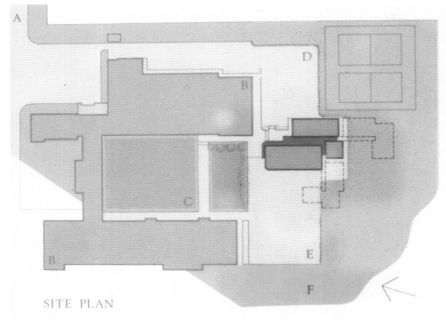

SITE PLAN

Top: The main entrance, with the performance hall, right, and teaching wing, left.

Bottom: Site plan showing the Arts Building in relation to the main school, with possible extensions in outline.

Top: View from upper playground, with the teaching wing to the left. The entrance is at the centre of the lower level, with the theatre/performance hall beyond.

Bottom: End detail of the performance hall with rear escape.

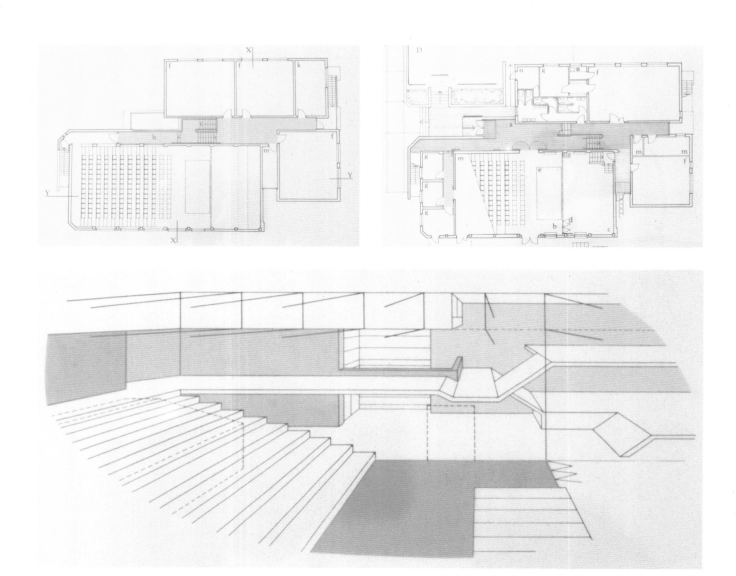

Top: Plans at lower and upper level.

Bottom: Diagram of the stair/performance hall entrance. The rehearsal room is on the right, with variable dais.

Opposite top left: The performance hall with view to the stage, and access gallery on the left.

Opposite bottom left: View to the rear of the performance hall.

Opposite right: Performance hall, view from rear showing removable wall to the rehearsal space, with variable dais in front.

Preparatory School
1989

The building is separated from the main school by a large playing field and has its own site entrance. Two floors of classrooms each served by a central corridor lit by clerestory on the first floor. There are stairs at either end, one of which is emphasised as a formal entrance where there is a long mural panel by Tom Phillips, RA, referring to the school motto and the founder Abraham Colfe. At this end spaces either side of the corridor can be thrown open to provide a large assembly room. A request to save something of the old pavilion which stood on the site resulted in the siting of six columns with connecting timber entablature, providing a link to an adjacent path and to the past.

Left: The old sports pavilion, showing the columns which were recycled to form the pergola.

Top right: The entrance end of the new building, with the stair on the left. The library at first floor is to the right, with the assembly space below.

Bottom right: The classroom facing the playing field.

Opposite left: The colonnade with the recycled columns, and the classroom wing beyond.

Opposite right: The corner detail adjacent to the pergola.

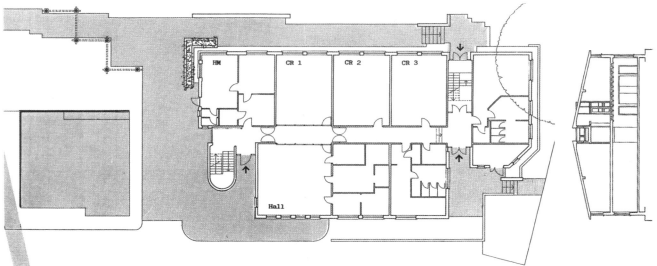

Top left: The mural in the entrance hall by Tom Phillips, RA, developed from the school's maxim.

Top right: The assembly space.

Right: General plan and section.

St Paul's School
Barnes, London SW13

Colin Dollimore, Trevor Dannatt
Colet Court Science Building 1981
Science Lecture Theatre 1983

These two independent buildings were sited against the main school built in the CLASP System. It was thought that any projected perimeter development should be in a more solid mode so that eventually they might form a 'crustaceous' rim to the bland expression of the main buildings.

Colet Court built for Junior School Science teaching makes its mark as a centenary building by virtue of its contrasting structure, 'traditional' materials and the play of forms between the linked lower and upper 'pavilions'. It provides two laboratories, preparation rooms and classrooms. The upper and lower copper covered timber roofs are largely supported off the window mullion system. Otherwise it is of brick load bearing construction, with concrete first floor.

Science Lecture Theatre. Although to some extent related to the science building in character it is more dominantly a brick building with a form that expresses the stepped interior. providing one classroom at entrance level and a lecture theatre for 80, which also doubles as a drama teaching space.

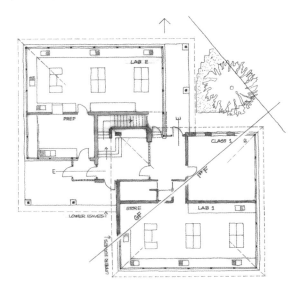

Top: General view of the Science Building, with the teaching spaces at two levels.

Bottom: The brick-built lecture theatre set against the CLASP System existing building.

Left: Plan, split between the ground floor and first floor.

SCHOOL P. 143 BL.

9   Campus

University of Greenwich Maritime Greenwich Campus Dreadnought Library, entrance from the south leading to the library concourse. Original Infirmary Building by James Stuart, 1768.

"A fixt intention for magnificence" on the part of its founder, Queen Mary, led Sir Christopher Wren and Nicholas Hawksmoor, the architects of the Royal Hospital for Seamen, to create one of Europe's finest architectural ensembles.[1] Residing within this magnificence is a range of spatial arrangements—a formal prose of repetitions and symmetries of double-banked rooms arranged around courtyards arising from humane responses to the original function—which has proved remarkably adaptable to different uses with minimal alteration—veterans' accommodation, naval training college, offices, residential, museum, hospital, and, now, a university.

Since 1980, Trevor Dannatt and Partners and Dannatt, Johnson Architects have designed and built many works for Greenwich University and its predecessor, Thames Polytechnic, on their various Campuses. In 1993, the opportunity arose to investigate the feasibility of the University using, initially, the Dreadnought Hospital and, subsequently, also the buildings of the former Royal Hospital. This led to the preparation of a master plan, by Dannatt, Johnson Architects, for the University's occupation of all the buildings on the site and, eventually, the regeneration of four of the five principal, and one of the subsidiary, buildings; each being the responsibility of a partner, under the overall responsibility of David Johnson, with all the buildings becoming fully operational in 2001:

Queen Anne Court—Carl Cairns
King William Court—Carl Cairns
Queen Mary Court—Jonathan Parry
Dreadnought Hospital—Dannatt and David Johnson
Dreadnought annexe—Dannatt and Jonathan Parry.

As discussed by Dannatt in his essay "Re-flections" 'regeneration' is the operative word—not 'conservation' or 'restoration' with their connotations of setting a building in aspic. Rather, the overall approach of minimal intervention arose from " the architects' belief that old buildings give a sense of depth and continuity of life, their sense of time and quality playing a crucial role in helping us to relate to our environment... [and] an understanding of the fundamental role which the framing discipline of architecture plays in our lives". There were to be no significant alterations, and as far as possible, the removal of internal walls/partitions was to be limited to later additions and those which had been removed earlier were to be reinstated. Where new work was required it was to be clearly transitory, contrasting with the robust continuity of the existing but matching it in quality.

A fit was sought between the existing patterns of space (and therefore of circulation and structure)—stripping back to the original, where possible—and the University's required patterns of use; the approach discussed earlier. In this search, it was found that the internal architecture of each building lent itself in a different way to new uses:

Queen Anne Court
(1699–1748—Nicholas Hawksmoor)
The original plan was characterised by large, open wards—four to each floor—with a central spine wall, the pensioners occupying individual wooden 'cabins' within the wards. In the late-nineteenth century, the building became partly a museum, openings being made in the spine wall to aid circulation. In 1936, the ward spaces were subdivided by partitions to provide small teaching rooms and other accommodation with a lecture theatre cutting through the spine wall. Now, the great ward spaces have been opened up again to form large classrooms and social/circulation spaces.

King William Court
(1698–1728—Nicholas Hawksmoor)
In the south wing, large cellular rooms were arranged on each side of broad, central corridors. To enable the circulation of air and the daylighting of the corridors, the wooden partitions between the corridors and the rooms stopped short of the ceiling. In the late nineteenth and twentieth centuries the partitions and walls were removed to form classrooms and a two-storey lecture theatre created at the east end. These earlier alterations increased the scope for the creation of new classrooms, computing suites and lecture theatres in the south wing, whilst retaining the original broad central circulation and

utilising the north–south central wider space as a 'break-out' social area—much as Hawksmoor had originally created areas for convivial gathering. The existing, small rooms in the more complex west wing are now offices, divided from the central corridor by the original, fan-lighted partitions.

Queen Mary Court
(1735–1751—Thomas Ripley)
Here, Ripley disposed uniform rows of cell-like, small rooms on each side of a central corridor—the rooms and corridors, on the ground floor and part of the first, being groin–vaulted and the partitions being solid rather than the timber as in the other two Courts. These now form offices (having earlier been proposed as student bedrooms) with the corridor lit by the original nineteenth century glazing above the partitions. The south–east corner rooms originally had lath and plaster partitions, making possible the opening out of administrative nodes, light and spacious.

Dreadnought Hospital
(1764–1768—James Stuart)
This building, originally two storey, was progressive for its day, being organised in two wings of well-lit, small wards on either side of a central corridor, around a courtyard, which permitted the separation of medical and surgical cases. Over its history, the building was much changed—the addition of another storey to east and west wings, the construction of sanitary towers to the east and west, the rebuilding of the central courtyard buildings to extend kitchens, baths and privies; and, more recently, the removal of some walls to provide larger wards and operating suites and general modernisation up to its closure in 1986.

This pattern of spaces and circulation has been skilfully and sensitively mapped onto the functional needs of the university library with the insertion of steel and glass structures within the two halves of the court to form the reception area on one side and provide a denser bookstack area on the other, where it was originally intended to locate a restaurant.

West Annexe
(1808–1810—John Yenn,
extended 1931–1933—Edwin Cooper)
This building was originally single-storey and known as the Helpless Ward. It has seen much change, including the addition of a central first-floor chapel in 1885, which was linked directly to the Dreadnought Hospital, the extension north and south of the first floor by Edwin Cooper and the destruction of the northern end by bombing in 1940.

The northern end has been rebuilt but not to its original extent. The resultant form is disposed asymmetrically about the original entrance position, which is on the east–west cross-axis of the Dreadnought Hospital—an axis which extends right across the site through the William and Mary Courts. The entrance is announced by the first floor projection of a concourse space within. Contrary to all the other works at Greenwich, which contrast new and existing work, here, Dannatt "enjoyed working in a sort of Edwin Cooperish manner".[3] Cooper's stripped classicism of the mid-1930s was a forerunner of that Janus-like position which Dannatt was to encounter and develop ten years later; that proximity in time perhaps enabling the sensibility seen here and the avoidance of the traps of pastiche and Neo-Classicism.

1. Bold, John, "The Royal Hospital Buildings at Greenwich", Maritime Greenwich Campus, London: Dannatt, Johnson Architects, 2002, p. 6.
2. Bold, "The Royal Hospital Buildings", p. 7.
3. Dannatt, Trevor, "A tree is not just for Christmas", 20th Century Society Presidential Inaugural talk, 11 December 2003.

University of Greenwich
Maritime Greenwich Campus
London SE10

The earlier practice and the present one (Dannatt, Johnson Architects) have been much concerned with campus planning. Early on Dannatt was involved with Leslie Martin at Leicester and in the University of London master plan.

Working for Thames Polytechnic (which was to become the University of Greenwich in 1992) studies and detail plans were made for Thames' Campuses at Woolwich, Dartford, at Avery Hill and Roehampton as well as extensive building development within the different frameworks.

Since its two main campuses were in the Borough of Greenwich the University designation was appropriate but it was considered that there should be a presence in 'historic' Greenwich, i.e. in the area associated with the Royal Naval College, Royal Park and Observatory. On the RNC site the Dreadnought Seamen's Hospital, formerly the Hospital Infirmary, had been vacant for some years after its closure. Leased by the NHS from the Greenwich Hospital Charity, negotiations for a transfer were instituted with a view to the building becoming the University's Centre of Governance and Administration. Planning permission for a full restoration/conversion had been approved when the then government announced that the main Royal Naval College buildings would be put on the property market and tenders would be invited.

The University led by the late Vice Chancellor, Dr David Fussey, responded and John McWilliam, Deputy Vice Chancellor, brought together a group of consultants and backers to further a bid for the group to become the central campus of the University. Dannatt, Johnson were appointed to prepare the Masterplan to demonstrate the viability of site and buildings for University use together with technical proposals for refurbishment throughout/providing space for administration, teaching, residential and social and full supporting services.

After much debate, the Jenkins Committee formed to consider future use and management of the site recommended the setting up of an independent Trust "charged with preserving the architectural and historic integrity of the site with the proper maintenance of the buildings and ensuring public access". Thus the Greenwich Foundation came into being and which among

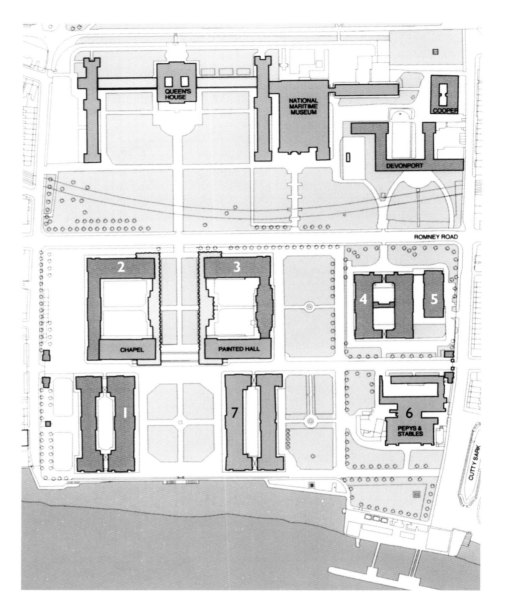

University of Greenwich Maritime Greenwich Campus [old Royal Naval College].

Key from top, south:
Greenwich Park
The Queen's House,
National Maritime Museum,
Old Royal Naval College, Romney Road

Clockwise, from bottom left:
1 **Queen Anne Court (UoG)**
2 **Queen Mary Court (UoG)**
3 **King William Court (UoG)**
4 **Dreadnought Library (UoG)**
5 **Stephen Lawrence Building (UoG)**
6 Visitor Centre (Greenwich Foundation)
7 King Charles Court (Trinity College of Music)

many duties leases the buildings to the University and to the Trinity College of Music which occupies King Charles Court.

Work commenced in advance of final negotiations commencing with Queen Anne and the Dreadnought which was to become the Campus Library. The work was done in close association with English Heritage and its Officers, especially Dr Michael Turner and his colleague Ms Paddy Elson.

Queen Anne Court

Despite extensive subdivision, it was found the original order of the building was virtually intact, except at one end where the spine wall had been cut away to provide lecture theatres, which gave opportunity to insert new more sophisticated theatres. The large wards either side of spine walls were cleared of all subdivision and were formed into two at the most classrooms with adjacent breakout spaces. Full circulation was achieved around each floor and electrical and heating services were totally renewed throughout. Throughout the design in all the buildings the intention has been to let the robust character of the building speak for itself and offer contrast where new elements were necessary by high quality 'lean' design.

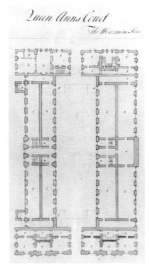

Queen Anne Court, first floor plan, c. early 1700s, showing ward spaces.

Part first floor plan, southwest corner after conversion.

Clockwise, from top left: Second floor of the west wing, with restored timber roof trusses over a multi-function space; The new lift in the space of a redundant early twentieth century stair, with glazed enclosure; Return glazing of the lift shaft to the double height space of the former stairwell; The new lecture theatre in the west wing, north end.

King William Court

"It is Hawksmoor we must thank for the resplendent architecture of the most wonderfully idiosyncratic building in England." (John Bold)

The building form embraces a large courtyard with the "Painted Hall" to the north, the architecturally highly charged wing to the west and the main accommodation wing to the south. Owing to major earlier alterations this wing offered the opportunity for more radical interventions. Thus two 200 seat lecture theatres are located at third floor level, requiring tiering making use of the roof spaces, where in one case it has been possible to expose the fine but massive roof trusses.

The second floor includes staff offices and two specialist computer labs whilst the first floor has two generous full width teaching spaces each with 100 workstations. In addition to a lecture theatre the ground floor includes three classrooms for 50 each plus a studio space.

The west wing is very dense with small spaces rather belying Hawksmoor's powerful elevation. Work here was essentially a conservation exercise but included the insertion of a new modern escape stair.

Clockwise, from top left: The west wing, new escape stair, in timber and glass; The south wing, first floor, open plan computer workstations; The south wing, third floor, east lecture theatre, with 200 seats, showing restored laylights with artificial lighting.

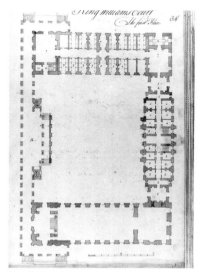

King William Court, Hawksmoor's plan of the first floor, c. early 1700s.

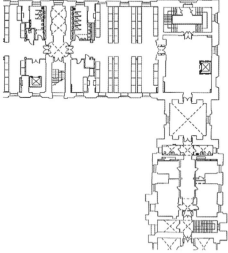

King William Court first floor, 2001, detail. Open plan computer work stations. Much of the internal structure had been removed during RNC occupation.

Queen Mary Court

Queen Mary is a much more cellular building. There are no ward spaces and work was primarily concerned with restoration, manifesting the original character of vaulted corridors with rooms off which had been compromised by insertion of suspended ceilings, crude partitioning and general malaise. All services were renewed, a new escape stair added, and complete re-decoration has transformed the building. It is largely devoted to offices, tutorial rooms and staff rooms. Originally it was to be residential as it was previously, but owing to King Charles Court, which was to be academic, being granted to Trinity College of Music, such use was not possible.

Clockwise, from top left: The southeast corner. Ground floor remodelling to provide a reception area; The new steel stair in the remodelled southeast corner; The first floor, east wing, with restored central corridor.

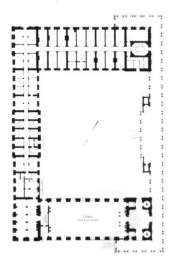

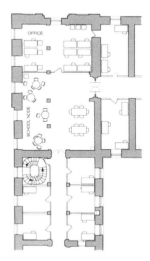

Queen Mary Court, plan, c. 1735, by Ripley, which replaced the Hawksmoor plan replicating King William—much as today.

Plan of southeast corner, first floor, showing the remodelled area with the new stair and school node.

Dreadnought Library
1995

Below: Ground floor plan as originally envisaged with Library concourse (1), restaurant (4), main corridors (2 and 3), Library entrance from the south (bottom), restaurant entrance (top), Stephen Lawrence building (to the left).

Opposite: The Library concourse, view to the south entrance, with reception counter and issue desk (to the right).

What is now the Dreadnought Library was originally built to replace infirmary wards in the Royal Hospital. As conceived by James Stuart the plan was a Courtyard (with central ablution block), narrow wings to the north and south and main wings to east and west on two floors and central corridors servicing small wards each with four beds.

Upon closure of the Royal Hospital in 1869 and creation of the Royal Naval College, the Infirmary was leased to the Seamen's Hospital Society. It superseded the converted "Dreadnought" hulk moored in the Thames nearby and cared for sick merchant seamen of all nations for over a century.

Early on the second floor was added and extensive rebuilding including repair of bomb damage and internal redevelopment occured throughout the life of the building. In 1986, as an NHS hospital after some years of neglect, a £10 million programme of regeneration and conversion was undertaken by the University. The building was in an advanced state of decay, necessitating wholesale replacement of timber and plasterwork, irretrievably damaged by wet and dry rot.

Many of the internal walls between wards were removed over the years to create larger wards and for requirements such as operating theatres. The renovation has retained many of these more open areas, as well as the few surviving four-bed wards plus the main staircases in the centre of each wing. Various archways within the building are part of the original fabric and the colonnade which links the main wings, sub-dividing the central courtyard, forms a significant retained feature.

The three floors of the building each provide approximately 1,000 square metres for library and information resource areas and the wings give easy access to library stacks and study areas on either side of the generous central corridors.

The two halves of the central courtyard between the wings have been infilled with a ship's deck-like structure of horizontal pierced steel beams supporting the main glass roofs. Originally, the North Courtyard was planned as a restaurant but became accommodation for library stack.

The entrance to the library is from the south side through the double-storey height archway. Here a low canopy links the archway to the library entrance doors in the set-back glass wall which forms one side of the library court, otherwise contained between existing walls and the colonnade to the north. The enquiry and control desk is central to the entrance; over to the left there is the library issue and enquiry counter. Users proceed to the colonnade where they can gain access to the main accommodation by lift or stairs. There was an existing link between the two main wings at first floor level, and this has been developed to include a link at second floor.

Apart from the restoration of the severely decayed fabric entirely new mechanical and electrical services have been installed. Heating is by LPHW radiators generally in a building of high thermal mass.

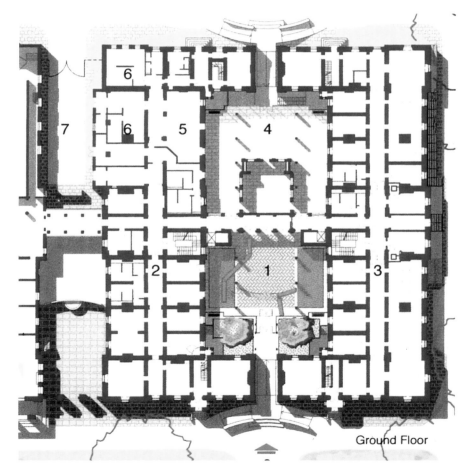

Ground Floor

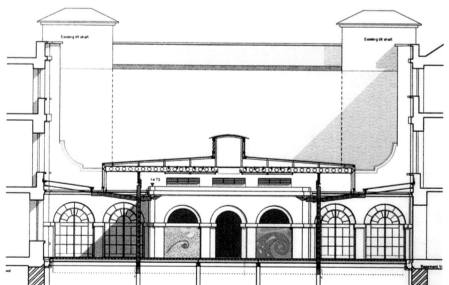

Early perspective view by Dennis Bailey of the north courtyard as proposed for a restaurant. The central 'pavilion' is part of the original building retained as a memento of its former use. The roof ceiling and structure are as built in both north and south courtyards. The section below shows the high central space with side aisles allowing natural ventilation to the first floor rooms in the main wings.

Clockwise, from top left: Structural detail showing the upper and lower roofs; Part view of the Library concourse showing the retained central collonade, which links the east and west wings; Detail of the columns and yard arms supporting the beam/gutter of the aisle roof.

Above: South glazed wall of the Library concourse, with the linking canopy through the open section of the court.

Top right: View to the south, over the courtyard roof, showing the central link between east and west wings.

Bottom right: The central link as seen from the south, showing the main roof with central ventilation monitor and aisle roof, bottom right.

The Stephen Lawrence Building

Known successively as the Helpless Ward, the Somerset Ward, the West Annexe and now named in memory of the local student killed in a racist murder. John Yenn's single-storey building (1810) became part of the "Dreadnought" hospital when various modifications took place over the years. The northern half was destroyed by bombs in 1940 and it remained a truncated and adapted part of the Dreadnought Hospital until closure.

Following the University's take-over there was temporary use until funding became available and it was decided to retain the existing part and rebuild the north end, but not to the full extent of the original building. This resulted in a format composed about the original entrance position. The new build includes the ground floor entrance hall with two classrooms to the north and adjoins the existing central corridor to the south—leading to a new escape stair. A main stair leads to a generous foyer at first floor, serving a 126 seat lecture theatre and the existing central corridor serving classrooms and offices. The building has been completely restored.

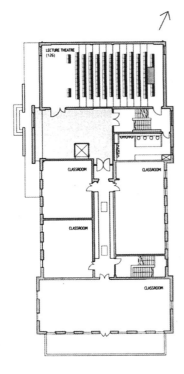

Above: Plan at first floor level.

Left: The rebuild of the bombed north end, with the main entrance and projecting bay of the lecture theatre concourse at first floor.

Top and bottom right: Upper and lower levels of the new lecture theatre at first floor.

10 Desert

Top: Concept sketch by Trevor Dannatt,
"Temple and Residential Hill", 1966.

Bottom: The Conference Centre and Hotel
seen soon after completion, 1974.

The conference complex in Riyadh provided the opportunity to create architecture in a very different topographical and cultural context and of a vastly greater size, scale, and monumentality than the other works but its success arises from exactly the same intentions, values and skills, not the least being an "understanding of proportion and scale".[1]

Won in a limited international architectural competition in 1966, this group of buildings is another form of campus, consisting of a conference centre, hotel, mosque and housing. Its location on the edge of the desert (as it was until enveloped by the growth of Riyadh) evoked a poetic response, adumbrated in Dannatt's generative sketch of a "temple and residential hill" for the "formal word" of the Conference Hall and the "common word" of the Hotel. This figure-ground contrast of a precise, geometrical, white figure standing four-square against a raking, flowing, organic, yet geometrically chiselled, brown ground/form was not just for architectural and symbolic reasons—the division of the brief into two distinct buildings also aided the production process in both design and construction.

The flowing geometry of the Hotel extends into that of the site, where it shapes the stone-faced flood control channels—the 'ground' in both a literal and figurative sense. Thus, the Hotel, with the enclosing slopes of its foyers faced with cleaved concrete blocks and its staggered bedroom wings faced in local stonework, appears to grow out of the landscape, whilst the conference hall stands in true temple manner on its horizontal podium of rusticated in situ concrete, with a colonnade of clustered columns carrying capitals supporting an entablature. The slight tilting upwards of the corners of the entablature (and of the fascia of the auditorium) to avoid the appearance of sagging is a flourish of classical entasis. The classical allusion is maintained further on the north–west elevation of the 'temple', where the pattern of gaps between the groups of vertical sunbreakers, themselves an allusion to fluting, suggests a colonnade in negative.

The two approaches to the Conference Centre are sharply contrasted: formal, axial, orthogonal from the road and subsidiary, informal, flowing, diagonal from the Hotel. The formal entrance, a grand propylaea, which announces the building, is an extension of the structure of the foyer. For the foyer, Dannatt had felt that "a grand scale and calm effect" was required—hence the slow, dignified rhythm of the large square grid, which is accentuated by the stately rise and fall of the vaulting; the square being essentially calm in its non-directionality but also, through its repetition, conducive to the milling movement of delegates.

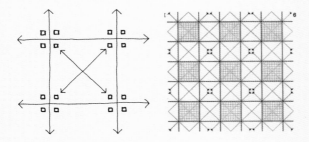

This ambiguous sense of repose and movement, which emanates from the square grid, is emphasised by the quadripartite column clusters, which also serve as ducts for the air conditioning from below by sealing the gaps between columns with glazed panels. The introduction of the conditioned air at ceiling level, but brought from below, obviates the orthodox need for plant and ducts in the roof and suspended ceilings. In this, and the pattern of the structure, the foyer anticipates Foster's Stansted Terminal by 25 years. But, whereas Stansted is a lightweight structure, this is concrete—the origin of which was the strength required to support rooftop parking, which, thankfully, was omitted, for security reasons, at an early stage of design development. However, the retention of the concrete provides both useful thermal mass and an appropriate quality of gravitas. The shaping of the capitals and pendant slabs in response to the structural forces, with the central slabs being lightened by coffers, which accommodate the light source, conspires with the giant order of column clusters and the secondary order of single columns to emulate a Roman grandeur, more Baths of Caracalla than temple—a sense of permanence in

the shifting sands. With this milieu, the Conference Centre contrasts sharply with the Royal Festival Hall (RFH), which had been so formative in Dannatt's development, and with which there are so many comparisons.

As at the RFH, the foyer and ancillary functions surround the auditorium, but, as Martin pointed out, Durand had shown in his *Recueil et Parallèle des Edifices*, published in 1801, this was an inevitable pattern in the anatomy of the building type.[2] The interest is therefore not only in the influence of the RFH but in how Dannatt recognised and responded to the differences between a concert hall and a conference centre.

The auditorium, as that of the RFH, is a separate, concrete 'basin'—the same element that was being used contemporaneously at Bootham School Hall and was to be used later at the Blackheath Friends' Meeting House. It shares with these two, but not the RFH, a 'floating' roof—here introducing boredom-relieving daylight through a clerestory. The roof is not supported on the walls of the auditorium, as at the RFH, but has its own structure of four diagonal piers, which are set beyond the confines of the hall and absorb thermal movement and wind loads.

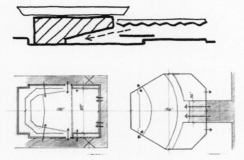

The undercutting of the auditorium and its spatial separation from the foyer, as at the RFH, opens views down to the lower foyer, which is extended as far as possible beneath the auditorium. The positioning of the principal, axial entrance at a split-level affords gracious, easy movement to both upper and lower levels of the foyer—the former by diagonal stairs recalling a flight in the original entrance vestibule to the RFH. Although

the foyer extends down the sides of the auditorium to give access to ancillary accommodation, such as committee rooms, it does not provide the RFH's multiple side entrances to the auditorium. In contrast, a single, broad, axial bridge flows from the upper level of the foyer dramatically into the centre of the 'belly' of the auditorium. Thereby, unlike the gradual build-up of individuals to form the audience for a concert, the delegates come together as they enter, disperse to their seats, and are then brought together again on leaving. Within, a further contrast between a concert and conference hall is revealed, for, on entry, it is immediately apparent that Dannatt has succeeded in his intention of creating "not an auditorium with desperately focused roof, rushing down to concentrate on the stage, but a spacious airy conference room... not theatrical in any way".

The interior of the auditorium also reveals a reversed figure-ground stylisation of the classical vocabulary of plinth, pilasters and entablature, which echoes that of the north–east elevation. Here is a further break with the orthodoxy of the time—a form of decoration, something the architects of the RFH had not been reticent about but which a later generation had rarely known how to handle, with a consequence which Michael Brawne identified in Powell and Moya's Wolfson College, where: "The eye moves from an understanding of [a] clearly structured space [directly] to the pattern of the wood grain: the intermediate hierarchies of space and surface modulation are absent and are missed."[3] As Brawne says, the classical vocabulary of pilasters or panelling and niches has a recognisable series of gradations which can aid an understanding of size and focus attention on the components of a space, as seen here at Riyadh.

The changing nature of the second, lesser, informal approach can be narrated thus—from the flowing movement initiated in the Hotel and extending into the landscape; into the quietening, imposing, calming, square grid of the foyer, with its views and opportunities for encounter and conferring opening in all directions; to the majestic, axial sweep into the laterally expansive repose of the auditorium.

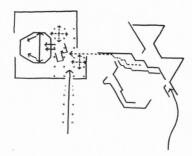

The generative geometry of the Hotel 's M-plan evolved from the desire to have all 200 bedrooms with patios facing north, with as much privacy between them as possible, and illuminated by reflected, hence softened, daylight. As can be seen in Dannatt's original design diagram, the plan reduces the length of corridor compared with a conventional single-banked layout by overlapping and echeloning bedrooms in a manner similar to that which was used at the Poplar housing to overcome its density/dwelling frontage problem. Another advantage is that there are no internal corridors, but balconies overlooking internal courtyards—the door to each room is directly related visually to the foyer—"a backdrop of bedroom wing and a fore scene of reception spaces, terraces, restaurants and the like". This was a new type of hotel building, the design of which predated John Portman's Hyatt Regency San Francisco, the so-called first of the atrium hotels, by several years, but was unrecognised as such, possibly because it was not completed until two years after the Hyatt Regency.

The concrete pendant reflectors, which suffuse the foyer with a soft light and exclude the sun are another variation of the suspended louvred ceiling. Externally, their heavy eyebrows—idiosyncratic but so right— show the sure touch of a feeling for scale and material and recall lines of geological strata upon a hill.

These dramatic foyer spaces, so appropriate in the Saudi context, where a hotel is tantamount to a public space, provide cool, but visually stimulating, oases, hovering, tent-like, between inside and outside. Unlike the Portman hotels, the soaring, high spaces are reserved for circulation and transitory activities, whilst the lounges and restaurants shelter restfully

under mezzanine floors of trabeated structures with hexagonal columns supporting a radiating system of beams in a hexagonal pattern of triangular segments. The non-directional grid again provides a spirit of calm as in the Conference Centre foyer, but here of an appropriately more relaxed nature. In the angles of the coffers are nests of timber slats, glowing with Trinity Hall's warm, patterned convivial light.

Thus, both the Conference Centre and the Hotel have what Dannatt calls " that substitute for external space which seems to me part of the Arab architectural tradition (whether done with or without architects)"— a tradition, perhaps with its roots in the tents of Wilson's "natural imagination", whilst a reference to tents proper occurs in the canvas entrance canopy.

In these two buildings, the integration of services and environmental control with the form, the use of geometry, and the play of the classical and modernism all recall the work of Frank Lloyd Wright; an architect with a classical training who, in the course of his long career, developed a congruency of structure and servicing systems in the classical, axial symmetries of the Larkin Building, 1904, and adopted angular geometries in section and natural/geological analogies as a means of relating to a desert site at Taliesin West, 1937.

At Riyadh, in the mosque and housing, another mode of architecture is also evident—yet all is held as a whole through the siting and consonances of scale, a material, structure and geometry.

The mosque is a place of great calm—austere but welcoming and rich in light and shade. It had occurred to Dannatt that mosques were "rather like congregational churches—the word's the thing, not the altar", and Sherban Cantacuzino describes how the eloquence of this Wahabi mosque, "... reflects Dannatt's non-conformist background and understanding of desert puritanism...".[4]

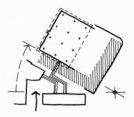

The mosque was originally planned parallel to the road but then skewed in its orientation after the intervention of the local Imam. The twist helps: it mediates between the geometries of the Conference Centre and Hotel and between the Hotel and the road, easing entry to the site. The rotation also opened up an additional, angular court, so that, "after the informal shape of [this] entrance court and the brilliant light-and-shadow play of the cloisters, the self-effacing character of the mosque proper is all the more striking".[5] This latter consists of a court and a covered area, at a slightly lower level, over which a tinted brown concrete slab 'floats', free of the walls, allowing (until later glazed) the flow of light and air. The character of this ostensibly simple place arises from the sophisticated interplay of simple elements, viz., a square grid of octagonal columns supporting a system of primary and secondary beams. The primary beams form a series of aedicules— the purest manifestation of the healing and comforting properties of the "natural imagination"—with each aedicule being centred by its pendant light fitting; whilst the secondary beams break down the scale of each aedicule to that of a group of four individuals kneeling below, each individual in their own corner of a square—the square being that most static and calming of shapes.[6] The secondary beams also, in their continuation, weave a tartan, interlinking each primary square within the whole. This relation of part to whole—individual to congregation— is also determined by the octagonal shape of the columns, their chamfered, softening shape promoting a flow of space which asserts the primacy of the whole space, whilst still defining each individual, square aedicule.

It is a building of minimal decoration—just thickenings of the wall surface—stripped to the bare bones of its painstakingly scaled and proportioned structure. Dannatt now reflects that it had "a certain Perret classical feel about it". In this can be seen "an easy commerce of the old and new", one of architectural cultures rather than buildings, and, even more significantly, an "easy commerce" of religions.

This "easy commerce" also arises from the reworking of two of Dannatt's tropes; the parti of a walled rectangle enclosing an interlinked covered space and court, conjoined as a whole, which was established at the Blackheath

Congregational Church in 1957; and the hovering ceiling plane, here in the L-shape seen at the Maze Hill Chapel, 1954, where, as here, it defined and sheltered the path to the place of worship. At the mosque, this latter takes the form of a pergola—a colonnaded kafess (sun grill)—which defines the courtyard on two sides, a variant form links Mosque and Hotel to one side of the Hotel ramp.

Adjacent to the mosque, and a further step down in scale, the terrace of three houses adopts the same ostensibly simple language of walled enclosure, part open as court, part covered with a slab roof and part covered by a timber kafass on a trabeated structure supported on columns, each, of course, with a fireplace and chimney for the cold desert nights.

1. Cantacuzino, Sherban, "Conference Centre and Hotel, Riyadh", *The Architectural Review*, April 1975, pp. 215–219.
2. Martin, Leslie, *Buildings and Ideas 1933–83: From the Studio of Leslie Martin and his Associates*, Cambridge: Cambridge University Press, 1983, p. 15.
3. Brawne, Michael, "Wolfson College, Oxford", *The Architectural Review*, vol. 156, no. 932, October 1974, p. 206–220.
4. Carolin, Peter, "Diplomatic Response", *The Architects' Journal*, 10th July 1987, p. 38; Cantacuzino, 'Conference Centre and Hotel, Riyadh'.
5. Cantacuzino, "Conference Centre and Hotel, Riyadh".
6. Wilson, Colin St John, "The natural imagination", *Architectural Reflections: Studies in the philosophy and practice of architecture*, Second Edition, Manchester: Manchester University Press, 2000; Kite, Stephen and Sarah Menin, "Philosophy and psychology of the *aedicule*—John Summerson and Colin St John Wilson", *ptah*, 2005:1, Helsinki: The Alvar Aalto Academy.

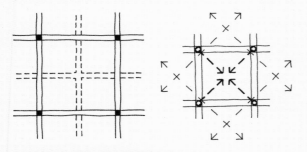

Whilst the minaret is liturgical in its origin and function, it also pinions the site in its original desert setting, marks an entrance to the site, and acts as a crucial element of the composition—counterpointing the essential horizontality of the other buildings and chiming with the vertical serrations of the echeloned bedrooms. In fulfilling these other purposes—analogous with those of the chimneys of Dannatt's houses—it is uncharacteristically tall and slender for Riyadh's unostentatious, Wahabian tradition of squat towers but, in being so, recalls Misha Black's advice to Dannatt to always add a third more height when designing a flag pole (advice, Dannatt also applied to his chimneys). This tall, slender minaret of white concrete with its balcony crown of oak and twisted gilded rods again recalls Frank Lloyd Wright, whilst the interplay of sticks and rods finds a different function in the almost contemporaneous Friends Meeting House.

King Faisal Conference Centre and Hotel
Riyadh
1975

This complex was the outcome of a limited competition organised by the International Union of Architects for the Saudi Arabian government. The competition design was developed and received the approval of His Majesty King Faisal in 1967. The scheme consists of two closely related but architecturally differentiated main buildings, as well as a mosque and three villas.

The Conference Centre comprises a hall with seating for 1,400, three meeting rooms for 150 each, two small meeting rooms, together with exhibition and refreshment areas at different levels and the necessary service spaces. A VIP entrance is reached by a spiral ramp at the opposite end to the main entrance and VIP reception is at upper level within the main foyer space. A large *porte cochère* breaks forward from the main front of the building and there is a link to the Hotel.

The brief called for a first class hotel on generous lines with 200 rooms, reception areas and lounges, dining for 300, private dining rooms and full service accommodation. The approach to the Hotel is via a curved, ramped roadway leading to the main entrance. The service entrance is between the two buildings behind the link and the central plant room is in the same area.

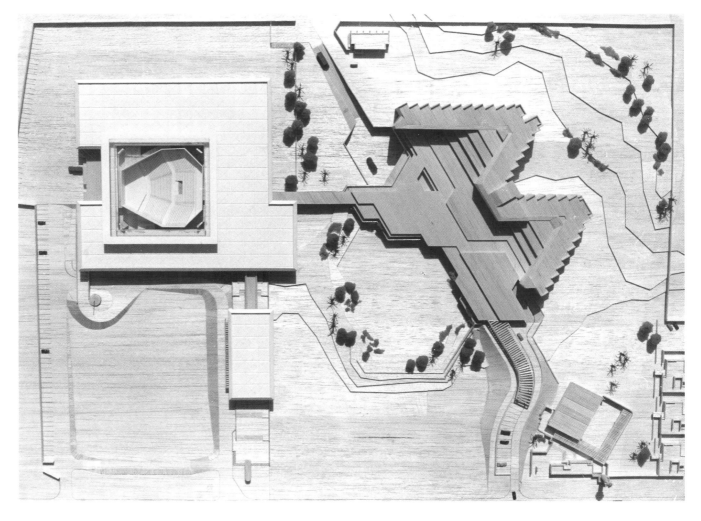

Opposite: Part view of the *porte cochère* of the Conference Centre, with the Hotel to the right beyond.

Right: Site model, 1967, with the Conference Centre (hall roof removed) (left), with *porte cochère* at the front, and the ramp to VIP entrance to the left. Hotel (right), with the main social rooms in front of the M-shaped bedroom wings. The Hotel entrance ramp next to the Mosque and Villas is at bottom right.

Following pages: The road view of the Conference Centre from *porte cochère* to the VIP ramp and entrance (left) at upper level, extending through the main foyer. The hall roof is beyond. The folded steel canopy over the car arrivals is to the left of the *porte cochère*.

Conference Centre
Trevor Dannatt and Partner Ronald Paxton

The Conference Centre is characterised by a formal, regular system of structure, providing large, free, internal, sun-protected spaces with the auditorium/hall at the heart. The Hotel is characterised by the accretion of carefully oriented individual rooms about two internal hall spaces. There is, therefore, a contrast between the Conference Centre, geometrically placed on the site—as a temple—and spatially generous for assembly and interchange, and the more plastic form of the Hotel that grows out of the site—like a residential hill and forming an indigenous building of unique character.

The foyer spaces around the hall are planned on three levels:
(1) An entrance area opposite the *porte cochère* which opens into a general foyer and exhibition space the full length of the building.
(2) An upper level, reached by broad flights of steps from the general foyer. From this upper foyer a wide group of doorways lead into the middle of the hall—a major architectural experience and one which enables participants to come together naturally before and after assembly. This level extends beyond the hall to serve as foyer to the range of meeting rooms.
(3) A lower level, reached by broad flights of steps from the main level. This area is a general space—which can be used for exhibitions as well as a refreshment area. Off this level are the principal toilets and service areas.

The 'hallspace' is square and covered by a space frame steel roof supported on four diagonally placed corner columns. The hall itself is set within this space and the enclosing walls rise to within one metre of the main ceiling, the gap being filled with heavy glazing. Thus there is effective spatial connection between the inside and outside of the hall which allows natural light into the foyer and the hall. However, blackout blinds are provided integral with the glazing between foyer and hall. To provide a calm room, the hall ceiling has been considered as a level but modelled plane (not a sloping plane focussing on to the stage as in a theatre or cinema). It is not a separate element but enmeshes with the structure—consisting of plastered coffers shaped into the pyramids of the steelwork. A number of the coffers contain 'spiders' which carry lighting and the air distribution.

Hotel
Trevor Dannatt and Partner Colin Dollimore

All Hotel bedrooms face on to private balconies, which themselves face away from the sun. The M-form arises from this arrangement and as a result there are no internal corridors—bedrooms are entered off galleries which overlook the covered courtyards formed within the arms of the bedroom wings. The entrance foyer connects the two courts that rise up through the full height of the building. The courts contain the principal lounges which at entrance level provide very generous spaces, open and in parts semi screened.

These courts, with their galleries at different levels, are the characteristic feature of the Hotel. They are sun-shielded, restful intermediate zones between private rooms and the outside, providing the luxury of architectural space in the 'grand hotel' tradition, rarely found in a modern hotel, but thought necessary in the Riyadh context.

Near the entrance is the stair down to the restaurant and adjacent is a walkway which extends as the link between Hotel and Conference Centre. Either side of this, at the Hotel end, space is provided for shops as well as the 'coffee shop', opening onto first floor terraces overlooking the extensive evening terraces at restaurant level below.

Left: The Conference Centre seen from the canopied ramp approach to the Hotel.

Opposite: Site plan, showing the Conference Centre (left) with the link to the Hotel (right). The Mosque is bottom right with the villas adjacent.
Note: Conference Centre—the detached *porte cochère* with the link to the main building, and the extended foyer space at two levels serving the five meeting rooms (top) and the central bridge to the Assembly Hall. The foyer extends along the front of the building with the upper level for VIPs with private car arrival via the ramp (left).
Note: Hotel—the curved access ramp to the Hotel entrance with the public spaces and two courtyards formed by the M-shaped bedroom wings.
Note: Mosque—the entrance court from the Boulevard, with service spaces to the right and steps down to the L-shaped pergola enclosing the courtyard, which fronts the enclosed space of the Mosque.

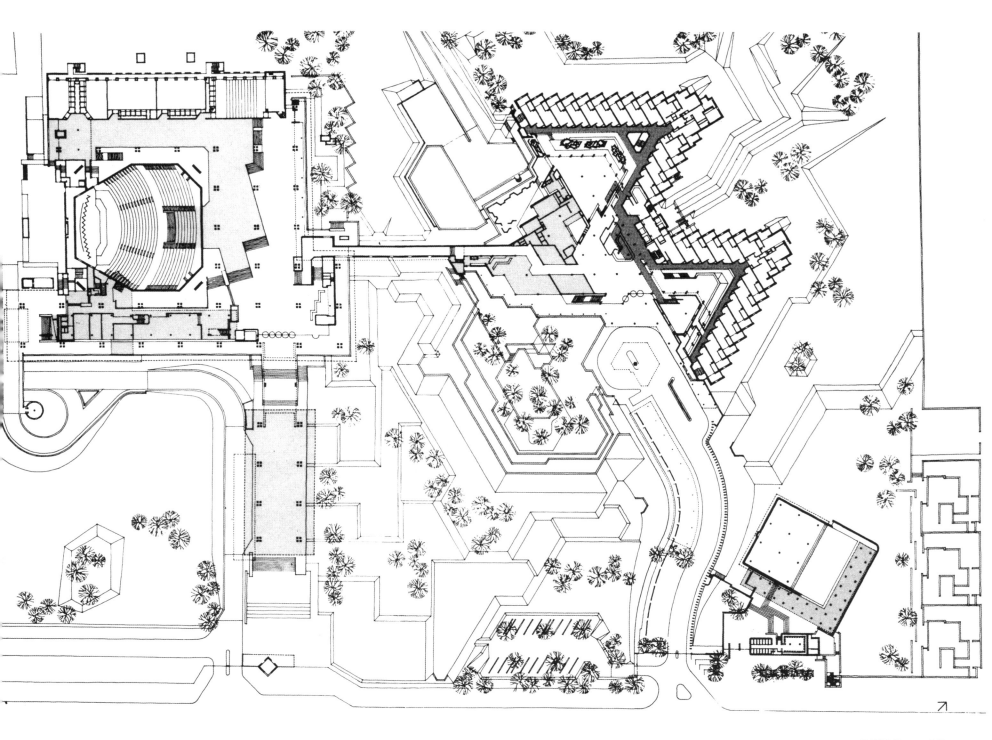

Opposite top left: The north–west facade of the Conference Centre, showing the roof over the Assembly Hall, and the Meeting Rooms block with windows screened by suspended sun breakers.

Opposite bottom left: Corner detail of the Assembly Hall steel roof, with part of the foyer structure below. Note the entasis on the 'cornice'.

Opposite right: Detail of the south–east facade, with the podium in in situ rusticated concrete (enclosing service rooms). The main foyer level, with the VIP upper level. The foyer cornice is finished in white mosaic. The metal assembly roof fascia is above.

Top: Link from the upper foyer level to the Assembly Hall entrances, with the lower foyer refreshment areas below. The rear Assembly Hall soffit is top left.

Bottom: Section through the Assembly Hall and the foyers—(1) main foyer level, (2) upper foyer, (3) Assembly entrance, (6) lower foyer, (7) refreshments.

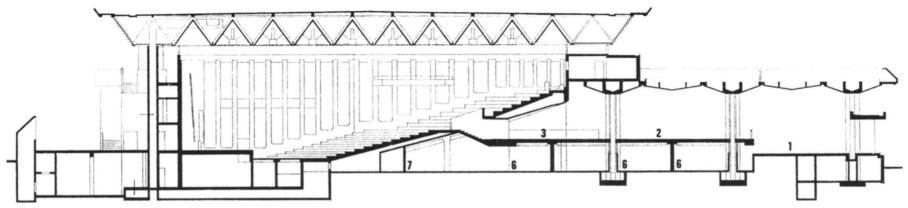

Opposite: The main foyer at entrance level. The steps to the left lead to the upper foyer and bridge into the Assembly Hall, with the slots beneath opening into the lower foyer. At the far end is the wall with the group of meeting rooms behind. The cluster columns with glass infill form ducts for conditioned air distribution.

Above: The lower foyer with refreshment areas. The upper foyer level is above.

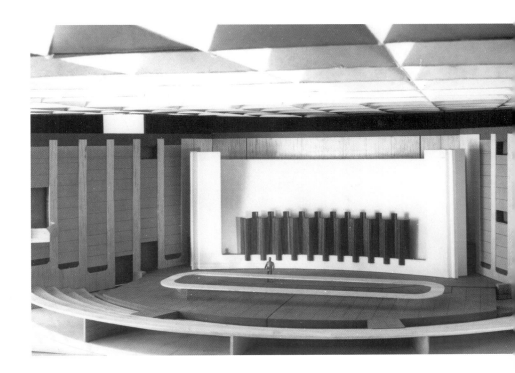

Opposite: The Assembly Hall interior with its upper tier of seating, and the steel roof with fibrous plaster coffers and lighting 'spiders' with central air distribution louvres. The enclosing walls with lilac blue fabric panels between travertine piers are shown, with the clerestory above (which can be blacked out). The light brown fabric seating contrasts with traditional white clothing.

Top right: Model of the Assembly Hall interior with the extended stage area, in conference format.

Bottom right: The Assembly Hall showing the central vomitory, the main cross gangway, and the coffered ceiling floating over the clerestory glazing.

Hotel
Trevor Dannatt and Partner Colin Dollimore

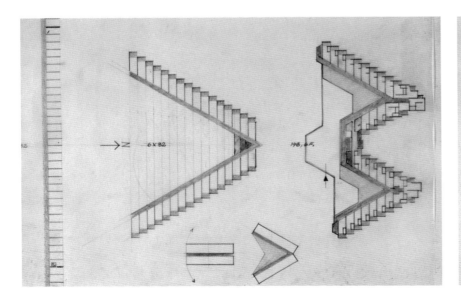

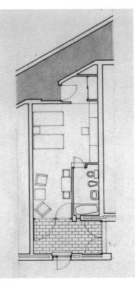

Opposite: The Hotel, showing general view of the central part, with bedroom wings receding to the left and right. The entrance level with terracing and the restaurant level below, opening on to private garden.

Above: The reception counter in the entrance foyer between the main concourse/sitting spaces. The private access gallery is above at intermediate level.

Left: Genesis of the Hotel plan—left to right: straight wing with rooms facing away from the sun; cranked plan with rooms opening to private balconies giving indirect light; double crank with central vertical access galleries serving bedrooms, overlooking enclosed courtyards.

Right: Typical bedroom plan—top to bottom: access balcony; lobby and wardrobe; bedroom area; bathroom; sitting area opening onto private balcony with outlook to the north and shutter opening to east or west.

Opposite, clockwise from left: Garden at the restaurant level, with entrance level above and arrival canopy. Also above bedroom wing with strip glazing to the court, with bedroom access galleries; Arrival area with the central canopy and linking canvas louvres; View from the terrace at arrival level, over the garden and Conference Centre beyond.

Right: One of the Hotel lounges in court with the screened access galleries to the bedrooms— looking toward reception. Suspended concrete louvres screen the strip windows.

Top: A bedroom access gallery looking into the court with the lounge below, and the sloping roof with concrete louvres.

Bottom: The extended lounge area in the second court beyond reception, with access galleries seen in the distance—before fitting out.

Riyadh Villas
1973

Built before the completion of the main buildings as part of the Hotel (management housing). These were used by construction staff during the development.

The normal Riyadh contemporary house is of Western type 'dropped' into a rectangular plot formed by a high wall on all sides, and surrounded by unresolved space. In traditional settlements houses are built with integral courtyards from which rooms are lit and ventilated.

The three villas develop this theme. They enjoy security and privacy and windows open into green courtyard spaces which can be enjoyed, the larger ones having slatted sun screening. External stairs lead to roof terraces.

Later schemes were prepared for larger clusters of similar plan-type villas.

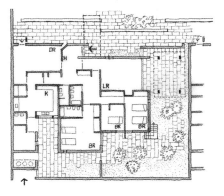

Top left: Development study for a cluster of villas on an adjacent site.

Bottom left: Plan of one of the villas. The access way is at the top, with the main entrance. The service entrance, bottom left. All rooms are courtyard lit.

Top: Villa roof-scape. The entrance canopy over the access way is in the foreground, with the canopy over the living room courtyard to the left.

Bottom: The living room courtyard with slatted canopy, and stairs to the roof terraces to the right.

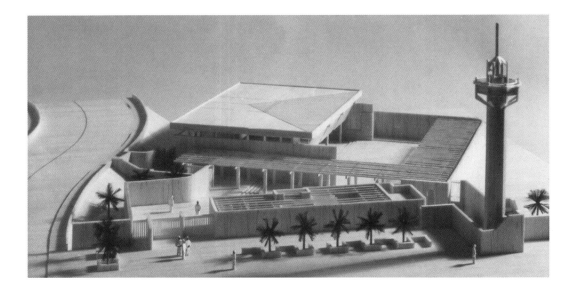

The Mosque
Riyadh
Trevor Dannatt and Richard Clarke

The competition design included a prayer room, then a separate Mosque was instructed with Minaret. As sited at the foot of the Hotel ramp, it aligned with the road geographically on the Mecca axis. To conform with precedent the siting was modified to good effect insofar as it broke a certain rigidity. An informally shaped entrance court steps down to the L-shaped shaded cloister that embraces the courtyard which fronts the open end of the Mosque.

The main space is enclosed by independent rendered walls separated by a gap from the coffered roof which floats over them and is supported by 12 octagonal fine finish concrete columns formed into two by three bays. The dialogue between wall and structure with its hints of Perret gave a measured and hallowed ambience responsive to the nature of earlier mosques in the Kingdom. Subsequent glazed enclosure with limited air conditioning gave more comfort but was less in accord with the spirit of the forerunners.

The Minaret stands on the road at the east corner of the site. It has a white concrete octagonal shaft and rises from dark brown lower walls and terminates with a steel and oak balcony structure in fragile contrast to the finite shaft.

Top to bottom: Model of the Mosque as built—from right: Minaret, service building (shoes, ablutions), entrance court from the Boulevard, forespace of the Mosque with L-shaped enclosing pergola, the Mosque with 'floating roof'; the entrance court seen from the Minaret, with steps down to the Mosque level and pergola (right). The service building in foreground; Long section with pergola, open courtyard, and the enclosed space of the Mosque.

Opposite top: Distant view of the Minaret, with floating roof of the Mosque.

Opposite bottom: The entrance court of Mosque looking towards the Boulevard.

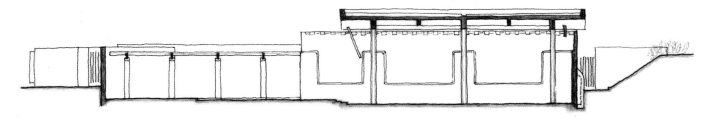

Top: Looking out from the Mosque to the open courtyard and pergola enclosure.

Bottom: The Mosque interior and part open courtyard.

Above: The Mosque interior, with detail of the column and beam structure supporting the floating roof, which is independent of the enclosing walls.

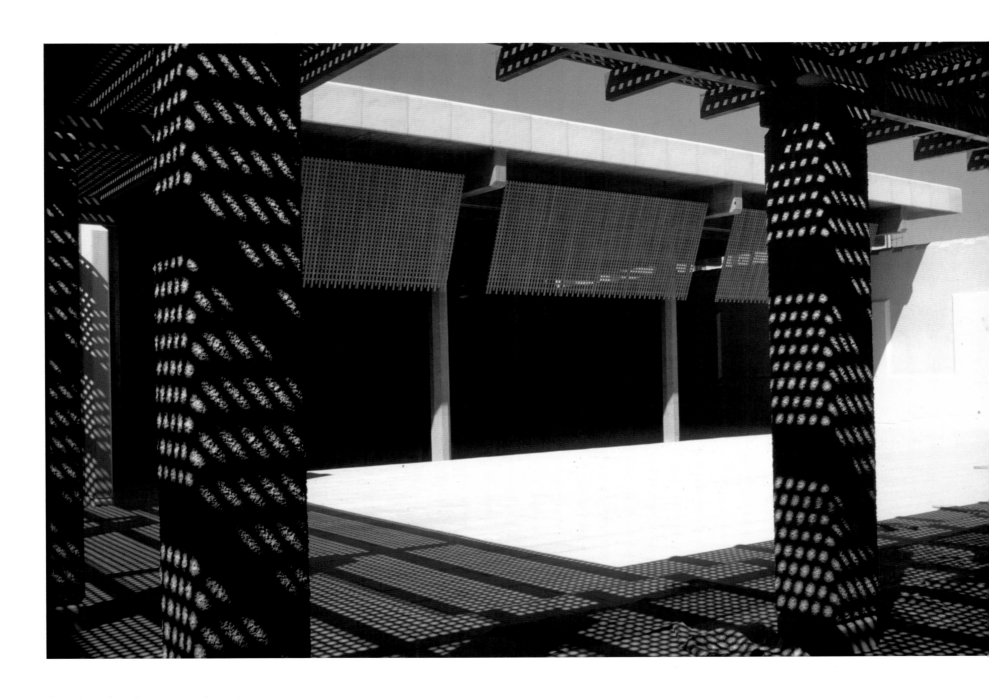

General view from the entrance, with pergola,
courtyard and the open side of the Mosque,
with hanging sun breakers.

11 Worship

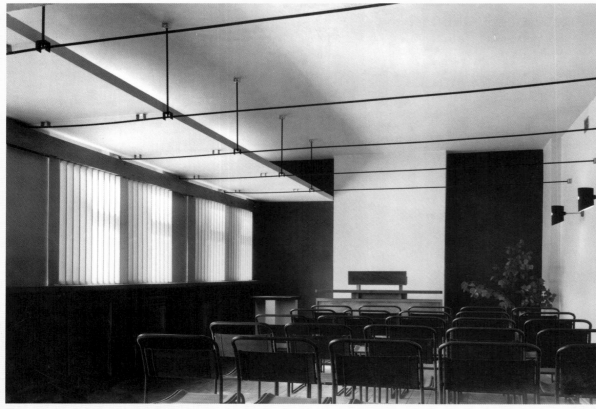

The small chapel, Greenwich, with a view to the pulpit and font stand at the end of the access aisle, with canopy over.

In *A Descriptive Note on the New Church* for the Service of Dedication of the new Congregational Church in Blackheath on 9 February 1957, Dannatt wrote:

> The architectural effect of the interior, like many a traditional parish Church, depends on simple forms carried out with ordinary materials (as poetry can be made from everyday words)....

This applies equally to the Riyadh Mosque and all Dannatt's other buildings for worship. Amongst other purposes, the poetry serves to create a milieu, an ambience, appropriate to the acts of worship and contemplation—a change of state of mind from the everyday, enabled in each case by the composition of the sequence of entry to the place of worship.

These intentions and the means of their realisation had first been built in 1954 at Maze Hill (Greenwich) Congregational Church, in the conversion of a school room into a temporary chapel—a conversion composed of fragmentary elements of an earlier design for a new, but unbuilt, church. The stepping and turning approach path; the free-standing planes of brickwork indicating movement and gradual enclosure; the swelling of the path to form a place of stasis and gathering before the porch; the hovering, horizontal plane above the porch; the stout oak beam—defined as an element in its own right (that figurative tie beam form embedded in Dannatt's "inner landscape"); the turn through 90 degrees on entering; the linear, hovering plane/canopy (that of the Festival of Britain Tea Bar, which adjusts scale, reflects daylight and conceals artificial lighting); the space-modulating rods (another renaissance church reference) which support the canopy; the counterpointing black cylindrical wall lights; the balanced asymmetry of the whole—all are elements and compositional means which consistently recur in various forms and are here combined in a deceptively simple interior of a calm, timeless quality: "In my beginning is my end...".

The earlier design for the unbuilt church had included a long L-shaped canopy which precurses the pergola at the Riyadh Mosque. This contingent nature of design, where an element or pattern, previously experienced or used, subconsciously finds its place again in a different context, was also seen in the Mosque's parti, which had its origin in the Blackheath Congregational Church of 1957. For Dannatt, this was "one of the few jobs where I had an instant mental vision of the design". Here again can be seen: the stepping and turning on entry, each event a potential pause whilst moving from street to court to porch to church; the balanced asymmetry, with the pulpit on the axis of the off-set ridge; the separated, sliding planes—that of the roof emphasised by the eaves detail; the horizontal scale-adusting, light-reflecting plane making a space within a space as at Trinity Hall; and the asymmetrical arrangement of objects—an Adrian Heath exhibition hanging projected into three dimensions.

At the Society of Friends' Bootham School, 1971, worship takes the form of a meeting—a gathering around (sometimes but not necessarily, a table) and therefore centralised, not linearly orientated to an altar. However, an adaptable building was required for both worship (centralised) and assemblies, concerts and drama (linear). Dannatt, with the engineer, Ted Happold, an old boy of the school (who was working equally closely with Dannatt at Riyadh in the development of the form and structure of the conference centre) resolved this conflict through a consonance of structure, form and light, which combines the centralised and the linear.

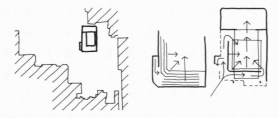

This is another school pavilion but here the need was for a sculptural form surmounting its figurative ground. It is another concrete (that plain, plastic, earthy everyday material) basin as at the RFH and Riyadh—with a floating roof. The L-shaped wrap of walls and stair—as at Needler Hall—divides and distributes circulation from the diagonal approach, forms a transition of gradual enclosure through a cloister, and subtly mediates between the axial and centralised foci required within.

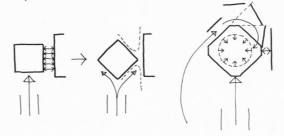

At the Maze Hill Chapel, the column supporting the oak beam at the entrance was rotated through 45 degrees, making it less abrupt and confrontational. The same rotation is used at the Friends' Meeting House, 1973, for similar purposes. Here it reduces the sense of formality, divorces the building from the adjacent hall and avoids a sense of congestion on the site. The rotation also initiates an entry sequence of increasing enclosure, in which the change from the external

materials of concrete and quarry tile to timber, plaster and cork signals the retreat from the outside world, but to which is allied an increasing sense of enlightenment and uplifting of spirit through the increases in ceiling height as the path ascends to the light-flooded meeting room itself—another internalised concrete 'basin'. The chamfering of the corners of the rotated square eases movement and asserts the centralised gathering of the meeting; whilst, externally, it restates the relationship to the adjacent hall and street—the pier facing the street being rotated through a further 45 degrees, thereby making the building appear less hermetic by opening up the undercroft, allowing the expression of the hall above as a separate element and relating base to crown through the axial correspondence of vertical arrises.

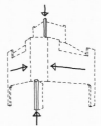

The chamfering also provides the means by which light can be brought down to wash the walls behind the worshippers, so again emphasising the enclosed, centralised nature of the space; a space which is crowned by the lantern—another congruence of structure and light, which is formed of the sticks and ties (those of the Riyadh minaret).

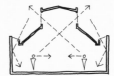

In the re-ordering of the chapel at St Paul's School, 1983, to achieve a more devotional atmosphere, it can be seen how an understanding of the essential qualities and order of the existing building—in particular, the nature of its section and the squareness of its plan—enabled the "tuning of the space" to create a place of calm, serenity and greater religious feeling. The

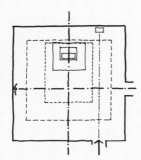
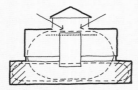

necessary strengthening of the altar axis by such means as the familiar hovering, louvred ceiling plane, which cuts out the glare, was balanced by creating a secondary axis from the side entrance to the repositioned crucifix, thus re-establishing the stable calm of the square. The higher, light walls of the central volume, flooded with daylight (or the equivalent, concealed, artificial source) shining down through the louvred plane, are contrasted with the lower walls (in the aisles) by painting these in a dark colour, warmly washed by concealed strip lights, to create a hallowed space within a space, and a contrast between the dark below and the heavenly light above, to which eyes are naturally drawn. The reredos, by Patrick Scott, is proportioned and positioned to overlap both the hovering plane and the fascia which surmounts the dark aisles, thereby bridging between all three realms. Thus, the building is tuned at all scales down to the level of detail, in, for instance, the replacing of the two forbidding, floorstanding candlesticks, which defensively marked the corners of the dais, with the pendant light fittings that eloquently and simply define this sanctum whilst allowing the flow of space which thereby encourages a sense of inclusion.

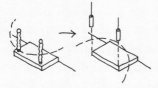

Although this tuning of the St Paul's chapel is so specific to the place, many of the elements—the balancing of primary and secondary axes; the emphasising of a space within a space; the linear, hovering, translucent plane; and

the contrast of light and dark walls—had been established in tuning another interior as a place of contemplation (of the paintings of Jackson Pollock) 25 years earlier at the Whitechapel Gallery.

In these adjustments at St Paul's Dannatt also drew heavily on his "inner landscape" of experience of worship and, in particular, of renaissance churches. Having flirted with the metaphor of a chapter house at the Friends' Meeting House (a significant departure from his earlier abstracted compositions), in the extension of Whittington College Chapel (1985) he drew directly on the precedent of a favourite painting, no doubt with a wry smile, imagining the congregation gathering before the new narthex which mediates between house and church, with its deep soffit recalling, and acting in the same manner as, the oak beam at Maze Hill Chapel, 50 years earlier.

Church and Chapel
Greenwich, London SE10
1954 (Chapel)

The nineteenth century neo-grec church at the bottom of Maze Hill was destroyed in the War but not the ancillary buildings. The proposed church (1952) featured a canopy stretching across the front of the churchyard and leading into the new building with 'nave' and one 'aisle' and an asymmetrical roof, the ridge centred on the pulpit. A small chapel was formed within the remaining buildings as a 'sanctuary' until the new church could be built. Being at the rear of the site and at a lower level, a raised canopy was used to mark the entrance. The approach was not direct and the visitor crossing the first terrace was 'turned' by a brick sculpture, then went by path and steps down to a brick paved terrace forming a small concourse at the entrance.

The chapel had an aisle on the window side with a lowered slab over, supported by rods from the ceiling and spanning the room. These and the slab, which reflected light on to the main ceiling, increased the apparent height and the horizontal rods helped to 'regulate' the space.

In the church design the free wall on the churchyard side was chosen by the painter, Ithell Colquhoun, for a projected work to feature in a Society of Mural Painters Exhibition.

Top: The canopy over the chapel porch, with the raised beam structure relating to the site as it drops to the entrance.

Bottom left: View from the porch back to the entrance off the street. The canopy is over, with the screen wall to the right.

Bottom right: Detail of the pulpit showing the zinc faced screen panel, with the plastered brick font stand and slate top.

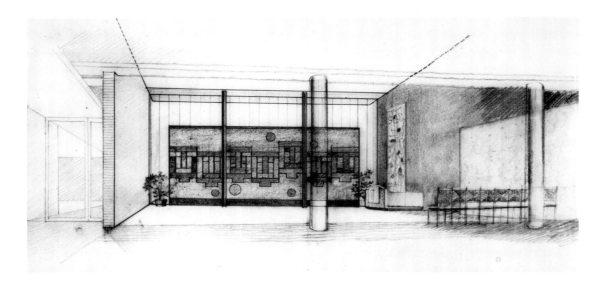

Top: Plan of the small chapel. The approach from the street on the left steps down to the entrance area with the beam and high canopy over. The porch, chapel, and aisle are on the left, with the pulpit and font stand.

Bottom: Plan of the proposed church—(from bottom) street, access path, marker wall, canopy over, leading to the entrance, with the main aisle to the right, and organ and choir seating. The main body of the church seats 160, with the enclosing wall on the left intended for the mural.

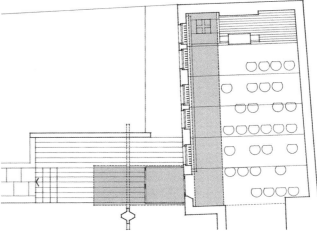

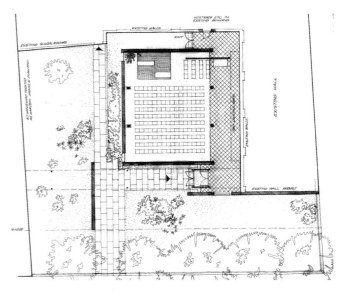

Top: Interior, with entrance to the left, showing the main body of the church with the wall for the intended mural, choir seating and pulpit to the right.

Bottom: View of the church entrance centred on the long canopy, with the street to the right.

Top: "Saints" mural design by Ithell Colquhoun, 1952. Courtesy of Dr Richard Shilltoe. © National Trust.

Bottom: The site model with the church (the chapel was in the old building, to the extreme left).

Congregational Church
Blackheath, London SE3
1957

Rather than demolish the war-damaged shell, a new church was created out of part of the old fabric, retaining sections of three walls and constructing a new roof over the reduced volume with axis at right angles to the old one. What was the end wall, with fine organ, became the side wall of the new building, the opposite wall consisting of glazing between two massive stone piers which support trusses carrying the low pitched slated roof. Thus the church is approached through a courtyard within that area of the old building not incorporated into the church, formed by retaining parts of the old walls as enclosing screens.

Seating is planned as a central block while the pulpit is central to the asymmetrical ridge line and set on a brick platform which also carries the communion table and the font. The main walls are left the white of lime plaster, and the timber trusses and roof construction are undecorated, providing a warm contrast to the walls. The side glazing is clear, the courtyard can be seen from within and in a sense the two spaces are united giving awareness of the relationship of old to new.

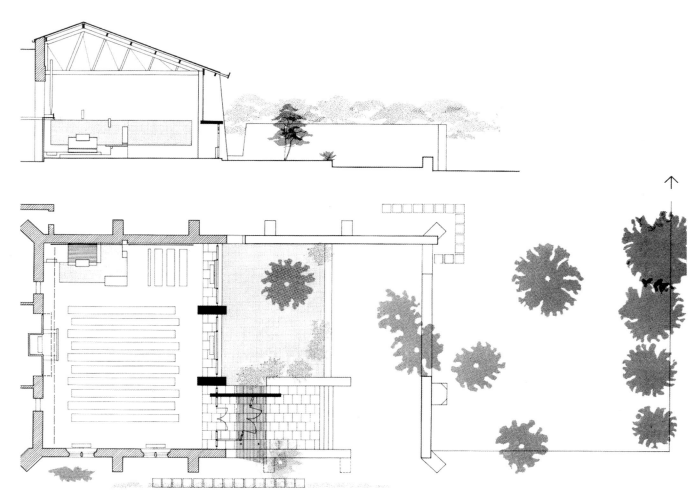

Top: Section of the church and courtyard.

Bottom: Plan. The original church seen in outline with retained walls (shaded) and the main piers supporting new trusses in black, the entrance courtyard formed within the old walls is to the right.

Opposite: Glazed side of the church to the entrance courtyard and garden. The church entrance is to the left, with canopy and porch.

Above: Details at the entrance.

Right: Interior showing the new stone piers to take the new trusses, connecting slab forming bays beneath, with set back patent glazing, above.

Opposite left: The new trusses and timber roof, with the saved/restored original organ.

Opposite right: View towards the pulpit, with the communion table and font stand seen from the entrance, with elm panelled wall behind, and existing pews restored.

Assembly Hall
Bootham School, York
1971

Bootham is a Society of Friends school. Detailed requirements were laid down which also indicated the critical problem—that of designing a building of form and atmosphere appropriate to daily assembly and Friends weekly Meeting, yet capable of being transformed into one suitable for dramatics—from serenity to festivity.

The hall seats 400 and is sited between the main school and outlying departments. A wish to preserve a view of York Minster gave reason for not attaching it to the main school. Also it was felt that the hall should be freestanding, pivotal to the complex of buildings, and that such a cardinal building should be fully modelled and of strong formal quality.

For Friends Meeting centralised space, top lit on four sides from a clerestory is defined by the walls that separate the crush hall from the main hall, by the side wall of the building and on the fourth side by a freestanding screen wall which stands in front of the stage curtains. For focused seating this screen wall remains for assembly but is raised out of sight for theatre. Directional lighting, related to shallow ceiling recesses change the emphasis of the interior, making it more elongated and bringing the stage to prominence. By means of movable sections various arrangements can be made for different events, e.g. conventional stage, stage with fore-stage, stage with orchestra pit.

The main enclosure is of reinforced concrete exposed externally. The roof is steelwork and consists of two trusses spanning from stage wall to columns at the rear and two cross trusses cantilevering out to carry edge beams on the long sides. These four trusses form a central 'box' carrying a high level roof, and clerestory light enters the hall through them. The lower roof, surrounding the 'box', spans off the trusses with a glazed strip between it and the lower structure, over which it hovers like a velarium.

General view—the existing school on the right, with York Minster beyond. The entrance end of the assembly hall, with stair to the gallery, and glazing to the front access route at the stage end.

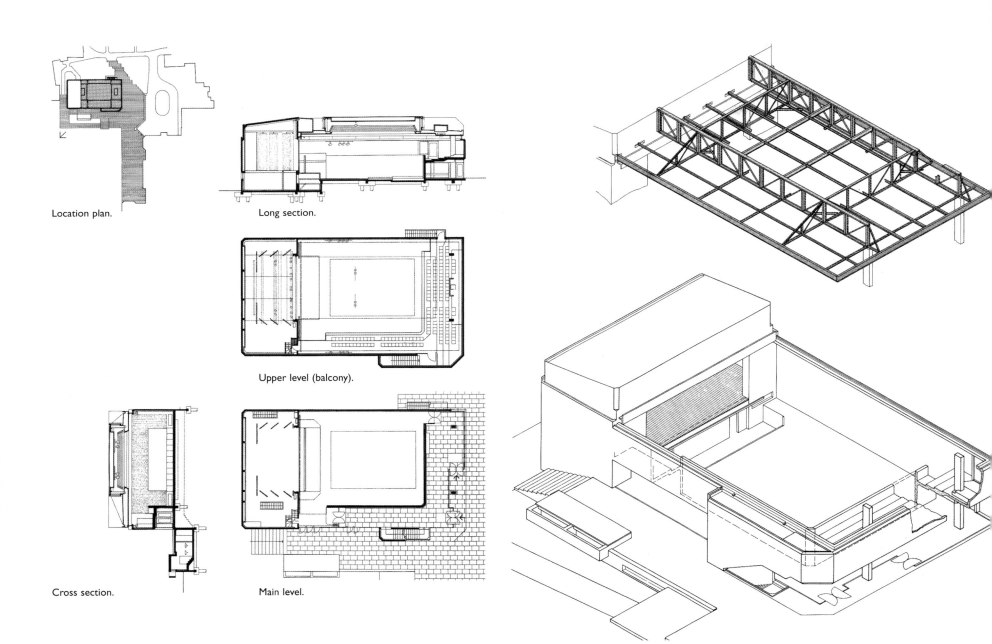

Location plan.

Long section.

Upper level (balcony).

Cross section.

Main level.

Top: Axonometric showing the steel roof over the concrete 'basin'.

Opposite: Stage end to the entrance, with copper cladding to the roof.

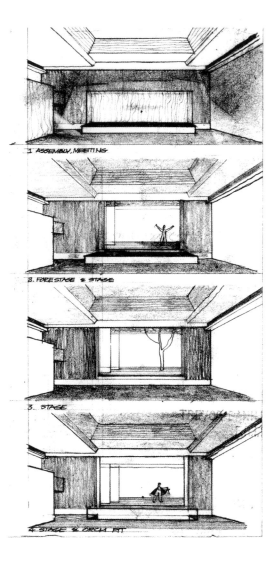

1. ASSEMBLY, MEETING

2. FORESTAGE & STAGE

3. STAGE

4. STAGE & ORCH. PIT

Top left: View from the gallery to the stage, with the removable background timber-clad wall.

Bottom left: Interior as a theatre.

Above: Drawings showing different combinations of the stage end.

View showing the front access to the hall, with the entrance beyond on the right, and the hall with gallery over on the left.

Friends Meeting House
Blackheath, London SE3
1972

The building provides a hall for Friends Meeting to seat 100 with associated entrance hall and concourse, approached from the upper level road. A kitchen and two committee rooms with lavatory accommodation also is provided and linked to the adjoining church hall at lower level.

A square plan for the main space was first considered, parallel with the line of the church hall, but an early decision was to rotate it through 45 degrees, avoiding congestion against the existing walls and windows and isolating the building as a sort of pendant, analogous to a Chapter House. From this originated the concourse with stepped walls and stepped ceiling leading to the calm inner space of the hall. Friends Meeting is formed round a square, and top lights seemed appropriate. A square lantern over a square space indicated four posts which in turn led to two parallel lines of support at right angles to each other, carried on the main enclosing walls. A combination of timber in compression and steel rods in tension thus supports the lantern in space and at the same time forms the main roof structure. The corners of the square room are cut off leaving space between roof and outside wall which is glazed and provides natural light on the perimeter wall. The walls at the corners carry up externally as turrets which receive the top of the glazing.

Opposite: The Meeting House as seen from Independent's Road. The access to the main space is from the higher road, seen on the left. Roofs of the old church hall are to the right. Photographed in 2007.

Top: Model with lower and upper roads, and showing the enclosed concrete 'basin' with the timber roof and lantern over.

Bottom: Plan view of the model—church hall (right), Meeting House (centre), showing the central lantern and roof lights at the corners. The entrance hall roof indicates the turning route into the Meeting House.

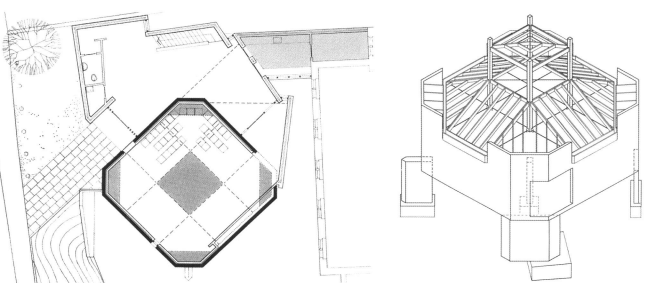

Opposite, clockwise from top left: The entrance hall, with the rotational space leading to Meeting House. The stair to the lower level is on the left; General view into the main space, with the timber roof construction and steel tie rods supporting the corner posts of the lantern below which the Meeting is centred. One window orients the space to the outside; The corner detail showing the junction of roof with wall and roof light.

Clockwise, from top left: Detail of a corner post of the lantern supported by steel tie rods; The lantern glazing detail showing tie rods and the timber-lined ceiling of the lantern; Isometric drawing showing concrete 'basin' with timber roof and lantern over; Plan at entrance level, showing the entrance hall and rotational space leading to the Meeting House proper, with the central lantern and corner roof lights.

St Paul's School Chapel
Barnes, London SW13
1983

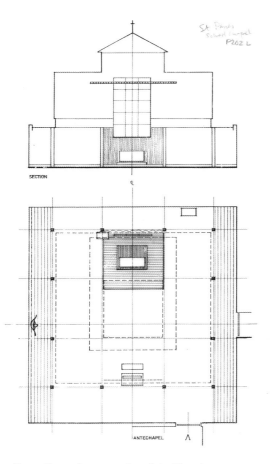

Above: Plan and cross section of the Chapel,
with the entrance at bottom right.

Right: Interior seen from the Chapel entrance.

An existing rather eccentric interior was extensively re-ordered to achieve more serene ambience. It was decided to strengthen the altar axis of the square Chapel with a lowered central louvred ceiling screening and softening harsh light from the central rooflight. New lighting was installed above the ceiling and two specially designed long octagonal light fittings were hung low to mark opposite corners of the dais.

The white upper walls are contrasted by the dark recessed lower ones, and, to link these and terminate the axis, a mural panel was commissioned from the Irish artist Patrick Scott—virtually a reredos built up from one by one metre raw canvas panels with rectangular motifs in gold leaf with areas of lines in thin white paint. The 15 panels are identical but are turned and composed together to form an entity. Only two panels are modified for central emphasis.

'The Reredos' by Patrick Scott. © Patrick Scott.

Woodland Chapel
Wellington College
1983

A study for a small chapel tailored into a woodland setting at the confluence of several pedestrian paths. The entrance and ancillary spaces (vestry, prayer room) form an L-shaped low wing that embraces two sides of the square space of the chapel. This is covered with a monopitch roof falling on the diagonal towards the altar behind which the corner is splayed.

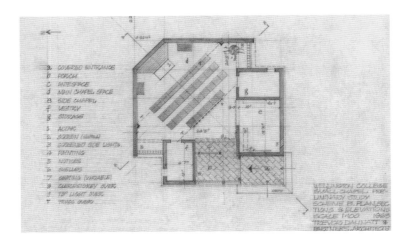

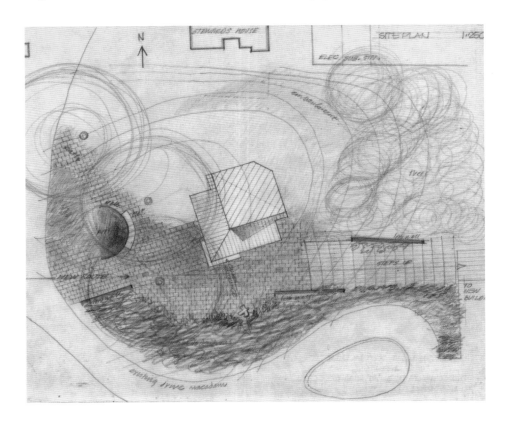

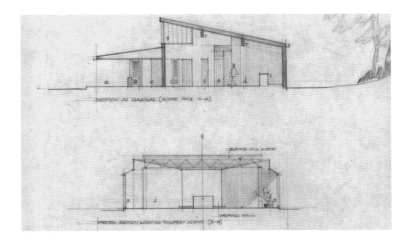

Clockwise, from above: Site plan; Floor plan; South elevation; West elevation; Section on the diagonal; Cross section, facing the altar.

Whittington College
Chapel Extension
1984

Whittington College was founded under the will of Sir Richard Whittington (1424) and the Charity is administered by the Mercers' Company.

In 1964 the College removed from Highgate to Felbridge where there are now three building groups. The ex-Highgate core of residences with Chapel, the sheltered housing group "Ebbisham Court" and Arkendale, elderly married couples housing.

With the increased number of Residents the Chapel had to be enlarged and this was achieved by removing lobby space which was partly within the volume of the building, replacing the end wall with a beam structure and building a new porch under a wide spreading pantile roof at the west end. At the same time some re-ordering was done within the Chapel.

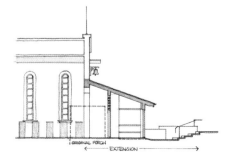

Clockwise, from top right: The west end of the chapel with Narthex extension; Interior from the new doorway towards the east; Interior showing the inserted structure to open up the west end; Part long section, the west end with Narthex extension; *The Nativity*, Piero della Francesca, © National Gallery.

12 Institution

Royal Botanic Gardens, Kew, Victoria Gate. Detail of the introductory trabeated structure which leads into the building and becomes the main element forming the central 'galleria'.

The British Embassy in Riyadh, 1987, and the Victoria Gate at Kew Gardens, 1992, are both required to present formal, ordered, public faces. The questions which distinguish the design of an embassy from other buildings were set out well by Peter Carolin: "Just what should an embassy building look like? Should it be imposing or informal? Representative of the architecture of the nation, or sympathetic to that of its host country? More like a trade fair exhibition building or discrete government offices? As in all good diplomacy the answers must take into account the traditions and expectations of the host country."[1]

The strategy for resolving the conundrum, in both the office building and the ambassador's residence, is sensitive and subtle and generally successful in its application. A restrained, quiet formality—that of Saville Row, perhaps—is combined with an immaculate detailing which exploits the colours and textures of local materials and the quality of the light. The sense of permanence and the 'presence' of the building—so important in an embassy—also arise from the thermal mass, thick 'double' roofs and walls with deep reveals—all in the local tradition—used in helping to control the internal environmental conditions, as opposed to the local, contemporary, ubiquitous glass box.

However, on occasion in the Embassy and Ambassador's Residence, Dannatt, uncharacteristically, drops his guard— "he had always wanted to do a symmetrical building"— with resultant notes of formalism. The assertion, with regard to the office building, that "the planners' limitation of three storeys [and] the brief... virtually dictated a symmetrical solution" cannot be valid, for it is always inevitable that there are many possible forms to be designed which can satisfactorily respond to a brief—it is in the recognition of one which is considered to be appropriate that values and intentions are revealed.[2] It is, however, not with symmetry *per se*, that the concern lies—for the Friends Meeting House is a fine and subtle essay in symmetry—but in the manner of the use and expression of the symmetry. In the principal elevation of the office building, the axis of symmetry—the axis of approach on which lies the main entrance—is marked not only too modestly but bathetically by the slit windows

of mere service rooms (the other potentially more evident signifying elements being the quasi-broken-pediment over the main staircase, which is set at the back of the building, and the *porte cochère*, which is recessive in form, detail and colour). In contrast, on the private, garden side, where a relaxed modesty would be appropriate, the axis is marked by inflating the main stair into an inappropriately grand and elaborate form of no significant meaning, again by incorporating service areas—minor, 'behind the scenes' functions. The precedent for this latter elevation was Robert Smythson's Doddington Hall—but its flamboyant entrance front rather than its restrained garden elevation.

Similarly, at the Residence—a classical tripartite composition—the central figure and focus of the principal elevation is a grand composition of plantroom and vertical duct (where Palladio would have placed a portico with its many contemporary significant allusions and messages). This is not a criticism of the classical composition—Le Corbusier's Villa Stein, 1927, and Frank Lloyd Wright at the William H Winslow House, 1894, and many related houses used variations of the same parti, as did the Laslett House—but of the divorce between form, content and meaning seen here; a rare lapse in Dannatt's work.[3] Architecture is indeed a tough game.

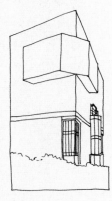

In contrast, the office building and its associated buildings in its compound are most successful when more relaxed—as in the interplay of formality and informality in the south-east corner of the office building.

In the absence of the need to present a formal, public face, the staff housing, for which Colin Dollimore was responsible, seamlessly achieves a happy consort between old and new architectural traditions in the range of house types for six different grades of staff on seven different sites. Each house is ordered around a central, top-lit court, which is cooled by a pool and planting and allows cross-views which enhance the spaciousness of the surrounding rooms; each house being composed of simple, indigenous, cubic forms adorned with gridded transformations of the vernacular forms of timber screens.

The Victoria Gate at Kew required a different character and presented a very different conundrum—a public face which had to be hidden behind the perimeter wall so as 'not to upset the neighbours'. The solution (prior to alterations 14 years after completion to accommodate increased numbers of visitors) is a witty, sensitive and skilful response, which takes the use of diagonal geometry and trabeated structure to new levels in an architecture echoing the geometrical patterns which structure form and growth in nature.

All that is visible on approaching the gate is a beam which frames a view of the gardens and is the beginning of a giant, trabeated pergola. On passing through the gate, the beam is then discovered to be the principal, dynamic element of a joyous, but formal, propylaea, which recalls those of the Riyadh Conference Centre and Martin's intervening Gulbenkian Gallery in Lisbon but is of a very different character. This dynamic propylaea, which also has something of a garden pavilion/gazebo about it, appropriates the existing campanile into a composition which balances horizontal and vertical—a composition with a deep sense of perspective (and therefore evincing a compulsion to

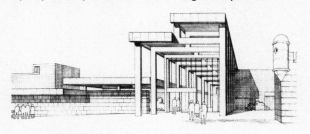

move forward into the pergola), which was magnified by the apparent doubling of its height by reflection in the pool (removed in the later alterations), and which shepherded visitors to follow the axis of the beam towards the building's entrance.

On approaching the building a second beam joins the first, both being parallel to the boundary wall, as the pergola takes the form of a concourse. Straddling the concourse, the secondary beams, set at 30 degrees, swing visitors from the forecourt on to the concourse, which is aligned with the campanile, and then off again, parallel with the side of the campanile, and on to the axis of the gardens' Broad Walk, where they frame a view of the Palm House—a stunning view, a big surprise, concealed until this last moment. Magic!

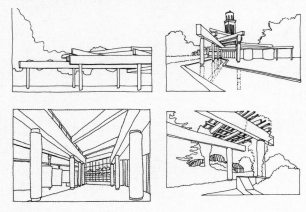

As Stephen Gardiner says, the pergola is the architecture, whilst the the 'lean-tos' are simple enclosures for the all-important commercial and educational sideshows, designed to pass unnoticed externally and eventually disappear into the vegetation. This is architecture which captures Kew Garden's peculiar poetic atmosphere with its likeness to the looking-glass world of Alice.[4]

"The architects could almost be onlookers, outsiders, as though observing from a distance certain factors relevant to the purpose and surroundings of their subject that have, it might seem, willed the various pieces of the puzzle into self-appointed positions..."—if only it were so simple![5] This is very

inventive and skilful architecture: of the classical tradition in its trabeated structure; of the picturesque tradition in its framing of views and the creation of surprises and discoveries through twists and turns; and of, what Wilson termed, "The Other Tradition" of modernism—that of Aalto, Scharoun and Asplund—in its use of geometry and materials and its humane response to the function and location.[6]

Whilst the Embassy, and in particular its housing, captures a poetry of the desert environment, Victoria Gate is a poetic garden architecture.

1. Carolin, Peter, "Diplomatic response", *The Architects' Journal,* 10 June 1987, p. 39.
2. Carolin, "Diplomatic response".
3. Rowe, Colin, "The Mathematics of the Ideal Villa: Palladio and Le Corbusier compared", *The Architectural Review,* March, 1947, pp. 101–104; Pinnell, Patrick, "Academic Tradition and Individual Talent", in Robert McCarter ed., *Frank Lloyd Wright: A primer on architectural principles,* New York: Princeton Architectural Press, 1991, pp. 18–58.
4. Gardiner, Stephen, "Open sesame to a once-secret garden", *The Observer,* 24 May 1992.
5. Gardiner, "Open sesame".
6. Wilson, Colin St John, *The Other Tradition of Modern Architecture: The Uncompleted Project,* London: Black Dog Publishing, 2007.

British Embassy
Chancery, Offices, Residence
and Housing
Riyadh
1985

Opposite: Chancery office building. Detail of the
boulevard elevation at the central entrance, with
its canopy.

Above: Chancery, and Offices, elevation to
the boulevard.

In 1981 the Foreign and Commonwealth Office interviewed
British architectural firms working in Saudi Arabia and
subsequently the practice was selected and appointed as
"lead" consultants for the design of the new Embassy.

Background
At that time the Saudi Ministry of Foreign Affairs and all
Embassies were in Jeddah, 600 miles from Riyadh. With the
advent of improved communications it was decided that the
Ministry should join all others in the Capital and Embassies
were required to move to a Diplomatic Quarter on the

northern outskirts. The Diplomatic Quarter was designed to
cater for an eventual population of 35,000.

Site
Planning regulations permitted only offices, Ambassadors'
Residences and staff amenities to be contained within a single
compound. Staff accommodation had to be located in
separate areas.

The British Embassy site is rectangular and bounded to
the south by a major boulevard which the main entrance and
the office building front. The Residence is at the opposite end,

off a secondary road and in between lie the service and amenity buildings. The centre and eastern side of the site remains free for gardens, swimming pool and tennis court.

As was required, the site is enclosed with high, limestone walls but open-fenced to the boulevard. The forecourt returns down the west side to provide parking spaces, and access to the ancillary buildings. From a side entrance a sequence of shaded open spaces include a 'street' between the service and amenity buildings to the Residence, a lower court giving direct access to a multi-purpose hall and, beyond, a linking walk with shading roof leading to the club entrance. A wall separates the amenity area from the Residence garden with a smaller swimming pool, two levels of lawn and planting.

Offices

In the ordering of the design there was an underlying predilection towards symmetry as providing a certain necessary authority while studies showed six equal areas of accommodation. Thus for formal and practical reasons the building was planned on three floors as required by the Planning Authority (for buildings on the boulevard) with one equal element on each side of the central stair. The symmetry

is primarily emphasised by necessary roof structures and a very positive canopy. Secondary emphasis is given by surface modulation which includes centering recesses on first and second floors which it was decided to glaze despite being only to minor spaces behind, but thought justified as telling inflexions of the wall surface.

Apart from the main entrance on the axis there is a public entrance to the west off a shaded court, to the Visa Section. To the east there is entrance to the Commercial Section off the colonnade which extends along the front.

The rear of the building is more expressive and the much admired principal elevation of Smythson's Doddington Hall influenced and encouraged the play of vertical elements. The central stair with paired service rooms forming a legitimate main feature where the modelling gives subtle light to the stair and discrete light to the service rooms. The central slit gives outlook, picks up the "wellhead" and channel to the pool providing a structuring line to the courtyard/garden.

The exterior is faced with beige Riyadh limestone, with horizontal bands of local granite, dark at the first floor level and for the colonnade, and lighter above. The building has a reinforced concrete frame on a 3.2 metre grid. Wide beams

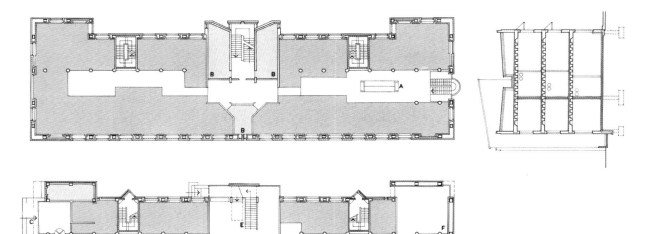

First floor showing the central stair composed with side lit service rooms (B). The stair to the commercial section is on the extreme right (A).

Ground floor
A Collonade
B Commercial entrance
D Entrance hall
E Stair hall with main stair and exit to garden at rear
H Visa Section

Cross section (right).

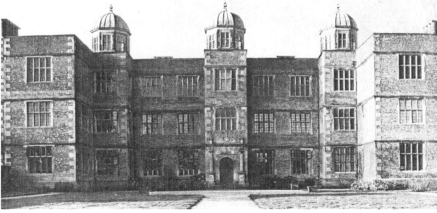

Top: Distant view from the north with the Residence to the right. The Chancery and Office building is beyond.

Bottom: Doddington Hall, c. 1600s, attributed to Robert Smythson.

Opposite left to bottom right: North side of the Chancery/Office building on its central axis, seen from the garden with the 'wellhead' and channel leading to the swimming pool. The club building is on the right; The 'well head' and channel to the swimming pool, with the pergola and club building on the left; Detail of the east end of the Chancery/Office building, with the stair to the commercial section.

are contained within the slab depths with coffers in between. This permits solid partitions to be varied in position for differing rooms. Well-insulated thick external cavity walls maintain a cooler thermal mass. Ceilings (coffers and beams) are fine concrete with white finish, as are the plastered walls. The brief required individual offices and excluded the use of suspended ceilings. The services are therefore generally justifiably exposed—for example circular air distribution ducts at high level create an elegant contrasting geometry in the central circulation areas.

The quality of the office spaces is enhanced by the use of good materials and the unique design of individual elements such as the bronze-finish windows with white marble cills, set in deep reveals with special fan coil units beneath. Doors and joinery are hardwood, beech and ash. Floors in the public areas are travertine, offices are carpeted.

Clockwise from top left: The entrance collonade; The stair to the commercial section at first floor, with coffered ceilings, and exposed ductwork; Detail of the main stair at half landing; The entrance hall, with collonade on the right.

Opposite top: The Residence seen from the northwest showing the entrance. The Chancery/Office building is beyond.

Opposite bottom: The Residence entrance with drive in, screen wall and canopy. The airflue is set back on the central first floor terrace, which gives side light to the two bedrooms and link at first floor.

Residence

The Residence

The Residence is also symmetrical by virtue of equivalent two-storey wings either side of the major single-storey Reception room.

The symmetry is very marked on the road side with central entrance screened by a required security wall composed with the plant room and air shaft at upper level set back on a central terrace and at the design stage regarded as valid architectural elements expressive of a consonant air conditioning system—analogous perhaps to the way chimneys became compositional elements in country houses—Coleshill for example.

On the garden side the building is more open, with recessed terraces at ground and upper level and a central terrace at first floor over the Reception room which articulates the building. The expressed structure is clad in Saudi granite, with infill of limestone.

To summarise, there are three zones. The central zone is 'public' with entrance hall and Reception room. The north zone is guests with dining room and attendant kitchen and guest bedrooms over at first floor. The south zone is private, Ambassador and family on two floors.

The Reception room ends in a semi-circular bay window and there is a recessed light coloured timber lined ceiling with elm paneled walls. The dining room opens off the Reception and part of the panelled wall can be slid back to give a combined L-shaped room for large functions.

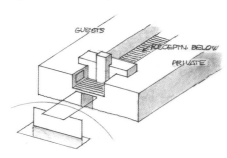

Opposite: The Residence, showing the garden side—two-storey private wing (left), the main Reception with semi-circular bay window and terrace over (centre), the two-storey guest wing with dining room at ground floor (right).

Clockwise from top: Semi-circular bay window of the Reception room with view to the garden, with the pergola and pool feature; View from the main entrance, with the split canopy focussed on the flag staff; The terrace over the front entrance, seen from a bedroom with central privacy screen.

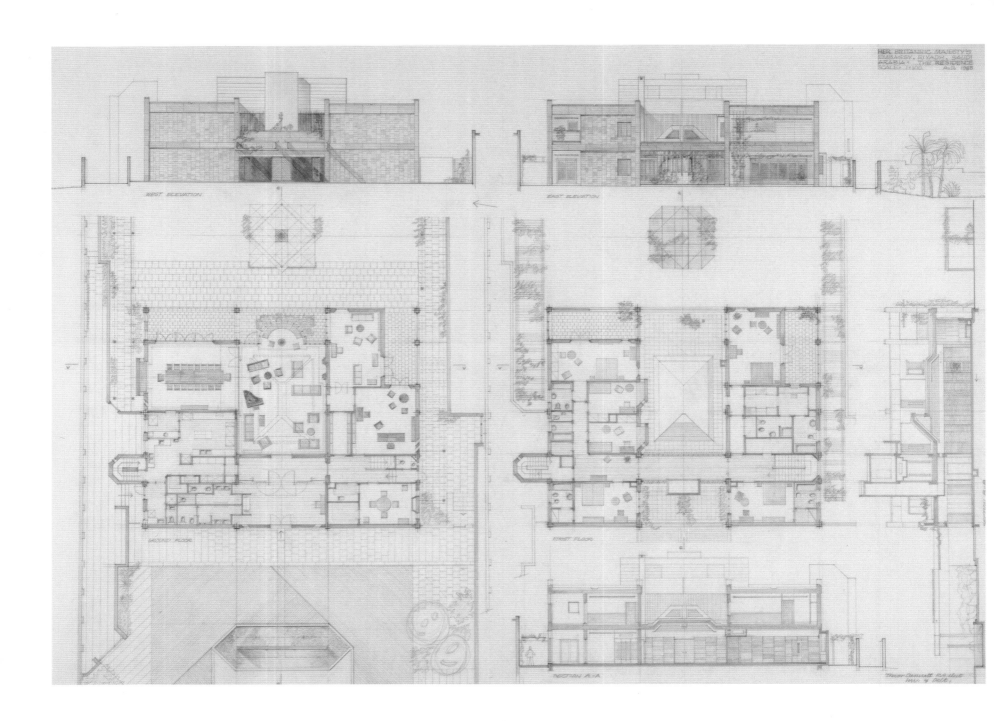

HER BRITANNIC MAJESTY'S
EMBASSY, RIYADH, SAUDI
ARABIA · THE RESIDENCE
SCALE 1:100   JULY 1981

WEST ELEVATION

EAST ELEVATION

SECOND FLOOR

FIRST FLOOR

SECTION A-A

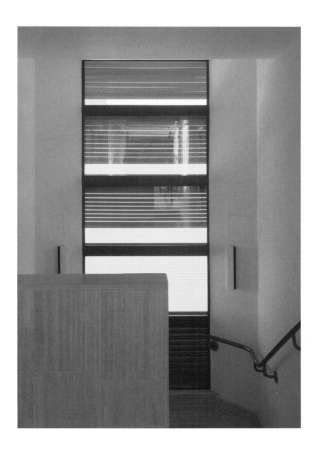

Opposite: Plans, elevations and sections of the Residence. Original drawing, Royal Academy Diploma work. Courtesy: Royal Academy of Arts.

Clockwise, from top left: Residence, window detail on the main stair; Reception room, fireplace detail; First floor, the central link between the private wing and guest wing looking towards the main stair; Mosaic pool feature in the bay window.

Staff Housing
Colin Dollimore, Partner

The housing is set to the north and northwest of the Embassy site in proximity to the Wadi Hanifeh and the 35 houses are in seven separate groups. The sites vary in plan and topography and some slope steeply to wadis; aspect, prospect and privacy also differ. Within these variations the two-storey buildings establish a common formal identity by the organisation of entrance hall and stair, and the disposition of rooms around internal courtyards open to the sky. The plan type responds to the wide variations in site gradient. The key element is the entrance hall which is treated as an intermediate platform between street entrance and courtyard—the base level about which the drawing room, dining room and kitchen pivot.

External block walls are finished with a beige Tyrolean render, and Riyadh limestone is used for plinths and special wallings at house entrances. Hanging timber lattice screens to balconies are a distinctive feature of the houses, providing privacy and shading and permitting air movement. Windows are provided with louvred timber shutters at first floor and varied shadings at ground floor. High front boundary walls screen the houses from the street, and entrances are formed in these walls, making a shadowed recess at the entrance gate.

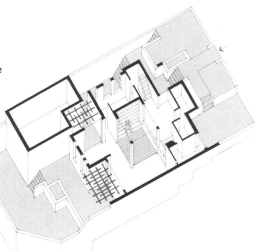

Opposite, clockwise, from top: Schema for a Minister's house, showing the central courtyard with fountain and planters; Entrance gates from the street of one of the larger houses, leading to the forecourt and front door; Street corner group of larger houses, showing both the main entrances and entrances to the parking spaces within forecourts.

Left: Part of the garden court side of a larger house. Sun screened terrace to a drawing room (dining room windows to the left). Sun and vision screened terrace to principal bedroom above.

Right: View across the court in a medium size house, towards a dining room, living room, with windows to the court on the right.

Victoria Gate, Kew
Royal Botanic Gardens
Richmond, Surrey
1992

Trevor Dannatt and Partners, later Dannatt, Johnson Architects, were Consultants to Kew from 1990 to 2004, appointed following a Design Competition for a new concourse and visitor reception at the Main Gates. This proposal was reviewed several times and a final scheme was approved with the intention of completion in 2000—however, this did not proceed.

Description of the Victoria Gate
as completed in 1992

The several priorities of the Development Plan included a visitor building at the more accessible Victoria Gate (Kew Gardens Station) and this took precedence since facilities there were negligible, for instance entry queues had to form in the busy road, outside the high wall that protects the Gardens.

Thus the provision of a gathering space within was a planning priority. Visitors enter freely through the old gateway, 1889, into a generous court with a wide prospect to the Gardens over the L-shaped pool, which separates them. The view is partially framed by the pair of beams, which extend right through the building, forming its principal structure and defining the central concourse or Galleria.

The parallel lines of beams and columns lead visitors in to the building and the long axis of the galleria with the main accommodation either side. It runs parallel to the boundary wall but turns at the further end to pick up the line of the Kew Broad Walk thus reconciling two important lines and locking the building into the existing landscape plan. To the left of the galleria there are free spaces with stepped ceilings

devoted originally to visitor orientation/interpretation, later to become primarily a cafe. To the right is the shop behind a glazed wall with (originally) the entrance at the further end. Here the 30 degree turn emphasised by additional top lighting directs towards the Garden Exit which brings visitors out adjacent to the Campanile with their first view of the Palm House and where turned by low walls they enter the Gardens, the Campanile behind them on the visual axis of the Broad Walk, across the lake. As planned, visitors leave the Gardens by the same route in reverse but are encouraged to exit through the shop, which includes staff accommodation, office, etc.. Also, public toilets close by.

The main structure is a concrete frame with Portland stone facings to main columns and beams, which carry cross beams at the angle corresponding to the line of the Broadwalk, carrying the flat roof and forming a clerestory to the Galleria. The main spaces either side of the Galleria are also framed as 'lean tos' of lighter character partly in steel supporting low pitched timber roofs, lead covered. External walls are light coloured brick matching the Campanile or glazing in steel frames. Internal walls are fair faced brick or plastered. Ceilings are boarded in western hemlock to the orientation and interpretation area or exposed timber joists with ply or acoustic panels between to the shop.

The entrance court is Portland stone paved as is the Galleria with underfloor heating as has the shop, which is paved with red ceramic tile.

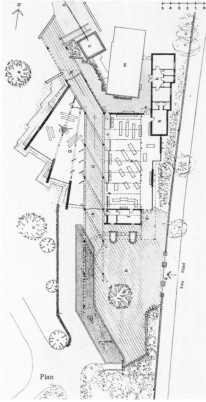

General plan of the reception building.
C—Campanile, E—existing plant room.

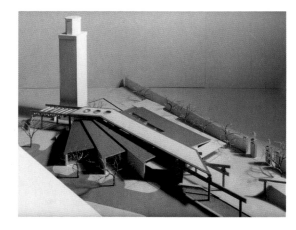

Opposite: View of the column and beam structure leading into the reception building as completed in 1992. The forgathering space is on the right, with the main entrance off street (not seen). The L-shaped pool separating the entrance court from the gardens is to the left. Ticket kiosks, with the shop roof behind. Portland stone clad main columns and beams.

Left: View of the model with the entrance (bottom), pool and structure leading into the building and forming the central galleria, with the shop to the right and stepped roofs over reception spaces to the left. The existing Campanile, with flues from the heating plant for the Palm House.

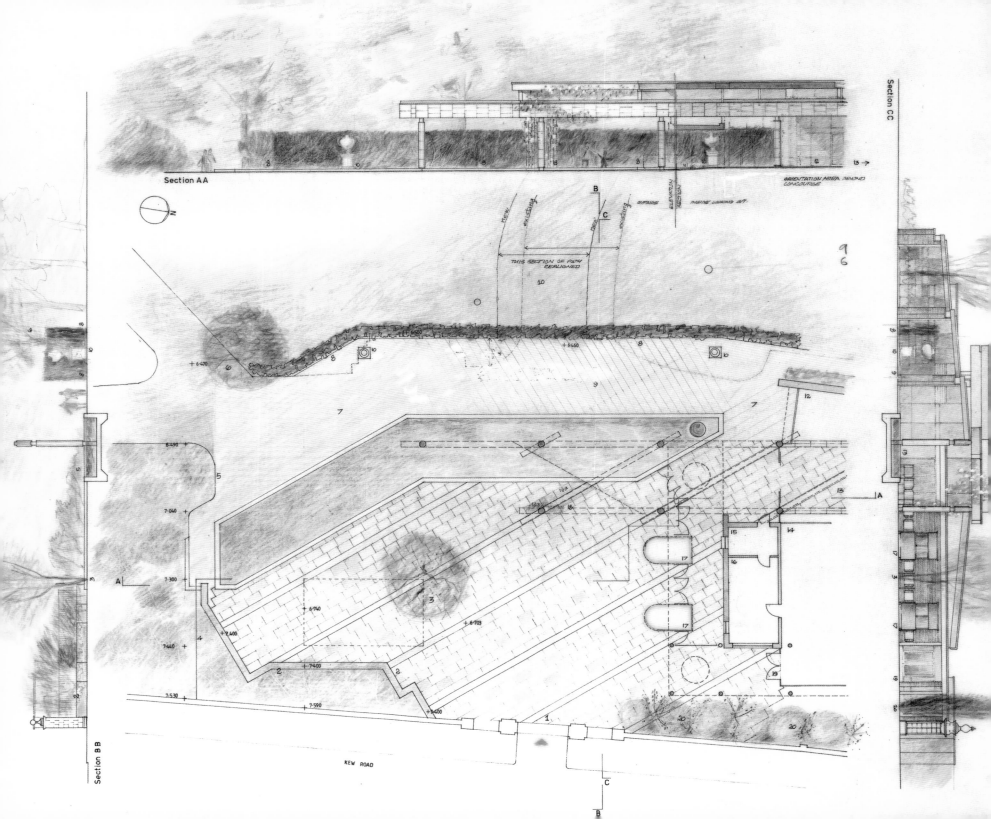

Section CC

Section AA

N

Section BB

ORIENTATION AREA BEHIND
CONCOURSE

ELEVATION SECTION
INSIDE LOOKING OUT

OUTSIDE

EXISTING

NEW

NEW

EXISTING

B

C

THIS SECTION OF PATH
REALIGNED

9
6

+ 6·470

+ 6·500

+ 6·460

6·490 +

7·040 +

7·300 +

7·440 +

7·530 +

+ 6·740

+ 6·703

+ 6·400

+ 7·400

+ 7·590

A

B

C

KEW ROAD

Opposite: Presentation drawing showing the plan and sections of the entrance and forgathering space, the separating pool with gardens beyond, and the column and beam structure leading into the building (to right), and entrance kiosks.

Clockwise, from top: General view from gardens with the Campanile, Galleria structure with clerestory showing the stepped lead-covered roofs over the visitor reception spaces; View along the Galleria, reception spaces to the left, shop to the right. Note the change of direction in the distance, where diagonal beams then align with the Broad Walk axis, leading to the exit to the gardens and the first view of the Palm House; Detail of the pool at the entrance end, with circular glass water source.

Description as re-organised in 2005

Over ten years the popularity of the Gardens and the Victoria Gate entrance and facilities brought congestion and delayed access at peak times, especially public holidays. It was imperative to increase the size of the courtyard arrival area. Numerous studies were made, including plans for more interior space, these were not pursued but a major recasting of the entrance court led to the removal of the pool (the memory of which has been retained in outline) to extend the area—reorienting the whole forecourt with four new kiosks to provide eight guichets (previously four) sheltered by a canopy supported on 100 mm stainless steel columns. These defined the routes, with all visually locking into the existing beam structure which intentionally started as one beam then increased to a pair, first in the open then leading into the building as Galleria. The courtyard is now defined by metal barriers which can be removed for special occasions.

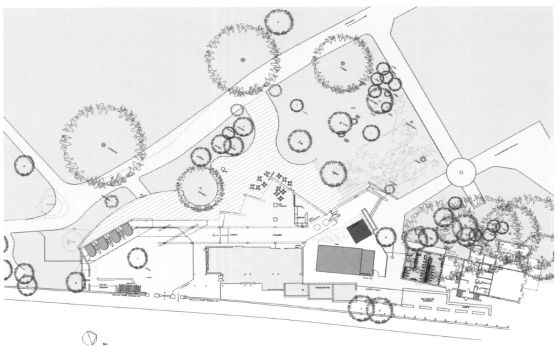

Clockwise, from top left: Entry to the Gardens showing the new kiosks with lower protecting canopy linked with the column beam structure of 1992; 2005 plan as modified for increased visitors numbers; Plan view of the model showing the Main Gate proposal, 2000, with pool screened by hedging directing visitors to the reception and entrance.

Opposite: View from the entrance to the galleria looking back to the forecourt and pool, 1992.

13 Exhibition

Weekend Exhibition, at Adrian Heath's Studio, 1952.
Main work, *Constructed Relief*, by Victor Pasmore.

Leslie Martin once remarked of a gardener: "she knew a lot about colour and species but very little about placing".[1] How typically succinctly and potently this summed up so much about the art of architecture—the appropriate and revealing placing of things in relation to an existing place and in relation to each other. A placing which is dependent on an understanding of the objects and of the nature and order of the context in which they are to be placed.

As has been seen in "The Complete Consort", the early placing of works of art for the exhibitions organised by Adrian Heath in his Fitzroy Street studio, the first being in March 1952, established new means of composition relating the art and the room. The exhibitions were curated on a shoestring and have become a significant event in the development of non-figurative art in Britain. The main spatial subdivision of the first exhibition was a large suspended screen painted black and white, related to a long canteen table, and some judiciously placed modern furniture. The show was composed around these and the various walls rails and features of the studio (including the gas fire as shown in 'Hearth') to create a very dynamic hang.

At the Whitechapel Gallery in 1959, in response to the deep ambiguity of Jackson Pollock's paintings—at once, dynamic yet calm, and ethereal yet expressly material (in the pouring, splashing and squeezing of the paint)—a deeply artful, ambiguous setting was created—dynamic yet calm and contemplative, metaphorical yet expressly material (in the rough blockwork and simple muslin). Both the paintings and the architecture play on that ambiguity which is essential to the existence of all art (poetry, in particular).

This setting is an abstracted landscape—the matting strip of 'grass' below, the rocky outcrops of blockwork, and the muslin clouds billowing above; it is also a church with a narthex, nave, aisles, transepts and chancel—art and religion being inevitably linked for Dannatt. In coming to understand how the existing space was ordered and then in its adaptation to receive the paintings, the same concepts were used as were to be rediscovered in the re-ordering of the St Paul's School chapel: the balancing of primary and secondary axes; the emphasising of a space within a space; the linear, hovering, translucent plane; and the contrast of light and dark surfaces. The 'reredos' is reserved for the placing of a major work, the focal point, immediately in the line of view on entering, the full length of the gallery away—thus the whole is immediately brought together but much is left to be discovered; all as in the nature of a traditional church. At the terminations of the cross axis are placed the earliest and latest works—beginning and end. A totemic work is placed on an angled board—the only diagonal.

Free-standing planes were a staple of modernism, as seen in the work of Mies van der Rohe and of Rietveld, who had used sliding partitions in a nascent pinwheel at the Schröder House in 1924 and planes of untreated blockwork in a looser configuration for an exhibition pavilion at Arnhem, published by Dannatt in 1956.[2] At Whitechapel, the inherent ambiguity of the precise pinwheel in which the planes are arranged suggests both stability, in the implied space of the central square, and dynamism, as the planes reach out, their extension creating a rotation of four separate but interlinked spaces and their unequal lengths impelling movement along the principal axis.

Albeit a temporary installation, it has stood the test of time and was recently analysed as an exemplar in *Art and the Power of Placement*.[3]

In the installation and placing of the works from his own collection at The Whitworth Art Gallery in 2006, Dannatt employs the same subtleties and the same understanding of the order and qualities of an existing place—so, *Now you see it!*

1. In conversation with author.
2. Wood, James, "Two Exhibitions 1955", *The Architects' Year Book 7*, London: Elek, 1956, pp. 100–101.
3. Newhouse, Victoria, *Art and the Power of Placement*, New York: Monacelli Press, 2005, pp. 175–176.

Architecture Exhibition
1956

The installation for the Arts Council was within an eighteenth century interior and attempted to create, by use of screens and velariums, spaces equivalent to the experience of modern architecture.

(Associated Graphic Designer Colin Forbes)

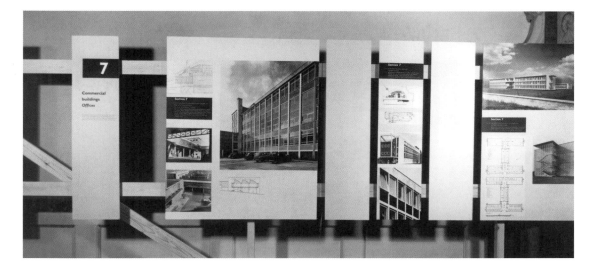

Top: One section of the exhibition showing the modular panel system.

Bottom: View of the main gallery with velarium at two levels. Special screens with modular panels, and large panels utilising the window reveals.

Installation, Jackson Pollock Exhibition
London
1958

Working closely with Bryan Robertson, the Director of the Whitechapel Gallery, a special layout and presentation was prepared to accommodate the travelling exhibition of Jackson Pollock's painting sponsored by the Museum of Modern Art.

An interlocking sub-division of the main space of the Whitechapel Gallery was generated by the placing of four screen walls of rough block painted white and forming an appropriate background for some of the paintings. Black and grey fabric was stretched over part of the existing wall areas and screens of untreated wood were introduced for special emphasis. A white fabric ceiling over the main area of the gallery helped to unify and emphasise the central space of the gallery, with the cross dimension emphasised by floor matting.

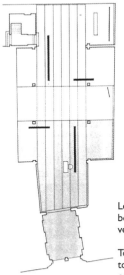

Left: Plan of the Whitechapel Gallery (entrance at bottom) showing disposition of the screen walls, velarium from front to back and cross carpet.

Top right: General view of the Gallery looking toward the entrance wall. To the left is a display on black fabric.

Bottom right: Special mounting for *Number 31*, 1950, showing a seat with lighting beneath.

Opposite: General view, just inside the entrance—(left to right) *The key*, 1946, *Number 32*, 1950, *Four opposites*, 1953, *Number 9A*, 1948.

France and Son
New Bond Street
London W1
c. 1960

Developed in association with Finn Juhl. A small ground floor shop provided reception and a new stair to a generous L-shaped first floor providing office space and a large gallery for exhibition of this Danish Company's furniture.

A simple rectangular timber ceiling grid defined and unified the carpeted exhibition space, bounded on the window side by continuous translucent curtain. A richly coloured abstract painting by Patrick Heron, *Cadmium Painting with soft lemon oblong*, 1959, terminated the vista providing a serene interior where furniture (including lines by Finn Juhl) was carefully grouped and displayed for consideration by both wholesale and retail customers.

Top: Main exhibition in the first floor showroom.

Bottom: Entrance from the street to the shop and the stair leading to the first floor showroom and exhibition area.

"Now You See It"
The Whitworth Art Gallery
Manchester
2006

Named thus since it was a pre-view of part of a collection of modern works—oils, water colours, prints and sculpture by British and European artists bequeathed to the Gallery. It was shown in a major space which has one long and one end wall in rich timber paneling with opposite walls painted white. While a V-shaped screen was installed at one end to provide a more intimate area for small works and some architectural

works. Another screen accented a change of level and showcases helped to articulate the space. The Exhibition was curated by the retiring Director, Alistair Smith, and the Curator of Modern Art, Mary Griffiths, with the donor's participation. It included works by artists such as Adams, Arp, bill, Buhler, Colquhoun, Gris, Heath, Heron, Kenny, Leger, MacBryde, Miro, Nash, Pasmore, Severini, Sutherland.

Overview of the exhibition installation towards the raised end.
(Original interior by Bickerdike & Allen)

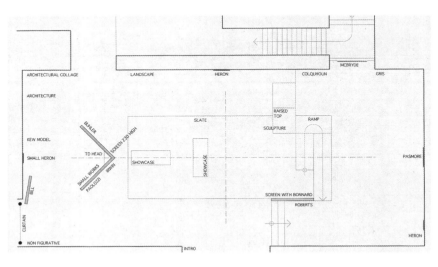

Top left: The V-shaped screen and view of the building display and route to the next gallery.

Bottom: Interior of the V-shaped screen with small works and portrait head.

Top right: Plan of the installation in the major Gallery space.

Words

Foreword to *Buildings & Ideas 1933-83*
From the studio of Leslie Martin and his Associates, Cambridge University Press, 1983

When Leslie Martin was chosen as the recipient of the Royal Gold Medal in 1973, the citation paid tribute to a truly outstanding contribution to architecture and planning, both through his private and public practice, and most notably as a leading figure in architectural teaching and research. That was the judgment of his professional colleagues. One writer commented that: *He could have won the medal for his architecture alone, or his research, or his contribution to education; but it is perhaps his attitude to the whole range of his endeavours and skills that is his most important facet. Leslie Martin manages always to maintain a consistent philosophy that holds true for the entire range of his involvements. It is his thought that is central.*"

In a long career in practice, he has worked with a number of associated architects and colleagues and he would be the first to acknowledge the part that they have played in the work of the studio that is included here. But colleagues have come and gone, and the continuing element, Leslie Martin himself, provides the consistency of thought and attitude that is demonstrated throughout this book and which, in the last few years, has flourished into one of his most creative and productive periods.

The idea and nature of this book has been discussed and developed over the last two years, and its structure is such that it demonstrates the architect's wide range of concern for the discipline of architecture in theory and practice. It represents his own rigorous selection of material both written and visual, and provides a comprehensive record, demonstrating the close correlation of idea and realisation in his work.

In one of his lectures Leslie Martin stated that he thought "every critic certainly and perhaps every lecturer has a duty to outline his own position in relation to his subject". I feel I should do so in relation to this introduction: write primarily as an architect who, as a student in the late 1930s and early 40s, was stimulated by the first published buildings of JL Martin (as he then credited himself)—two or three houses and the Northwich School. I had *The Flat Book* and, more important, *Circle* (where perhaps I 'read' the illustrations with more understanding than the text). He was one of the architects for whom I wanted to work, and did—followed by an association in work, friendship and shared interests over some 30 years, a period which has seen the development of a grave and eloquent architectural language, personal yet within the developing movement (now a tradition) of constructive architecture.

Recently, the ideas and the buildings of the movement have been under attack, and although some critiques at least may have exposed the corrupt slogans and thin arguments of the 'social architecture' wing, yet they have left—in my view—the central ideas (and major buildings) more than relevant. At the same time, we have seen a simplistic historicism (and or vernacularism) promoted almost as a packaging solution to the problems of design and style. If content as well as form is valued, if we believe that form and image have to be sought through an understanding of their historical relationship rather than based on an easy pictorial reading, we can see in the best work of past years a true achievement in this direction. Today we can see new developments that are manifestly creative, enriching and diversifying the language of architecture. It is this sense of contributing to development—not change for its own sake—that shows a continuing thread through Martin's thought and works.

In no way is this book another 'practice brochure'; rather it is a record of architectural endeavour that also, I believe, could be a source of new creativity in the underlying theme of continuity and ideas in development. Through varied presentation the genesis and essence of the buildings is made known, while the related texts and essays clarify the foundation of the work in general and specific thought about building and the Modern Movement and its intention towards an architecture that is responsive to changing requirements. Thus the emphasis is on context and the underlying order of each development and its relation to others of that type (and indeed, to other types). Yet underneath differing forms, forms that have sprung from the need of function—use, environment and structure—there is manifest the architect's concern with the primary qualities of architecture; the interdependence of these primaries is demonstrated but also the underlying integrity of the architectural idea.

I feel it appropriate to try to identify aspects of the architect's philosophy and approach to the order that is manifest in the buildings. Firstly, at a broad level we might see in the designs or the buildings how needs have been analysed, digested and restated in total terms—the building is from early on seen as a whole rather than put together. The idea may often seem deceptively simple but behind it there is, among other things, a conceptual ordering that does not dismiss precedents but draws on and revitalises them. The university residential buildings restate the elements of the traditional college courts and then elaborate these in relation to different room clusters around staircases and differing sites. The auditorium buildings always coordinate planning requirements with a vision of movement—spatial flow and connection leading to central volumes. Or, to take a specific example at Oxford, we see three libraries of different size and volume brought into relationship around the central organising flights of the external staircase.

These examples illustrate a central theme of all the work, the sectional planning principle—not, of course, peculiar to Martin, but rarely found developed with such grace as an architectural generator rather than an intellectual exercise or ingenious device, whether in a modest house such as the one in Portugal, giving a fresh and spacious interior in a small space, or in a large development such as the Zoology/Psychology complex at Oxford, where it is tuned to circulation and the economic provision of varied spaces and future extension as well as spatial diversity.

Secondly, we may study with satisfaction how the conception has been brought into a total system, a consistent formal and structural language to which all parts respond. For example, in the Bristol competition design the 'post and beam' construction is part of the spatial and plastic system and orders the whole conception without strait-jacketing it. Or, at a more modest level, in the conversions, existing structures are respected and clarified and consonance between idea and means is attained in a most limpid manner.

Thirdly, the main body of work shows a sureness and fine sensibility in the handling of elements and materials that can be enjoyed almost for their own sake, conjunctions perhaps of brickwork and metal roofing, or brick, timber, glass and plaster, innately pleasing but enjoyed also because there is such a satisfying conjunction of whole and part. There is a sense of style that runs throughout from overall concept to, say, the way the doors are put into openings, in the quality of panelling and fittings, in the detail of a fireplace—all responding to the same aesthetic.

It is here, finally, that one touches on the question of other values and I would like to define the delight and satisfaction that comes from the perception of, say, one of the buildings as a total experience. Perhaps one can only make comparisons with other artists. If painters, then Nicholson comes to mind, for whether in two or three dimensions there is a common sense of serene spatial relationships, just scale and proportion, cool harmonies of colour. William Feaver used the word *gravitas* in connection with a Moore head and spoke of the same quality being achieved by elimination in Barbara Hepworth's *Three Forms* and repeatedly in Ben Nicholson's carved reliefs. With all these artists Martin has had long association and the same quality of gravitas seems evident in his architecture, showing a consistent threefold harmony that demonstrates a clear intellectual ordering, deep understanding of space and form and the craftsman-like handling of materials. Behind it all there is the sense of structuring buildings about ideas of wholeness rather than the domination of, say, planning arrangements or preconceived expression or technical or sociological obsessions. A sense of consonance brings due importance to each and every part and structures the whole organically in relation to the greater whole.

In the catalogue of the 1930s Arts Council Hayward Gallery Exhibition, 1979–1980, the point is made that "At the end of the war modernist architects found the means available to put their ideals into practice. The tragedy was that these ideals had been so narrowed and hardened in the ideological conflicts of the 1930s and so little tested or refined through the practical processes of building and development." No doubt such testing would, but for the war, have occurred. However, in the

Leslie Martin with view of Gulbenkian Centre for Modern Art, Lisbon, 1984.

Martin and Speight, House at Ferriby, East Yorkshire, 1940. Courtesy *The Architectural Review.*

case of Martin's own work we can see the steady development of an architecture and building mode that has its roots in those ideals of the 1930s but has not become rootbound. For example, if we look at the nursery school at Northwich of 1938 we can, among other things, enjoy the structure for its clarity (as well as its material) and see that it is part of the grammar of the building rather than just a new way of building or, as now seems the case in so many 1930s buildings, merely a pictorial reference to functionalism'. Similarly, looking again at the Bristol proposals, the structure relates closely to planning needs but is also integral with the spatial idea. As in the earlier building it seems natural and inevitable.

When Martin received the Gold Medal in 1973 one perhaps thought his work complete. Gratifyingly, since then, a decade has seen the design and often the realisation of a number of outstanding buildings, as well as some significant lectures and essays.

There has been a steady development of earlier and new ideas and their realisation in specific projects or buildings of varied scales. Especially one should mention the enrichment of Cambridge by the recently completed music school building group with its serenely lit concert hall and surrounding necklace of linked smaller spaces and courtyards. Then there is for the future the possibility at least that Glasgow may be enriched by the City Halls and shopping precinct which create a new nodal point within the city grid, and the new home for the Royal Scottish Academy of Music and Drama where a significant building is emphasised by its setting and its form. In this particular project again, a clear linear arrangement of the elements of the plan is enlivened by the development of the section which achieves a separation of the working levels of the Drama and Music Schools but provides also the flowing spaces that unite the main volumes of the auditoria.

Both these projects have evolved through a series of studies that have been subject to continuous development, both as a result of external changes of programme and also because of the review of designs as they have developed. Surely one of Martin's great strengths lies in this reflective re-appraisal of work in progress, as all who have worked in his studio will testify; the sense of not being satisfied with what was thought to be the right solution and the illuminating discovery that further development and new combinations are always possible.

Almost as an aside, at the private level, the Walston house or the Church Barns conversion renew the dialogue of spatial flow and natural lighting so evident in the earlier Kettle's Yard Gallery. There, through a poem of light and space we can relax, receive a sense of calmness that releases the spirit and enhances life— while in the more domestic works, through material and colour a reassuring warm environment is achieved for human delight.

The Gulbenkian Gallery in Lisbon is likely to be one of his most eloquent works, for it unites spatial and structural concerns in a building type where the dialogue between plan and section, between form and light, is of primary consideration. There is particular revelation of the architect's method in the way the section of the building is 'brought forward', modified and given significance to become the 'portico' entrance. The total nature of the design is such that it reaches the point where it could be regarded as a paradigm of the architect's artistic philosophy. The architecture is serene and independent, yet entirely sympathetic to the subject. One feels how appropriate it is that this late work should be in a region where the architecture has been of such abiding interest to the architect and is also a building that is devoted to those arts with which he has had such a long and deep involvement.

The book gains wider significance for the inclusion of what Martin would deny was architectural history. It represents him as architectural essayist and teacher, notably with his recent reflections on the architectural ideas of the 1930s, "Notes on a Developing Architecture". This, together with reflections on his own background (the Arts and Crafts Movement, Lutyens and the end of Beaux Arts training), shows the varied influences on his development—the context of about 50 years' work of someone who was committed to the search for the principles inherent in the ideas of CIAM and the MARS Group rather than the ideology and slogans that went with the fight for work and recognition in those heady days.

In the writings, there is a demonstration of the way ideas in architecture develop from analysis of tasks, from precedents and concepts, to realisations. The illuminating essay on some drawings of Leonardo is particularly relevant with respect to our understanding of the process of design, a process equally demonstrated by the selection of completed work or projects, showing how forms have been ordered round particular problems and then developed in a 'flux of mutation', and how parts can be brought together into a total solution—demonstrating that we are not concerned with either/or but with a whole range of factors that have to be brought into a harmony, art and science, and that this constitutes the theme of architecture in our time.

In writing these notes I have followed to some extent my address given at the RIBA in 1973 when Martin received the Royal Gold Medal. That touched on his wider contribution; here I have only attempted to define some aspects of his work and approach to design. Concluding now, as then, I draw on Martin's own words at a previous Gold Medal occasion: of Aalto he spoke of distinctions between architecture of his kind, which is ordered, controlled, worked for and not just accidental; between the detail of his kind, which is the result of the completeness of a great idea and not just a trivial end in itself: between his kind of architecture, which cannot easily be drawn but rests in the building itself... and that which looks well only on the drawing board.

"Reflections", from *The University of Greenwich Maritime Greenwich Campus*, monograph, John Bold and others, published by Dannatt, Johnson

Re -pair, -store, -habilitate, -build, -furbish, -new, -construct, -generate. Regenerate seems the most appropriate word, the life has gone out of a building, the wind "shakes the wainscot where the field-mouse trots". Even in the humblest buildings there is a sort of pattern, in great buildings usually a clear pattern, of a total concept, though perhaps modified by time. A new use can, by adaptation and compromise be made to fit in or, by analysis and thought a template for new use can be achieved and reviewed against the existing template of use or beyond that the one that structured the building originally. These have to be discerned and by love and knowledge of what existed and care for what might be they must be encouraged to be in sync.

Such architectural opportunities need not be judged as separate from new build, as an entirely specialist concern, although because of the conservation element the tendency exists—as in other fields of work where 'track records' are required before that particular field can he entered.

On the contrary, success in one field should invigorate thought in another field. For surely, the common denominator, the architect's specialty, is in the organisation of space, the manipulation of form towards a coherent entity.

The Old Royal Naval College group exemplified this beyond measure, to the point where it is categorised as "one of the most important and inspiring ensembles in European architecture" although stigmatised by Dr Johnson as "too magnificent for a place of charity, and that the parts were too much detached to make one great whole". John Gwynn declared "it wants a proper centre".[1] This latter view is common enough and yet is more than questionable and what *is* satisfies infinitely in mass and composition and in the flow of space to the Queen's House and beyond to the high edge of the Park with the Observatory, pleasing to the latter-day romantic eye. As for magnificence, Hawksmoor protectively declared magnificence was part of the architect's brief, noting Queen Mary's desire "to have Greenwich built with great magnificence and order".[2]

There it is and this is what through "times Strange reverses" two higher education foundations, well-established but of modest origin, have come into, laying a new pattern of aspiration and use over two previous

patterns. At the functional level, the level of daily use, both bodies have attained appropriate accommodation, generous space horizontally and vertically, with that surplus which enhances, rarely attained in 'new build' and with a matching quality, hard to define, of robust construction with simple conjunctions of material, conveying the sense of depth in time, to the feel of history and for students, memorable years.

In early days of the University's bid, critics questioned the aspirations of such a young body to occupy such grand buildings. This, on the whole, reflected a certain establishment attitude but it was a question that raised in our minds the representative role of architecture. The buildings had fulfilled the needs of a Hospital but by their position and 'order' represented the Senior Service, the Royal Navy. Could they represent their new tenants?

The perception of the University is perhaps over-coloured by Oxford and Cambridge with their disparate academic and residential buildings: no College, however wealthy, attained the grandeur of Greenwich except perhaps at All Souls. Rather, we have to refer in the UK to later foundations for precedents, for example Edinburgh University or University College, London, where there is classical grandeur and a sense that the University is part of the civic order, "a whole body of teachers and scholars engaged in the higher branches of learning in a certain place". We might ask if the order of such building is relevant to a modern University. In contrast, there are good examples of new universities where there is a consonance between what is done and what it is done in, but unlike the above examples the sense of high purpose has not been realised.

That sense exists at Greenwich. How will the two Institutions be affected by the noble expressive buildings they occupy? Environments shape Institutions and vice-versa.

How are we as architects affected by involvement in major works in major monuments—or for that matter lesser ones, where a new pattern of use has been established over an older one but where the representative order is unchanged? How does this relate to the design of new buildings? Particularly now

Former Royal Naval College buildings. Queen's House, National Maritime Museum at top. The University of Greenwich occupies Queen Anne (bottom left), Queen Mary (above), King William (right). Trinity College of Music occupies King Charles (bottom right).

when diverse needs can be compounded behind all embracing facades or within seemingly wilful over-expressive structures that attempt to satisfy aspirations or the need for promotional identity.

Contact with historic buildings leads to reflection on, amongst other things, the creative act whether in old contexts or new build. Is there such a gap? Perhaps not, for what we build new is likely to be the outcome of a series of propositions, the construction of a hypothetical building and its regeneration through stages to a final transformation. Time for reflection, for discovering the essence of the task is needed, and not always available. The genesis of Aalto's Viipuri Library comes to mind, from neo-classical concept to its final modernity, the process is fascinating and stimulating.[3] One might also cite the Gothenburg Town Hall extensions of Asplund, or in our time the design progression of the British Library from its inception on the Bloomshury site to its eloquent completion at St Pancras.[4]

Certainly involvement with historic buildings enhances one's perception of the timeless quality that generous buildings provide. The case for creative conservation is more than established and needs to be considered by government and all who need buildings and would build. Consideration should include, whoever supplies it, a vision of what might be achieved and a statement of aims. This was the condition at Greenwich and the Client, represented by John McWilliam, conveyed the necessary broad definition of objectives as a guide rather than a strait-jacket enabling all concerned to work with zest towards their achievement.

Such a philosophy needs to be more widely addressed considering the stock of existing buildings and the too easy way of facade retention and hollow space within. The creative embraces what exists, as the springboard for a new order that identifies and respects an older one—to the advantage of both.

1. London, *Wesminster improved*, 1766.
2. Bold, John, *Greenwich*, London: Yale University Press and English Heritage, 2000, pp. 104 and 105.
3. Spens, Michael, *Viipuri*, London: Academy Editions.
4. Stonehouse, Roger and G Stromberg, *The Architecture of the British Library at St Pancras*, London: Spon, 2002.

Ove Arup 1895–1998

The architectural landscape has lost a number of outstanding features recently and Ove Arup's death removes yet another—though perhaps he was more of a climate than a feature, a climate that encouraged others to grow.

In 1945 a bold request from the Editor of the *Architects' Year Book* for an article on reinforced concrete elicited a long piece from him with a characteristic opening: "This article is supposed to be about 'Reinforced Concrete'. Here I take this to mean 'Reinforced Concrete as applied to building', or to be more specific 'the right use of Reinforced Concrete in building. There were definitions and a response beyond the subject and an attempt to assess 'rightness' in an equation. Thus Rightness equals 'basic commodities' plus 'excess commodities' plus 'delight' divided by cost. (Basic commodities form the basis of the building programme—the minimum needs. Excess commodities are those provided in excess of the basic ones.)"

This article, still pertinent, was a good introduction to Arup's philosophy of architecture/engineering. Subsequent meetings in the generous atmosphere of the Fry, Drew practice increased my understanding as well as affection for this Dansk/Engelsk phenomenon. I remember a long afternoon when unstinted time was given to translating texts on Danish buildings we were

publishing. Later, working on the Fry, Drew housing schemes in Lewisham, there were rather alarming site visits with Ove driving his fluid-flywheel Daimler over south London tramlines, head mostly turned towards one and no reduction in the flow of speculative talk or speed. In this case he had a strong personal interest in the then topical box frame structure.

Much later, in my own practice and with a more significant commission, I sought an engineer. I discussed a half formed idea for the building, with one of fairly close acquaintance but with negative response. I went to see Ove, and explained what was growing in my mind, the need for a reaction to the ruins of a Roman building, its scale and grid and the idea of a massive structure for an open lower floor forming a table for a lighter structure of cellular spaces. There was immediate response, the offering of alternatives and a structural/architectural dialogue followed.

"Well, you know, you could do this... I don't know, perhaps... yes, it is possible, maybe." His elliptic method, open-minded response and generative power seemed to lie in this willingness to speculate, to see alternative structural potentials in any architectural task. He offered solutions that nourished one's tentative search for structural consonance and, in his words: "Did try to produce additional values by judicious disposition of the various parts."

Left: Ove Arup in later life. Courtesy ARUP.

Right: Kingsgate footbridge over the Wear, Durham, 1962–1963.

Of course, it became the 'Firm' with whom one dealt, first and second generation partners, but method, sound practice and concern for quality persisted, as well as the knock-on effect of Ove's charisma. This had special and wide appeal, the calculator, the man of science, yet vague, the slightly absent minded professor image with his strong Danish accent, chopsticks in his top pocket; a warm persona, concealing perhaps the shrewd Dane who inspired what remains for our and other practices the benign empire of Ove Arup & Partners—which perhaps did not always follow, again in Ove's words "the engineer's sad duty of restraining the enthusiasms of architects for new structural forms".

The Architects' Journal, 17 February 1998.

Colin Dollimore 1932–1993

Colin Dollimore's architectural roots were in the modern movement which he saw as a continuing and evolving language of space and form, matching needs with a coherent order inwardly derived, not imposed. As a teacher, Dollimore differed from academics who allowed students to indulge in wilder flights of fancy or modish abstractions; his counsel was to seek for poetry in proper order and argued that good architecture emerges from concepts that recognise necessities in

Sheltered housing, Arkendale at Felbridge, part of Whittington College, 1981.

University of Greenwich Avery Hill Campus, Norbert Singer Lecture Theatre, 1992–1996.

structures that are derived from thought and crafted with care. This he did in his own work.

Born in 1932, he studied architecture at what was in those days the Polytechnic, the original institution in Regent Street, central London. Its school of Architecture had exemption from both intermediate and final exams of the Royal Institute and was noted for its many eminent part-time practitioner staff and the standards achieved by its students in both design and constructional knowledge.

Dollimore's early experience included housing work with the 'Planning Design Team' Group headed by Harley Sherlock and time with Arup Associates, particularly working with the engineer Derek Sugden on the original Snape Maltings Concert Hall, a building for which he had a deep and abiding affection.[1] Most of his too short professional life was as my partner, working at first with the then other partner Ronald Paxton on the King Faisal Conference Centre in Riyadh. He was particularly responsible for the Hotel element, skillfully resolving the problems of building on a 60 degrees/30 degrees grid arising from a plan form responding to the climate. A few years later he was partner responsible for the British Embassy Staff Housing in Riyadh: 35 houses in several clusters individually structured round the Arab courtyard format, with massive walls and contrasting finely detailed sun screens over openings, mediating the

harsh climate for interior comfort.

Over some 15 years he took the leading part in work for Thames Polytechnic, now the University of Greenwich. A remarkable range of projects on several campuses: classrooms, staff rooms, laboratories, workshop, lecture theatres and libraries. One of the happiest and most sensitive was the re-ordering of the great ballroom at Avery Hill into a most elegant library. At St Paul's School, in west London, the new Colet Court Science building was his, as was the Arkendale housing for the elderly at Whittington College, in Felbridge, for the Mercer's Company, beautifully tailored into the existing landscape.

Dollimore was a thoughtful and inspiring teacher. After an invitation in the 1970s to act as visiting critic at Washington University, School of Architecture, St Louis, he returned there regularly as visiting Professor running several studios. He also taught at the Mackintosh School, Glasgow, and was instrumental in establishing links between the two schools. He pursued quality with that persistence needed on any building project and was thoroughly professional in all he did. He was on the Council of the Association of Consultant Architects and an active member of the Highgate Society and was Vice-President from 1975 to 1978. He was a long standing member of the Environment Committee and much involved in the refurbishment of Lauderdale House after the 1967 fire. This Grade One listed building in Waterow Park is now a Community Arts Centre. He advised the Friends of Highgate Cemetery on its care and fittingly he is there buried.

The Independent, 20 August 1993.

1. Sherlock, Harley, *An Architect in Islington*, London: The Islington Society, 2006.

Jane Drew 1911–1936

In 1943, through an introduction from Peter Moro, I went to 2 King Street, St James, 'The office of Jane B Drew'. Put at ease in terms of comfort on a sheepskin-covered Marcel Breuer long chair, I was interviewed and appointed. I started soon after, my first real job. A heady place in which to work in 1943, optimistic, we never doubted the war would end successfully and Sir would "... Look shining on new styles of architecture, a change of heart."

We were an odd group, for various reasons not liable for call-up. Myself, ex-Regent Street Polytechnic and somewhat innocent, Kurt Linden ex Architectural Association, devoted to finding the best cakes in war-time London, Denis Roberts, our senior, devoted to filing systems and office organisation, who nailed Jane's 'In' and 'Out' trays to her desk and jumped up and down at her frequent abuse of this simple system, our secretaries, Miss L, all lipstick and knees and the irreplaceable Miss B who did the salaries and everything else and kept the show on the road.

We all tried to channel Jane's inexhaustible energy and compensate for her refusal to accept the realities of war-time building. She pursued the modern in everything. Assured it was not available Jane would intervene and go to boundless lengths to have stores searched for forgotten stock or new inventions and would generally get what she wanted. We were in a small Georgian building, an L-shaped first floor furnished with amongst other goodies two Picasso etchings (*The Dream and Lie of Franco*) and a considerable Ivon Hitchens. We had some factory work, a few private clients and four farm worker's cottages to build.

Jane Drew and Maxwell Fry married in 1943. Maxwell was then in the army but in due course was seconded to the Colonial Development Corporation as planning advisor for a number of African towns and set off for West Africa with a team of young enthusiasts. Soon after Jane got a Gas Council appointment and we were deep into post-war kitchens. Jane was in and out of the office, with boundless enthusiasm, nudging the appliance manufacturers into the twentieth century. Soon she was off to the US courting the American gas industry, the main outcome being an enormous trunk full of glossy brochures and the five volumes of Sweets Catalogue.

With Jane often away, I and the Berlin architect FL Marcus—dearest of men and an architect of immense integrity—ran the practice. Arriving one morning we found the office a pile of rubble. A melancholy group trooped up to 12 Bedford Square, was received by Peter Gregory and offered Lund Humphries basement, we occupied the front, while in the back lurked Padmore their Commissionaire, usually with a friendly bottle. We continued there for some while through V1s and V2s and past VE day. When Jane was around there was an incessant stream of visitors, from all walks of life from Le Corbusier to able-bodied seamen encountered en voyage.

We started *Architects' Year Book*, the brainchild of the emigré publisher Paul Elek. Jane rallied her friends and press-ganged others and a mélange of articles resulted. The format came from *Circle*, Peter Ray designed volume 1. I was assistant editor, later joint editor and, at volume 3, Jane generously passed it over to me entirely.

As for the post-war kitchens our five prototypes were embodied in a lavish brochure, where surprisingly all the perspectives (by Helen Riehm Marcus's wife) showed women in domestic roles, men waiting to be fed, and in an exhibition at the Dorland Hall designed by Bronek Katz with kitchen colour schemes and a mural by John Armstrong. I moved over to Katz's office to bring kitchens and exhibition together and stayed until I rejoined Fry/Drew when the overseas planning contract ended and the Partners set up at 63 Gloucester Place.

The war well over, the practice burgeoned building extensively and mostly in West Africa. Jane and Max disappeared for stretches at a time leaving a big office to run itself in some remarkable way. When at home architectural, social and domestic life interlocked. A regular stream of visitors, architects, writers, musicians, poets, businessmen and engineers passed through the Fry/Drew salon. At the same time Jane's dynamic, with Max's Liverpool-trained yet instinctive feeling for site planning, coupled with a suitable building mode for West Africa, produced many appropriate and pleasing buildings.

Although I left the office in 1948, I continued to visit Gloucester Place for *Architects' Year Book* Editorial meetings. These were rather diffuse and difficult to convert into action. Peter Gregory, ex-officio member, enthused about some young painter or sculptor he had discovered. Herbert Read smiled wryly in the background, while Ove Arup philosophised, usually commencing with a "Well, you know... it might be...." Max inveighing against endlessly repeating mechanistic architecture, Jane free ranging as usual. We got some good contributors and they stayed with us despite

Client meeting. Playwright Ben W Levy, Jane Drew, Maxwell Fry at 66 Old Church Street, Chelsea (in 1950s).

Elek's reluctance to pay them.

It was my good fortune to have worked with Jane and Max and through that association to have joined a wider architectural community, to have had my interests and understanding widened and through that extraordinary office to have formed deep and lasting friendships.

But above all, from that first week at King Street in 'The office of Jane B Drew' to have been trusted and given responsibility was great encouragement. There was a mythical and sacred quality to her life, work and allegiances. Truthfully, she saw herself as an architect, not a woman architect, and so did we. Of course she preferred men and said so and wives and lovers suffered her indifference, with few exceptions.

She generated a climate where creativity could blossom but her own design was more a matter of hunches and assemblies. Monopitch roofs were adopted a few days after ACP's work in the West Indies was published, Max vainly objecting. In developing the Daneswood Avenue five-storey building, Jane suddenly discovered maisonettes and box frame construction and the main wing was tortured into shape with five projecting concrete framed elements forming expressive features on the main facade. Architecturally Jane was a collagist and the discipline of ordering plan/section, space, form and structure was not for her. Others did that—as Max said—with constant interruptions from Jane.

Although sometimes erratic, it was a great and generous office. Nevertheless, in 1948 it was a relief to move into the philosophic aura of Leslie Martin and Peter Moro in the Festival Hall Group, at the LCC while keeping a foot in 63 Gloucester Place through the *Architects' Year Book*, and lasting friendship with the Partners.

From *Jane Drew Architect, a tribute* Bristol Centre for the Advancement of Architecture, 1986.

Edwin Maxwell Fry 1899–1987

In 1938/39 the standard 'new architecture' tour started in Hampstead and ended in Highgate. High on the list was the Sun House, off Frognal, which John Summerson regarded as Maxwell Fry's outstanding work of the 1930s, showing "a relaxed confident mastery of the new ideas, telling variety in its proportions and the play of projecting elements". Elsewhere there was the much earlier Kensal House, the Ladbroke Grove flats, the Cecil Home in Upper Gower Street, other houses such as Old Church Street, Chipperfield in Kent and the big Kingston house and of course, Impington Village College. A considerable oeuvre considering the time. These buildings were imagic, assimilable, as fresh as one's first discovery of Impressionism and after.

Gropius and Fry, Impington Village College, model, 1938.

Kensal House flats, 1936, detail. Maxwell Fry with James and Wornum as steering committee with housing consultant. Denby.

Maxwell Fry was a sort of talisman and I thought it awesome to seek employment in his practice. But later, in wartime, circumstances lead me to the office of Jane Drew and, amazing moment, I met 'Major Fry'. Maxwell and the School of Architecture hero did not disappoint. I wobbled a bit, though I was soon put at ease by his approachability and charm. But he was much abroad and it was not until 1946 when the combined office got going at 63 Gloucester Place, that I had any close association.

Chatting about those days with a former colleague, we agreed how lucky we were, for we did not then realise how much trust and responsibility we were given. There was much larking about but, ultimately, we were committed and serious and the prevailing austerity was full of hope. The two Partners, the central nervous system of the office, radiated hope. Max's sprightly spirit never let us down and bore us through every crisis: Even a roof blown off did not daunt him and that client came back with one of the office's largest UK projects. Confidence radiated; confidence that brought in an amazing number of West African building projects and which helped to realise them successfully.

The mechanics of that office still mystify. How did it keep going with so little formal structure and how did it remain solvent? A lot was built even though our building experience was limited and there was little time for reflection. We were imbued with enthusiasm, with loyalty to the practice and loyalty to the idea of architecture that Max transmitted. There was goodwill all round from clients, consultants, contractors, and sub-contractors. For many years Max declared his antipathy to professional indemnity insurance!

I was involved in some minor works in West African buildings and the design stages of housing schemes in Lewisham. The Daneswood Avenue development, now listed, is authentic Max and still has that freshness of the early work. Other Lewisham work followed, and the social aspect echoed Fry's deep awareness of that dimension of architecture, as does the work in West Africa.

In Britain one should mention the Pilkington building which seemed in my view a fine achievement of Max's later years. There, and in West Africa, Max showed his considerable art and skill in site planning. His Liverpool training under Reilly and his time with Adams and Thompson shine through in his disposition of buildings and landscape. The picture I have is of long weekends at the drawing board. Then, late on a Monday, would appear a delightful crayon perspective, plans, sections and elevations with all levels worked out, often for projects on extreme African terrain. At my LCC Architects Department interview in 1948 I showed my best set of working drawings done at Fry/Drew, designs for an Ahenfie, a chief's house with bedrooms for several wives. It was remarked that there was an Arabian night's atmosphere about the work of the practice. There seemed some truth in this. Max did imbue work with a sort of magic; he rubbed the lamp and a new job would arrive or a stale one would be transformed. Or Jane and Max would materialise after an African visit, beating tom-toms and wearing outlandish gear, or our ex-stoker caretaker would turn out to be the local burglar, Aalto would appear, or Ernesto Rogers, or Constance Cummings and hosts of other notables.

Architects such as Jack Howe, Bronek Katz, Reggie Vaughan, Arthur Ling who had worked in Max's pre-war office, all spoke of Max with regard and affection. Indeed he inspired affection. It was a delight to meet him, for his bright spirit always showed and his love of architecture and urbanity was boundless. I admired his diverse talents, his fluent writings, sometimes prolix, occasionally messianic, but often wise, full of clear judgments, generous and supportive of other architects. At heart there is a continuing concern, about the place of art in a technological society and the relation of the individual to the mass. He wishes for "technics to be commanded by humanity". On new office buildings, "the machine triumphs in commercial captivity" or, to me he wryly quoted "put not your trust in Princes". anent my commission in Saudi Arabia

Kevin Roche declared how inspirational it was to be in the Fry/Drew office in the late 1950s. Earlier and later generations found stimulus in Fry's power to communicate his enthusiasm for the arts, for buildings, for towns, and ultimately for the Mother of the Arts.

To quote: "I say once again that the aim of life is its continuation and that we continue where we find a form for life that allows it to be best expressed for us by the organisation of our life on the earth's face and for this we must adapt and modify the hard and resisting facts of nature to our ends and scrutinise her enigmatic face. This is the task of science. But we must live ideally and religiously and for this we must lay ourselves open to revelation and await the intimations of immortality of which Wordsworth spoke. This is the way of art."

The Architect, October 1997.

Finn Juhl 1914–1989 A personal note

I first met Finn Juhl in London and in 1947, at his invitation I went to Denmark and thereafter regularly. We enjoyed a continuing friendship founded, initially, on my side on respect for his work and his revelation of the qualities of the Danish/Scandinavian tradition plus his critical acumen (even if this was often sharply expressed; there was a bit of the *enfant terrible* about him).

He was something of an anglophile, very well read in English literature and history. We shared a love of Mr Pickwick as well as the humour of Bertram Wooster. We did honour him in England with the award, eventually, of honorary Royal Designer for Industry, and he liked that, especially the Royal bit.

Finn Juhl graduated in architecture at the Royal Academy in Copenhagen in 1934 and then worked for Vilhelm Lauritzen especially on the Radio House until, in 1945, he opened his own studio. At the same time he became Principal of the Frederiksberg School of Interior Design. At home his furniture was at first critically received, for it questioned the tradition of Klint, the rational productions of Fritz Hansen's factory as well as the 'craft' school, but it soon gained international acclaim, being thoroughly modern in its structural clarity and articulation of the main elements and also appealing in its sensuous sculptural qualities and cultural resonances.

His Bing and Grøndahl showroom, 1947, at once showed a new voice in a clear and well organised response to needs, plus an acute feeling for space and colour, as well as general and detail furbishment, creating a serene ambience characteristic of all his subsequent interiors: for example the notable Trusteeship Council Chamber at the United Nations, various SAS offices, the Danish Embassy in Washington, many private interiors and numerous exhibitions worldwide

His few houses are in a relaxed mode and I see in them something original, very much ignored by architectural critics or historians. It is difficult to find precedent for what he did. Perhaps Danish vernacular

The "45 Chair".

Summer house in Asserbo, 1950.

building, which his underlying sensibility appreciated as much as it was engaged with the classical, or with such buildings as his much loved Liselund, a delightful blend of the vernacular and neo-classic in south east Denmark. (Møn). His own house in Charlottenlund, was a place of magic. I admired the spatial organisation, the relaxed mode of building. It was immensely sympathetic with a quiet poetry of space, light and colour, a total artwork.

These were private buildings, not public ones, and occasion now demands a statement and architecture becomes more expressive, sensational, theatrical and at the extreme puts form before content. To speculate, had we been fortunate enough to have had, say, an art gallery by Juhl, I am sure his priority would have been the subject not the object and he would have discovered a form from within not imposed an image from without. An analogy might be the very sympathetic Kröller-Müller Museum in Holland by Van de Velde as opposed to Bilbao, which is to be admired more as an urban pivot than a gallery.

He was a linguist with a wide cultural awareness, much engaged with Greece and Italy, yet loving the artistic riches of his own country, in context and as part of a fine tradition. Pictorial and sculptural experiences enriched and stimulated his work which followed a strong personal direction. Imitators, alas, abounded and then other lines prevailed for he never really engaged in 'the Market' and remained a singular artist of exceptional sensibility. His classic works are mainly of the period 1945–1965 and in a country where architects are especially honoured he will enter their pantheon, and also survive wherever visual imagination and quality are valued.

Based on various texts, 1989, 2004.

Denys Lasdun 1914–2001

We exchanged Christmas cards for years, met at gatherings from the MARS Group to the Royal Academy of Arts, gossiped and talked seriously about issues for which we both cared. These occasions were a source of pleasure and for me often brought a renewal of commitment. Once by chance, meeting in Tuscany, characteristically DL enthused about the Benedictine Abbey Church of Sant' Antimo, and demanded we visit, which we did and were rewarded. Similarly, he insisted one should read Panofsky's "Gothic Architecture and Scholasticism". The historical dimension of architecture was a potent generator for him evidenced in his lifelong interest in the architecture of Hawksmoor "so singular and so profoundly concerned with the roots of architecture and the nature of space". (Curtis)

There was so much to admire in the man and the buildings. Admiration was again reinforced on a recent valedictory tour of his London buildings, particularly in the core space, the central circulation of the Royal College of Physicians, a building esteemed and loved by all especially the President of the RCP at the time of its making, "Bill" Hoffenberg, who paid immense personal tribute to DL. He must have been a good client as its consonance seems to indicate and DL's return years later to build an extension is a credit to the client body and architect relationship.

There is an architectural density in that generative central space of great potency, a similar density in the core space of the National Theatre, and surprisingly in the Claredale Street housing where at the confluence of access galleries there is an extraordinary poetry of space and material with slots of view extending into the city.

Designed as social housing, at risk for a while, and saved by the efforts of DOCOMOMO, the 20th Century Society and English Heritage and admirably restored by Lincoln Holdings as Keeling House. Not so far away at Usk Street there are two earlier examples of this pattern and these 'cluster blocks' exemplify the search for new housing patterns with which Lasdun was much engaged, in CIAM/MARS and the TEAM X dialogues to which Lasdun made considerable personal contribution.

After leaving the Architectural Association School Lasdun worked for Wells Coates, (his "temporary artistic mentor"), on Palace Gate (the 3:2 section), and with his second commission, number 32 Newton Road Paddington completed, Lasdun joined the Tecton practice led by Lubetkin in 1938. Curtis quotes Lasdun as saying of Tecton, "Here I found a professionalism, a classical attention to detail and a continuity of attitude to concrete which had its roots in the work of August Perret." The Lasdun/Lubetkin relationship is an engaging area for speculation. No man is an island and

Royal College of Physicians, 1959.

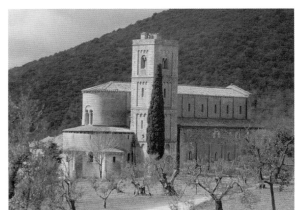

Abbey Church of Sant'Antimo, c. 1120.

Lubetkin by all accounts was a powerful influence on the Tecton members, much younger, much less experienced. Lasdun, some 13 years junior must have recognised in Lubetkin an authority that was based on clear principles and critical awareness, qualities that he also embraced, together with an underlying admiration for Le Corbusier and response to his works and words. Lasdun's genesis and genius is well served by William Curtis, as is Lubetkin's by John Allen. They were both strong characters and inevitably, there was a divergence in later years.

Two close friends of mine were Partners of Lasdun and both spoke of the authority and charisma which he possessed. Only such authority could have achieved projects like the National Theatre, and the European Investment Bank building. Behind that authority was the powerful discipline of a committed and loyal office. Graham Lane has said there was a constant questioning of aims and achievements and DL was certain "true architectural art could only be achieved by struggle". There was debate and fierce argument and in work there was nothing so simple as the common practice of producing a valid sketch design and then working it up.

Lasdun saw every building as a piece of true research intensively conducted at every stage. From John Allen it is clear that the Lasdun method was close to that established by Tecton. Lane speaks of the distinct stages in which Lasdun participated to a greater or lesser extent, the study of all those facts which impinge on a building project objectively and subjectively. The objective was to find the *genus locii* of a place and in Lasdun's words "the soul of the building". At some stage all the main elements of the building were put into model form. From this emerged a clarification of the concept and its development in greater detail, so that functional and architectural needs were reconciled and the language of the building was completely coherent, the elements of space, structure and form brought into harmonious relationship.

London has enough building by Lasdun to satisfy any architectural enthusiast. From Bethnal Green, Bloomsbury, South Bank, St James' Park, Regent's Park

to Paddington with the Hallfield Estate, and its lively coda Hallfield school) and in Newton Road the 1937 House. Here I remember its pristine freshness (well captured in *The Architectural Review* of March 1939), its sophisticated character and much more considered construction than most houses of that period. And this by an architect in his early 20s! It was job number two out of some 30 realised projects, five listed in London alone, apart from a range of outstanding competition entries.

Although my lazy predilections are for a looser sort of architecture, especially in the domestic field, I cannot but hold my breath in awe of his achievements, his singleness of purpose, the outstanding ability to extract a formal architectural order out of so many diverse building tasks and heighten it to the level of eloquent dominance, as is so evident at the National Theatre against an intractable bridge. A timeless architectural language exemplified in Corbusier's magical sentence "Le jeu, savant, correct et magnifique des volumes sous la lumière." For me, from days of awe I moved on to days of deep personal respect and affection for a great architect and a most lovable man. *The Architectural Review*, March 2001.

Peter Laslett 1915–2001

Peter's last gift to me was a rarish English edition (about 1779 I think) of Lewis Cornaro's "Discourses on a sober and temperate life—The method of preserving health to extreme old age". This was characteristic of the last of his vast range of interests—I think from being his architect I had become a working exemplar of longevity, an interesting case history into which he was always probing, to my entertainment and pride.

It's not quite 50 years since Peter and Janet engaged me as their architect. Introduced by their landlandy, a former co-student of mine Rachel Wallis, later Rachel Rostas, in the Cambridge scene. It was my second house commission, though completed before the first. It was opportunity to put ideals of architectural design into practice. Ideals gained through student years in contact with Peter Moro and later at the LCC, with him and under the creative, benign and refined eye of Leslie Martin, subsequently Cambridge's first Professor of Architecture.

These ideals I think most concerned the resolution of the living needs of what I suppose Peter would have called a nuclear family, on a site with modest natural features (strip lynchets) and to a limited budget—I wasn't concerned with architectural rhetoric.

Peter Laslett at No. 3 Clarkson Road.

However, Peter's wish, I inferred later, was more perhaps towards making a statement of the 'modern' in the then stuffy architectural climate of Cambridge, the College having just rejected a scheme by Powell & Moya. Had I known this, I think I might have been more inhibited in my approach for I preferred the architectural statement to grow from within, expressiveness being the function of right order. Anyway, the expression and the content immensely pleased Peter and Janet and family then and now.

Rarely has an architect had a building so well looked after and such a happy relationship with clients who turned into friends. As patron, Peter in his more seigneurial style liked to parade me as his architect, sometimes to my embarrassment, I must admit, but rarely so—and exceptionally he and Jan would not do anything to the house without full consultation, whether it was a new cooker or a work of art or the typography of "The World we have lost", and Peter and Jan became good patrons in so many respects, such that the house became a sort of *Gessamtkunstwerk*. Though it has been 'modernised' in a least two respects, over the years, it has remained intact and for me has always been a pleasure to visit, though its owners were foremost in my regard.

As friends Peter and I had some amusing and extending times, exploring bits of London and Cambridge mostly, and for me meeting various Laslett friends and colleagues and always learning something. His probing interest always made one feel good. I found myself on these expeditions somehow protecting Peter, his interests dominated and he seemed unaware of the manifest dangers of roads, buildings under construction, or pieces of furniture for that matter.

Of course talk dominated and continued regardless. I remember in the days when he sported a pipe he dropped it under our dining table, where he had difficulty in retrieving it—words continued to flow from beneath the table, like some Delphic oracle. Another pipe encounter liberally smudged his face and I had to clean him up before he gave a passionate address to the Listeners and Viewers Association. I was somewhat allergic to what one of the founders of that association called "Idiot's Lanterns", Peter thought my young son deprived and produced a TV for him from somewhere a neat critique and nice gift even if it didn't work very well!

Generous in the extreme, full of enthusiasms, an immense stimulant and wonderful guide to Cambridge and his College, which he loved dearly, even while being highly critical of arcane rituals. I remember his groans when his much loved 'open university' went in for the panoply of robes and beadles and what he called "all that jazz". There was always this love-hate relationship around the panoply of power but his College tours were a joy and bore repetition, usually ending in the Chapel where I always extolled the virtues of the two types of space, light and dark while he talked of Newton and Barrow—one of his specialties, and Wordsworth's response to seeing Newton's statue through a chapel window from his room in St Johns ("The Evangelist St John my patron was") was a favourite quotation of Peter's, which might well conclude this modest tribute to a true patron and very dear friend. I find it relevant, for they were loved words and Peter's Cambridge life spanned St Johns and Trinity.

Trinity College Memorial Service, 8 March 2002.

Frederic Lucas Marcus 1888–1975

The Berlin architect always known as Marcus, who died in Hampstead which he called 'beiunski land' was born in Dessau and studied architecture in Munich and Berlin, where he was later in practice, one of the group of distinguished architects in that city who were evolving a clear and austere style that made Berlin one of the key centres of Modern Architecture in the 20s and early 30s. His work there was mostly domestic and especially notable for its artistic economy and directness.

He left in 1933 for Paris and then Spain (Tossa del Mar), where he also built, particularly the 'Hotel in Spain' of Nancy Johnston's best-seller of that title, prototype of the escapist genre. He and his wife, Helen Riehm an artist, reached England in 1939 through the efforts of the late Richard and Katya Church, who became close friends and for whom he designed an elegant oast house conversion in Kent.

As happened to many refugees, a dreary round of internment followed at the outbreak of war but ill health led to release and after a period of war work, through the good offices of Herbert Read in 1944 he joined the then small office of Jane B Drew, where he was especially involved in post-war domestic planning and design.

In 1946 he was appointed Head of the Department of Interior Design and Furniture at the Central School of Arts and Crafts (under William Johnstone), an appointment of which one feels Lethaby would have approved, for he held it with wisdom, engaging several distinguished part time teachers and showing great support and affection for the young. His hatred of design indulgence and sense of style influenced a considerable number of students to whom his use of English was salutary in its directness, yet deeply endearing.

He retired in 1953 and in private practice he completed houses and many domestic and shop interiors, all marked by innate simplicity and style in the best sense. A Fellow of the Society of Industrial Artists, he was known to, and respected by many fellow architects and designers and will be remembered with deep affection as a person of indomitable spirit, an architect and teacher of

Marcus and his House in Berlin.

profound integrity who, like many of his generation, survived to reach this country to our good fortune.

Helen Riehm wrote a moving account of the vicissitudes of their life together following their escape from Germany, *Still alive with Lucas* published by Peter Davis, 1940, and which went into a second edition.

The Architectural Review, December 1975.

Peter Moro 1911–1997

In 1941, as a student then at the Polytechnic School of Architecture Peter Moro's arrival heralded a new era, one where his strong personality, his continental aura, work with Tecton and his evident achievement in the elegant and sophisticated house at Birdham provided a lodestar. He taught best on a one-to-one basis where, untying knots, his three-dimensional skills were dazzling, while on the broad front his searching 'crits' and acerbic comments on student complacency were salutary, persuading all to do better. At that time, received wisdom was 'form follows function'. Moro declared he learned more from Lubetkin than in all his school years and, like him, eschewed the 'functionalism' of the day and believed in the form- giving role of the architect as well as the organising one.

Following his LCC years, as Associate Architect on the Festival Hall, he achieved notable success with his Nottingham Playhouse, radical in its day, the finest of the first tranche of post-war theatres, and in which he achieved a contemporary richness of experience to match that of traditional theatre.

Although he and his partners worked in several fields, the theatre was a major interest for him, and work included refurbishment at the Bristol Old Vic, The Queens University Theatre at Coleraine and, in 1982, the Plymouth Theatre notable for its variable capacity to suit winter repertory and big summer shows as well as providing a notable architectural presence in the city. At Hull University, the Gulbenkian Centre provided a practical range of studios for media

students wrapped in an envelope of refined architectural character.

Whatever the subject, his architecture was deeply rooted in the bedrock of the programme, where he sought to organise space and volume for convenience and delight, aiming to create humane environments. He was deeply involved with the niceties of use, the pleasures of movement, the delight of material to sight and touch. He pursued building design with a rare honesty of approach. He was rational, with a clear understanding of how to put things together and, perhaps, faith that in designing well, resonances would emerge from unconscious springs.

Latter-day practice did not suit Moro's maestro temperament, and retirement was a pleasure. He enjoyed life in his Blackheath house, (listed grade 2) the visits of friends, tennis, and writing trenchant letters to the press. He made delightful relief constructions, fastidious in design and execution, which showed him as the visual man he was, through and through, not really in tune with English prejudice towards literature.

His pictorial sensibility inclined to the ordered rather than expressionist, and he had in architecture and design a sort of pantheon to which admission was highly selective, but over a wide field. Here his yard-stick was rigorously applied and just as in his own work characterised by strong 'modern' visual appeal and a love of quality.

The Architects' Journal, 22 October 1997.

Peter Moro at the Royal Festival Hall, 1951.

Theatre Royal, Plymouth, 1982.
Courtesy of Andrzej Blonski.

Book Review
Out of the Ordinary

Without rhetoric: an architectural aesthetic 1955–72,
Alison and Peter Smithson. Latimer New Dimensions, 1973.

Of the different definitions of 'rhetoric' it is, I think, that of 'language' characterised by artificial or ostentatious expression which the authors believe architecture in our time can do without. This is the underlying theme—the achievement of ordinariness (Perret's 'banal') using the word in a non-depreciatory way. Thus *"... why we think about the Hochschule für Gestaltung at Ulm—of its ease, of its ordinariness that has a kind of understated lyricism which is full of potential and does not disturb the peace of the hillside...".*

An unsympathetic critic while enjoying their prescience might cavil at certain aspects of the authors' earlier writings and pronouncements (often gnomic without being lapidary), the cryptic style, the ingenuous self-documentation, even a certain arrogance. But this has disappeared leaving only a trace, in the blurb, where they are described as "being instrumental in the development of the thoughtful approach to modern architecture" and in the text, perhaps the generous self-quotation and certainly the ambiguous use of 'we'; sometimes at first construed as architects in general but always ending up as no one but the authors. On page ten we have it clear; *"Gropius wrote a book on grain silos, Le Corbusier a book on aeroplanes, and Charlotte Perriand—it was said—brought a new object to the office every morning; but in the 'fifties we collected 'ads'."*

But this is marginal in reading the book I found it entirely sympathetic—a long essay which had to be consumed at one draught, for there are no resting places and it proceeds from theme to theme with deceptive ease until suddenly, to one's regret, it ends. There are, in fact, three strands: the essay proper, the nicely juxtaposed illustrations and then verbal illustrations (contained in ruled boxes) which perhaps check the pace more than they should. Read separately or together they contribute to make a total greater than the sum of parts.

Three months after having read an advance copy, I re-read it with an enjoyment which on reflection I can only compare with the delight I have had from certain, for me, extending books—for instance Adrian Stokes' *Smooth and Rough* or Michael Tippett's *Moving into Aquarius.* Each has a common characteristic—the compelling quality of literate artists writing about their art and other artists with sympathy and understanding.

In a short review of an essay which scatters much seed by the way (so full of 'quotes') it is not easy to single out examples, but for one I was especially taken by the discriminating account of Mies, why he is important, why significant repetition is not to be confused with endlessness, for;

The Economist Building, St James, London, 1962–1964.

"The elements repeated seem to derive from the intention of the whole of which they form the part... [his buildings] are to be seen as a vehicle conveying the self-construction, the self—control and the reticence now needed by an architect."
Then on services:
"It has always taken a very long time for a useful thing to become an idea—to acquire formal value.... Since the late middle ages the best architects have been able to deal with fire, the fireplace as idea. The removal of the fireplace (in 18th or 19th c buildings) destroys the meaning of the English domestic room.... To have an architecture now our machines and services must become idea."
Again some discerning reflections on architectural elements as metaphors (reminiscent of the 'subjunctive architecture' in Summerson's 1948 essays) are beautifully put—and what better support for the necessity of architectural history?

And then, on housing;
"All of us want the sort of house we can make our own, within the limits of the fashion of the time, and without feeling any pressure either to communicate our trivial uniqueness or to conform absurdly."

Out of context these quotations may appear flat, not showing the roundness or concentration of the whole: let it be said, the authors are revealed as working yet reflective architects concerned with wholeness in their craft and in their philosophy and which they succeed in communicating with authority. They illumine many things that one has seen but, hitherto, as in a glass darkly. Full of observation and comment on the present state of architecture it is a most mature and lucid work in writing, from that multidisciplinary team of two which gave us in building, the Economist Group—that diamond among the paste of commercial architecture of our time.

The Architects' Journal, September 10 July 1974.

(James) Trevor Dannatt RA
Dip Arch MA FRIBA Hon FAIA
Doctor of Design, *Honoris Causa*, 2002,
University of Greenwich

B 1920 London
Education: Colfe's School, Lewisham Hill, then at the School of
Architecture, Regent Street Polytechnic, London, 1938–1942

Practice
1943–1948: Office of Jane B Drew, subsequently Fry, Drew
1948–1952: Architects' Department London County Council,
Festival Hall Group
1952: commenced private practice
1970: with Colin Dollimore and Ronald Paxton formed
Trevor Dannatt & Partners
1978: with David Johnson formed Dannatt, Johnson Architects
2004: Consultant, Dannatt, Johnson Architects, with Partners David
Johnson, Jonathan Parry, and Carl Cairns

Works 1957–1984
• Congregational Church, Blackheath
• Laslett house, Cambridge
• Dobbs House, London
• Plante House, London
• University of Leicester, Women's Hall of Residence with Sir Leslie
Martin. Also London University Precinct Master Plan
• University and City of Leicester, Vaughan College and Jewry
Wall Museum
• Old Library refurbishment and Council Chamber,
University of Leicester
• Needler Hall Men's Residence, University of Hull
• Fellows Common Room, Trinity Hall, Cambridge
• Science Building and Gymnasium, Rosa Bassett School, London
• Eltham Hill School new classrooms, and science labs, London
• Pitcorthie House, Fife
• Housing, Poplar High Street, London
• 1968–1973, King Faisal Conference Centre, Intercontinental Hotel,
Mosque and Villas, Riyadh, Saudi Arabia
• Old People's Homes, Lambeth
(Cedars Road, and Union Road, London)
• Assembly Hall, Bootham School, York
• Ebbisham Court at Whittington College, Felbridge,
(Mercers' Company)
• Children's Reception Home, Southwark, London
• Society of Friends Meeting House, Blackheath
    During this period various interior works including conversions or
interiors domestic. For AL Lloyd, Dr Bertha Malnick, Tom Hopkinson,
Lord Elwyn Jones, Robert Donat, Mrs W Bowman, G&A Dannatt.
Interiors commercial: for Wm S Ellis (catering), Primavera, J Walter
Thompson, Lund Humphries, Georg Jensen, France and Son, Dickins
and Jones, Van den Burghs (Spry), Coach interiors for British Rail, etc..

Works 1984–2006
• Lecture Theatre, Laboratories and Chapel re-ordering, St Paul's
School, Barnes, London

• British Embassy, Riyadh, Chancery and Office building and
ancillaries, Ambassador's Residence, (Staff Housing Colin Dollimore)
• Arts building, Preparatory School, Colfe's School, London
    In the two practices Trevor Dannatt was particularly involved
in the following. In 1988 (initially Trevor Dannatt and Partners,
subsequently Dannatt, Johnson Architects) were appointed
Consultant Architects to Thames Polytechnic (later the University
of Greenwich) for master plans and for new buildings and
conversions which have included numerous lecture theatres,
libraries, laboratories and classrooms, Student Union buildings.
    In 1993 the practice was commissioned to prepare the Master
plan for the University for occupation of the old Royal Naval
College, Greenwich. Subsequent works included conversion and
refurbishment of three of the four Grade 1 listed historic buildings,
Queen Anne, Queen Mary and King William Courts. Also the
Dreadnought Seamen's Hospital and adjacent West Annexe.
    In 1988 the practice was appointed Consultant Architects to the
Royal Botanic Gardens, Kew for new buildings and restorations
which included the No 1 Museum, the Aroid House, Constabulary
and storage building, extension and restoration of the Orangery,
the Victoria Gate Visitor Reception and Facilities building.
    In 2003 renewal and development of the Marylebone Campus,
University of Westminster. Currently Dannatt, Johnson Architects are
involved in a wide range of works both new build and conservation
for public and private clients, including the Universities of Greenwich
and Kingston; English Heritage, The British Museum, the Barbican
and The Royal Academy of Arts, Northwood College, the London
Borough of Greenwich. With the practice Trevor Dannatt is
designing a large country house near Petersfield.

Exhibition Design
1950: Exhibition designs and installations including architecture
exhibitions for the Arts Council and Group shows (notably
"weekend exhibitions")
1958: At the Whitechapel Gallery with Bryan Robertson "20th Century
form" subsequently, "Jackson Pollock" and, "Mark Rothko". Recently
"Now you see it" at The Whitworth Art Gallery Manchester, 2006

Academic Posts
1975–1986: Professor University of Manchester, School of Architecture
1976 and 1986: Visiting Professor, Washington University St Louis
1995–2005: Professor of Architecture, the Royal Academy of Arts

Professional Services
• Assessor for Council of Industrial Design (C.O.I.D) Design Awards,
Architectural Design project awards, Civic Trust and RIBA Regional
Awards, and various architectural competitions, UK and overseas
• RIBA External Examiner
• Modern Architecture Research Group (MARS) Hon Sec, 1952–1957
• Served on the Cathedrals Advisory Commission, 1986–1991
• English Heritage Post-war Listing Advisory Committee, 1986–2003
• Fabric Committees of Cathedrals: Lichfield, Portsmouth and until
recently St Paul's Cathedral.
• DOCOMOMO (Documents of the Modern Movement) Trustee
1991–present
• President of 20th Century Society 2003–present

Publications
Principal Publications
• *The Architects' Year Book*, (10 volumes, 3 initially with Jane Drew),
Elek, 1948–1962
• *Modern Architecture in Britain*, Batsford, 1959
• *Trevor Dannatt: Buildings and Interiors 1951–1972*, Lund Humphries
1972 (Foreword by Theo Crosby)
• *Buildings and Ideas 1933–1983 from the studio of Leslie Martin*,
Editorial Advisor and Foreword, Cambridge, 1983
• *Architecture, Education and Research* (Leslie Martin), Joint Editor
with Peter Carolin also a contributor, Academy Editions, 1996
• Monograph *Maritime Greenwich Campus*, John Bold and others
Dannatt, Johnson, 2002

Press and otherwise
(in addition to what is published herewith)
General
• *Architects' Approach to Architecture* (lecture), *RIBAJ*, March 1969,
available at www.trevordannatt.co.uk
• Aalto, *Manchester Guardian*, 8 April 1957; *AD*, April 1957; *RIBAJ*,
September 2008
• Denmark, Early publications on travel, exhibitions, furniture, etc.,
A&BN, 25 July 1947, 30 January 1948, 5 March 1948, 12 November
1948, 24 June 1949, 10 March 1950, 14 August 1952, *AR*, June 1948,
AD, June 1954, *Politiken* (Dk), 20 May 1968
• Homes for the Elderly, "In Memoriam", *20th Century Soc. Newsletter*,
Autumn 2005
• Leslie Martin, Trevor Dannatt address at Royal Gold Medal
presentation, *RIBAJ*, April 1973
• Obituaries: Theo Crosby, *RA Magazine*, December 1994
• John McWilliam, *The Independent*, 4 April 2007

Reviews
Books
• "About Wright", Tafel, Wiley 1993, *RSAJ*, December 1993
• "Building Environment—hot, dry lands", Saini, Angus & Robertson,
1975, *AJ*, 2 April 1975
• "Modernism", Christopher Wilk, V&A, 2006, *20th Century Soc.
Newsletter*, Autumn 2006 (includes exhibition)
• "Shaker life, Work and Art", Sprigg and Larkin, Cassell, 1988, *AJ*, 2
November 1988
• "The Villa Mairea", Pallasmaa, Aalto Foundation, 1998, *ARQ*, vol.3
no 4 1999

Exhibitions
• *20th Century Form*, catalogue Introduction, The Whitechapel Art
Gallery, April 1953
• *Ten Years of British Architecture*, catalogue, (with John Summerson),
Arts Council Exhibition, 1956
• "Now you see it", catalogue Introduction, The Whitworth Art Gallery,
February 2006
• "Jensen jubilee exhibition", Copenhagen, 1954, *AD*, May 1954
• "Halsingborg 55 exhibition", *AD*, August 1955
• "Alan Irvine " Heinz Gallery, 1989, *AJ*, 26 April 1989
• "Frank Lloyd Wright Gallery V&A", *RSAJ*, March 1993

Press references to Works
Following the order in the book
- Richard Church House: *A&BN,* 27 March 1952; *HG,* April 1952
- Eynsford Interiors: *AR,* November 1966; *MD,* February 1964; *AD,* May 1965
- Furniture: Terrace Chair, *A&BN,* 22 July 1949; Radiogram, *AD,* March 1954
- House Designs: Dewar Mills, *A&BN,* 20 December 1946
- Rees House, *A&BN,* 20 December 1946
- Laslett House, *AD,* March 1959; *A&BN,* February 1960; *HG,* April 1960; *MD,* August 1960; *CL,* 21 July 2005
- Dobbs House, *AD,* March 1959; *A&BN,* 30 November 1960
- Plante House, *AD,* April 1961
- Pitcorthie House, *MD,* July 1967; *CL,* 30 May 1968
- Vicarage Avenue Housing, *AR,* December 1978
- Union Road Old Peoples Home, *TA,* August 1978
- Ebbisham Court Felbridge, *AR,* December 1978; *BW,* May 1979
- Childrens Home, *AJ,* 10 October 1973
- Poplar Housing, *AR,* January 1965
- Union Road Housing, *TA,* August 1978
- Coffee Bars, *AD,* June 1954, December 1955
- Primavera, *AD,* January 1954
- Dickins and Jones, *AD,* August 1955, December 1955
- J Walter Thompson, *AR,* November 1966
- Lund Humphries, *A&B,* September 1958
- Greenwich Building Soc, *AD,* December 1959; *AJ,* 29 January 1975
- Hall of Residence Leicester, *AR,* June 1961; *AD,* April 1962
- Needler Hall, *AD,* June 1965; *MD,* February 1966; *BMeist,* December 1965, *ID,* January 1965
- Vaughan College, *AD,* May 1965
- Trinity Hall, *AD,* June 1966
- Rosa Bassett School, *A&BN,* 26 April 1967; *BMeist,* May 1960
- St Paul's School, *AJ,* 19 September 1984
- Univ Greenwich, *CL,* 23 November 2000, Monograph Maritime Greenwich Campus. John Bold and others. Dannatt Johnson 2002
- Riyadh Conf Centre and Hotel: *AR,* February 1968, April 1975; *SE,* December 1975; *IIC,* November 1979; *IDC,* April 1980
- Riyadh Mosque: *AR,* April 1975; *RIBAJ,* June 1976
- Maze Hill Chapel: *AD,* August 1957
- Blackheath Cong. Church: *AD,* August 1957
- Bootham School: *AR,* March 1967; *AD,* March 1967
- Friends Meeting House: *AR,* April 1973; *CC,* June 1974
- St Pauls Chapel: *AJ,* 19 September 1984
- British Embassy Riyadh: *AJ,* 10 June 1987
- Victoria Gate Kew: *BD,* 04 September 1992
- Weekend Exhibitions: (Adrian Heath and others) *BM,* December 1990
- Ten Years of British Architecture: *AJ,* 16 February 1956
- Jackson Pollock Exhibition: *BM,* December 1958, Newhouse " Art and the Power of Placement" Monacelli Press NY 2005; *MD* March 1960
- "Now you see it" Cat. The Whitworth Art Gallery February 2006

Key: *Architect & Building News (A&BN), Architecture & Building (A&B), Architects Journal (AJ), Architectural Design (AD), Architectural Review (AR), Building Design (BD), Burlington Magazine (BM), Country Life (CL), Concrete Quarterly (CC), House & Garden (HG), Interior Design (ID), Structural Engineer (SE), The Architect (TA), Bouen&Wohnen (BW), Baumeister (B.Meist), Mobel&Dekoration (MD), Industria Italiana del Cemento (IIC), Industria della Construzione (IDC), RIBA Journal (RIBAJ).*

Photographic Credits for Works
Most photography was instructed by the two Practices who hold the copyrights.

Photographers commissioned include: Martin Charles (MC), Peter Cook (PC), John Dewar (JD), Frank Donaldson (FD), Keith Hunter (KH), Edgar Hyman (EH), Sam Lambert (SL), Mann Bros (MB), Henk Snoek (HS), Colin Westwood (CW), Uncredited photographs generally by Trevor Dannatt. Following the order of the works, credits are as follows:

Model Photos:
All by (MB).

The Complete Consort
p.8 *R* (MB), p. 13 *B* (KH).
Hearth
p.34 *L* (JD), p.35 *L, TM, TR, BR,* (CW), *BC L&R* (PC), p.36 *TC* (MB) *TR* (EH) *BC* (PC), p.37 *TL&C* (SL) *TR* (JD) *B* (EH).
Domestication
p.39 *BL* (PC) *BR* (MB), p.40 (CW), p.41 (EH), p.42 *BL* (MB) *BR,* (PC), p.43 *BL, BC, BR* (MB), p.45 (CW).
House
pp. 55, 56, 58, 59 *TR* (PC), pp. 57,59 *BR* (MB), p. 60 *T* (CW), p. 61, 62 (SL), pp. 68/9 (courtesy Homes and Gardens).
Communal house
pp. 72, 76, 77 (CW), pp. 78,79 (CW), pp. 81, 82 ,83 *T* (CW), pp. 85, 86, 87 (CW).
Housing
pp. 88, 90, 92, 93 (CW), pp. 94, 95 (CW).
Commerce
pp. 96, 98, 99, 100,101 *T* (MB), 101 *B* (EH), pp. 102, 103 (CW), pp. 104 *R,* 105 *L* (MB), 106, 107 (CW).
Collegiate
pp. 111, 112, 113 (EH), p. 116 *BL,* p. 117 *R* (FD) 117 *L* (CW) pp. 118, 119, 121, 122,123 *RT&B* (SL) 126 *L, TR* 127 *R* (EH).
School
pp. 128, 129, 130, 132, 133 (CW), pp. 134 *B,* 135, 136 (CW), pp. 137, 139 (CW), pp. 140, 141, 142, (PC), p. 143 (MC).
Campus
pp. 144–155 except 154 *TR* (PC)
Desert
pp. 160–177 except 168, 170 (HS), p. 178 *B,* p. 180 *TL* (HS).
Worship
pp. 182, 183, 185 (MB), pp. 189, 190, 191 (MB), p. 195 (FD), p. 197 (CW), pp. 198, 200 *R* (PC) p. 200 *TL* (EH), pp. 202,203 (EH).
Institution
pp. 206, 208, 209, 211, 212, 213, 214, (PC), pp. 215 *T,* 216, 217, 219 (PC), pp. 220, 221 (PC), pp. 222, 225, 226, 227 (PC).
Exhibition
p. 229 (SL), pp. 230, 231 (MB), p. 232 (CW), pp. 233, 234 (PC), p. 241 *L* (CW) 241 *R* (PC).

Key: Left *L,* Right *R,* Top *T,* Bottom *B,* Centre *C,* Middle *M.*

Acknowledgements
Many committed individuals contributed to the realisation of these works and it is right but only practical to make a collective 'Thank You', considering the time span, but it is possible to thank

My Partners
Roger Stonehouse, who engendered the book and
Dennis Bailey who designed it

I am also grateful for the help of
Andrzej Blonski
Peter Cook (Photographer)
Adrian Dannatt
William Dawkins
Eleanor Gawn
Kate & Susanna Heron
Richard Shillitoe
and Jenny Woodcraft

Trevor Dannatt May 2008

Also one must acknowledge the contribution and support over the years of certain Consultants

Structure:
Ove Arup & Partners
Buro Happold
Michael Barclay Partnership

Services:
Dale & Goldfinger
Engineering Design Consultants

Quantity Surveyors:
Widnell & Trollope
Monk & Dunstone
Gordon Fanshawe & Partners
(early Practice Names)

Index

© 2008 Black Dog Publishing Limited, London UK,
the architect, authors and photographers
All rights reserved

Texts by Trevor Dannatt, Roger Stonehouse,
John Tusa
Design by Dennis Bailey
Artwork by Rachel Pfleger@Black Dog Publishing

Black Dog Publishing Limited
10A Acton Street
London
WC1X 9NG
UK

t.   +44 (0)207 713 5097
f.   +44 (0)207 713 8682
e.   info@blackdogonline.com
w.   www.blackdogonline.com

All opinions expressed within this publication
are those of the authors and not necessarily of
the publisher.

British Library Cataloguing-in-Publication Data.
A CIP record for this book is available from the
British Library.

ISBN   978 1 906155 21 6

Every effort has been made to trace the copyright
holders, but if any have been inadvertently
overlooked the publishers will be pleased to make
the necessary arrangements at the first opportunity.

Black Dog Publishing Limited, London, UK is an
environmentally responsible company. *Trevor
Dannatt: works and words* is printed on Lumisilk,
an ECF and FSC certified paper from an ISO
14001 and ISO 9001 accredited supplier.